Historic Storms of New England

Historic Storms of New England

Its Gales, Hurricanes, Tornadoes, Showers with Thunder and
Lightning, Great Snow Storms, Rains, Freshets, Floods,
Droughts, Cold Winters, Hot Summers, Avalanches,
Earthquakes, Dark Days, Comets, Aurora Borealis,
Phenomena in the Heavens, Wrecks Along the Coast,
with Incidents and Anecdotes, Amusing and Pathetic

Sidney Perley

COMMONWEALTH EDITIONS
Beverly, Massachusetts

This edition copyright © 2001 by Memoirs Unlimited, Inc.

First published in 1891 by the Salem Press Publishing and Printing Company, Salem, Massachusetts

Front cover: *Rising of a Thunderstorm at Sea,* oil on canvas by Washington Allston, courtesy of Museum of Fine Arts, Boston. Back cover: Sidney Perley photograph, courtesy of Phillips Library, Peabody Essex Museum.

Library of Congress Cataloging-in-Publication Data

Perley, Sidney, 1858–1928.
   Historic storms of New England / Sidney Perley. -- New ed. of an 1891
     classic. p. cm.
   Includes index.
   ISBN 1-889833-27-4 (alk.paper)
   1. Storms--New England--History. 2. New England--History.
     3. Storms--New England--History--Anecdotes.
     4. New England--History--Anecdotes. I. Title.
   F4 .P47 2001
   974--dc21

                                 2001047028

Copyedited by Orion M. Barber
Indexed by Dan Connolly
Art researched by Peter Nelson
Art developed by Susan VanEtten
Cover and text designed by Jill Feron/Feron Design
Printed in the United States of America by Patterson Printing Company

Commonwealth Editions is an imprint of Memoirs Unlimited, Inc.,
21 Lothrop Street, Beverly, Massachusetts 01915.

Visit us on the web at www.commonwealtheditions.com.

Contents

Introduction

Sidney Perley

'Tis pleasant, by the cheerful hearth, to hear
Of tempests, and the dangers of the deep,
And pause at times, and feel that we are safe;
Then listen to the perilous tale again,
And, with an eager and suspended soul,
Woo terror to delight us.

Some of the readers of this volume after they have finished its perusal will probably pronounce it a series of tales of horror, and even those who are supposed to thoroughly understand the history of New England will be liable to think that the facts are overstated. It does indeed present a series of instances of varied natural phenomena, often resulting in great and terrible disaster.

New England lies between the torrid and the frigid zones, and its climate often suddenly changes from that of one zone to that of the other, having at times the hot wind and air of the south, and again the snow and ice and cold of the north.

The average temperature of the year is about forty-six degrees above zero, but it is exceedingly variable, ranging between fifty degrees below zero in winter to one hundred and two above in summer. The changes are frequent, great and sudden, the mercury sometimes falling fifty-five degrees in twenty-four hours.

The prevailing wind is the northwest; and when it blows from that quarter the weather is generally pleasant, and the air pure, dry and invigorating. The most uncomfortable wind is the northeast, which is much felt and complained of along the coast and in the interior as far as the Connecticut River, especially by those people that are affected by pulmonary disease. West of the Green Mountains it is rarely felt. This wind is strong and often attended with rain, sleet or snow, according to the season.

The climate is generally conducive to health, strength and longevity, and to that high moral tone, and the active, enterprising spirit of the New Englander, that has had so much to do in influencing the world in modern times. The climate is not a dry one by any means, as more rain falls here than in Europe, but in much less time, so that we have a larger share of clear, pleasant weather than the old world in the same latitude. Even "sunny France" does not have as many days of sunshine as New England. By a record kept here for many years, it is shown that the annual average number of pleasant days was one hundred and ninety-seven, three-fifths of them being very pleasant.

The summers of New England are generally dry and delightful, and when the air reaches a state of oppressiveness from the heat it is purified by thunder showers. The lightning attendant upon these showers has destroyed life and property nearly every summer and in some seasons has been very disastrous. In ancient times in the old world it was supposed that the objects that were struck by lightning were sacred, and bringing to mind the old superstition Cotton Mather said if that be true then "this is a sacred country indeed."

A season peculiar to New England is that known as the Indian summer, which occurs in October and continues only two or three weeks. It comes after the early frosts, when the wind is southwest, and the air is delightfully mild and sweet. The sky is then singularly transparent, pure and beautiful, and the fleecy clouds are bright with color. The Indians believed the season to be caused by a wind that was sent from the southwestern god Cautantowwit, who was regarded as superior to all other beings in benevolence and power, and the one to whom their souls went when they departed from the earthly body.

The winter season generally begins the first of December and continues into March, being usually cold and rigorous, and the temperature often below zero. On the mountains and high hills snow falls earlier and remains later than in the lowlands, the wind driving it with great force into the long and deep gullies of the mountains so solidly that it is not quickly dissolved during the warm days of spring, and is seen on the highest peaks even in July. Snow falls most deeply during the northeast storms, which are the most violent, and of longest duration. It often falls also in the southeast storms, which are sometimes more violent, but much shorter than the northeast ones, the snow usually turning to rain after a few hours. On the seaboard the temperature is several degrees warmer than in the interior, which is probably due principally to the presence of the warm waters of the Gulf Stream.

For periods of several years each, there have been series of severe and rigorous seasons, which have been followed by another series of mild winters, when little snow remained upon the ground, and the temperature was comparatively high for much of the time. After a series of mild winters, one of which series is now about closing probably, people think that a change must have occurred in the climate. There are very slight records of such series of mild winters, for people are not as apt to record pleasant seasons as they are those that are rigorous and stormy, in which they have suffered, and which are indelibly impressed upon their memories. Nevertheless, each century has had them. The winter of 1774–75 is a good illustration of one of those seasons when no snow came to lie, and farmers plowed their land, flowers bloomed, and fruits grew and ripened. It will be remembered how early the next spring was and how the grass waved in the wind in Massachusetts on the nineteenth of April. The mild winters that have been experienced here during the last thirty years have rarely or never been wholly moderate. Perhaps those of 1869–70 and of 1877–78 are the two mildest that there have been in recent times. It will be remembered that the first two months of each of those winters were warm, no snow falling to remain on the ground, and it seemed that, as an early writer put it, "winter was turned into summer." But the latter part of each of those seasons was stormy, and the springs that followed were late and cold. The old saying that "Winter never rots in the sky" can generally be relied on.

Storms frequently pass through New England and at all seasons. Often accompanied by strong wind, they have many times proved very disastrous to forests and buildings and to the shipping on the coast. Thousands of vessels have been wrecked, and many lives lost. The great easterly storms have also wrought many changes on the sandy portions of the coast, especially at and near Cape Cod, where the great force of the wind and waves have opened and closed harbors, causing the shifting sand to move hither and thither, even far out from the shore, on which many a craft has been cast away.

Many of the rainstorms have produced great freshets that have proved very disastrous to life and property. The Indians here had a tradition that away back in the ante-historical days there was a flood which rose so high that it destroyed the entire human population of New England, with the exception of a chief Powwow and his squaw, who saved themselves on the top of Mount Washington in New Hampshire.

It is said, and with much truth, that New England has more tornadoes and cyclones in proportion to its area than any other part of the United States. They occur with comparative frequency, and are often terrible in their effects. Tornadoes and kindred winds have always blown from a western to an eastern direction, and often at a speed of more than one hundred and thirty-five miles an hour. They are undoubtedly caused by rapidly shifting winds, and are associated with bad weather. General Greely advises that it is safest to go as far as possible to the cyclone's left side, as that is the inside of the circle, and on that side the wind is least strong.

The country has not been without those subterraneous convulsions generally known as earthquakes, of which more than five hundred have occurred here since the Pilgrims landed, several of them being frightful and disastrous. Although none of much severity has been felt since 1755, it is not certain that no more will come. Agassiz believed that earthquakes had elevated and depressed portions of this continent, and that it was very probable they would again.

—Salem, Massachusetts, 1891

Historic Storms of New England

Chapter i.

THE GREAT STORM OF AUGUST 1635

In the summer of 1635, the few English settlements scattered along the coast of New England were struggling to gain a foothold in the New World. Plymouth had indeed existed for fifteen years, but most of the villages had been founded only a few months, or a few years at the longest. On the Connecticut coast there was not a hamlet, and in the whole state in fact no settlement had been made, except at Wethersfield on the Connecticut River. There, a few men had spent the preceding winter, their number having been increased this summer by some new colonists, who suffered for awhile with the others, and finally travelled across the wild country to Saybrook Fort, the nearest place of refuge. Not another settlement could be found nearer than Plymouth, which was more than a hundred and fifty miles away, and separated therefrom by an unbroken wilderness inhabited only by Indians and wild animals. Following the coast of Massachusetts Bay, the next town beyond Plymouth was Scituate, then came Bear Cove (now Hingham) and Weymouth. The several settlements at or near the mouth of the Charles River, most of them now being included in the city of Boston, came next. A short trip up the river, and a turn to the right through the woods brought Rev. Peter Bulkley and his small company to the site they had chosen for their new home—this being the first colony that had penetrated the forest so far. In this summer of 1635 they marched into the woods and took possession of the clearing they had made, building for their shelter huts covered with bark and brushwood. Farther along the coast was Saugus (now Lynn), then came Salem, Ipswich and Newbury. At the mouth of the Piscataqua River stood Portsmouth, and up the stream was Dover. Nine miles from Portsmouth and also on the coast was York. With the exception of these few, small, defenceless settlements in the clearings of the forest along Massachusetts Bay from Plymouth to York, and of Wethersfield, in Connecticut, the entire region now included in New England was the pathless, dangerous wilderness.

The planting of the seed and the cultivation of the crops had been concluded, and some of the hay had been gathered and placed under cover for the support of the cattle during the coming winter. The whole of the second week of August the wind had blown from the direction of south-southwest with considerable force. At midnight of the fourteenth of the month its course was suddenly changed by way of the southeast to the northeast, and before daybreak a northeast rain storm was in progress. The wind had greatly increased in violence, blowing terrifically, and the rain fell in torrents, sometimes with such fury that the insecure houses of the settlers seemingly could not withstand its force. After the gale had continued five or six hours, the wind changed to the northwest, and the tumultuous elements gradually subsided.

The wind caused the tide to rise to a height unknown before. At Boston it measured twenty feet, and was brought in twice in twelve hours. The Narragansett Indians were obliged to climb into the tops of trees to save themselves from the great tide in their region. Many of them failed to do so, and were swallowed up by the surging waters. Had the storm continued much longer the water would have submerged several of the settlements.

An inconceivable number of trees were blown over or broken down, the stronger being torn up by the roots, and the tall pines and other brittle trees were broken in the middle. Slender young oaks and good-sized walnuts were twisted like withes, and Indian corn, the main dependence of the colonists, was beaten down and much of it destroyed, while it was hardly in the milk.

Some houses were blown over, and the roofs of several were torn off. At the plantation of Manoment at Plymouth, the wind took off the roof of a house and carried it to another place.

Among the many incidents of the storm is that of an old man in Ipswich, who had a small boat in which he was accustomed to go to sea, his only companion being a dog that he had taught to steer. As the storm came on, he hoisted his sail and started off down the river in his boat. He was warned of the approaching tempest, but he replied, "I will go to sea, though the devil were there." He continued on his way, but neither he nor his boat was ever heard of again.

Several shipwrecks were caused by the storm, for there were at this time large immigrations of settlers, and a number of ships were near the coast, having on board many passengers and goods for New England.

The *Great Hope,* a ship belonging in Ipswich, England, of four hundred tons burden, was in Massachusetts Bay when the storm came on. The gale drove the vessel aground on a point near Charlestown. The wind suddenly changed to the northwest, and the ship was blown out into the bay, but soon came ashore at Charlestown.

Burial Hill. From *The Pilgrim Fathers*, by Arthur Hall, Virtue & Co., London, 1853.

The ship *James*, of Bristol, England, having on board about one hundred passengers, who were from Lancashire, was near the Isles of Shoals when the gale came on. The vessel was run into a strait among the islands, the master thinking probably that he had secured a harbor; but when well in he found that it was an unprotected passage. The anchors were lowered, and all three of them were lost, the violent and almost irresistible wind snapping the cables and leaving the anchors at the bottom of the deep. The vessel was then placed under sail and run before the northeast gale, but neither canvas nor ropes held, and she dashed through the foaming crests on toward the rocky shore of Piscataqua. Instant destruction seemed inevitable. But lo! as if a mighty overruling hand controlled the angry elements, when within a cable's length of the ledges, the wind suddenly veered to the northwest, and the ship was blown away from the deadly rocks back toward the islands again. The wind in its change seemed but as mocking them after all for here they were plowing along toward rocks as dangerous as those they had just escaped. When about to strike in a last fatal plunge a part of the mainsail was let out, which caused the vessel to veer a little, and she weathered the rocks, almost touching them as she plunged past. The desired harbor was finally reached in safety. As they sped on their way havenward, they saw tossing on the still boisterous waves, goods of shipwrecked immigrants, which testified to the thorough work of the storm-king. On board this ship was Rev. Richard Mather, the pastor of the other passengers, and his family. Four of his sons were afterward eminent clergymen. Another of the passengers was Jonathan Mitchell, a mere youth at the time, who became a worthy and useful minister.

Another ship of Bristol, called the *Angel Gabriel,* arrived on our coast in season to encounter the storm. From the time of setting sail from their native land, it is recorded, the passengers observed many things about the vessel as ominous of some great disaster. The feeling certainly took form and grew into fact when the precious freight reached our inhospitable shores. The storm struck the vessel off Pemaquid Point,[1] and dashed it against the foam-covered rocks. The passengers were all saved, but their goods were lost.

At this period there was a boat, belonging to Isaac Allerton, sailing regularly between Piscataqua and Boston. It was a pinnace in build. On Wednesday, two days before the storm, the boat sailed from Ipswich, where it had stopped, on its trip to Boston. The passengers were sixteen in number, and consisted of Rev. John Avery, his wife and six children;[2] Mr. Avery's cousin Anthony Thacher, who had been in New England but a few weeks, his wife and four children;[3] and another member of his family, and one other passenger. There were four mariners. Mr. Avery had been a minister of good repute in Wiltshire, and came to Newbury, in New England, which had been settled the preceding year, with the intention of becoming the pastor of the little colony, but concluded not to remain, after being advised and urged by his friends and the magistrates and his brothers in the ministry to settle in Marblehead. He decided to go to Marblehead, and on this Wednesday took the boat at Ipswich for that purpose.

The loaded craft sailed down the placid river, while behind them

Pleasant, lay the clearings in the mellow summer morn,
With the newly planted orchards dropping their fruits first-born,
And the homesteads like green islands amid a sea of corn.

Broad meadows reached out seaward the tided creeks between,
And hills rolled wave-like inland, with oaks and walnuts green;—
A fairer home, a goodlier land, their eyes had never seen.

After entering Ipswich Bay the course of the shallop was changed more southerly, but it was soon discovered that progress in that direction was

---

1. Pemaquid Point is a promontory in Lincoln County, Maine, extending into the ocean near Muscongus Bay.
2. Winthrop and Mather say six, Hubard five, and another writer says that there were eight children.
3. One writer says that Mr. Thacher had nine children drowned at this time.

much impeded; and, as they proceeded farther into the face of the wind, it blew so strongly that no advance could be made, tacking being useless though it was tried again and again. On the evening of Friday, the fourteenth, after striving for two days to round Cape Ann, they had not succeeded in doing so. The wind became stronger during the evening, still blowing in the same direction. At ten o'clock, a fresh gale was rushing over the waters, their sails being rent by it, and the vessel was anchored. At midnight, the direction of the wind changed to the northeast, and the storm came on in all its fury. The vessel dragged its anchor, and drifted about at the merciless control of strong winds and mighty waves.

Blotted out were all the coast-lines, gone were rock, and wood, and sand,
Grimly anxious stood the skipper with the rudder in his hand,
And questioned of the darkness what was sea and what was land.

And the preacher heard his dear ones nestled round him weeping sore:
"Never heed, my little children! Christ is walking on before
To the pleasant land of heaven, where the sea shall be no more."

All at once the great cloud parted, like a curtain drawn aside,
To let down the torch of lightning on the terror far and wide;
And the thunder and the whirlwind together smote the tide.

The vessel was driven nearer and nearer to the rocky shore. Then came a shock, the vessel had struck, and the sound of breaking timbers added to the thunder of the storm. The pinnace was upon the rock off what is now Rockport, which has since been known as Crackwood's Ledge.[1]

When the vessel struck, Mr. Avery and his eldest son and Mr. Thacher and his daughter were thrown into the seething waters and carried by a mighty wave upon the rock. When they found themselves there, they called to those in the pinnace to come to them. During the few moments they were upon the ledge, expecting every instant to be washed from their footing into the raging sea, Mr. Avery raised his eyes toward heaven, and uttered these memorable last words: "Lord, I cannot challenge a preservation of my life, but according to thy Covenant I challenge Heaven." Hardly had the words

---

1. The fatal rock for more than two centuries was supposed to be that called Avery's Rock; but later investigations have brought about the conclusion that Crackwood's Ledge is the place. This is located about a hundred yards distant from Thacher's Island.

been spoken, when a gigantic wave lifted the pinnace on high and dashed it as with giant arms upon the rock, washing from the ledge those who had gained a momentary foothold upon it. Thus passed Mr. Avery and all his household to their eternal rest. Whittier has put the incident into poetry calling it the "Swan Song of Parson Avery," from which extracts have already been made. Of this portion of the story, he wrote the following lines:

There was wailing in the shallop, woman's wail and man's despair,
A crash of breaking timbers on the rocks so sharp and bare,
And, through it all, the murmur of Father Avery's prayer.

From his struggle in the darkness with the wild waves and the blast,
On a rock, where every billow broke above him as it passed,
Alone, of all his household, the man of God was cast.

There a comrade heard him praying, in the pause of wave and wind:
"All my own have gone before me, and I linger just behind;
Not for life I ask, but only, for the rest thy ransomed find!

"In this night of death, I challenge the promise of thy word!—
Let me see the great salvation of which mine ears have heard!—
Let me pass from hence forgiven, through the grace of Christ, our Lord!

"In the baptism of these waters wash white my every sin,
And let me follow up to thee my household and my kin!
Open the sea-gate of thy heaven, and let me enter in!"

When the Christian sings his death-song, all the listening heavens draw near,
And the angels, leaning over the walls of crystal, hear
How the notes so faint and broken swell to music in God's ear.

The ear of God was open to his servant's last request;
As the strong wave swept him downward, the sweet hymn upward pressed,
And the soul of Father Avery went singing to its rest.

The pinnace was such a small vessel and its destruction had been so complete there were few timbers for the drowning men, women and children to cling to. After having been beaten about in the surging waters for a quarter of an hour, hope having left him—for what could save any of them now!—being now and then thrown against the rocks, Mr. Thacher felt a firm footing. He soon found himself standing with his head above the water, his face toward the shore, which he soon reached in safety. He felt so grateful for his deliverance that he thanked God for it, and then looked about him to see what he could do for his companions. In the midnight blackness of the storm, his gaze was greatly restricted, and his voice was thrown back to him in mockery by the raging winds or drowned in the thunders of the waters. At first he could discern nothing, nor hear any human cries, but after a few moments he saw some pieces of the frame work of the pinnace being washed toward him, with a woman's form entangled in them. After a severe struggle, the woman extricated herself from the timbers, and before he could get to the place where she struck the shore, she had reached it in safety. It was his wife.

The storm raged on.

Mr. Thacher and his wife watched there in the rain and the blast for signs of their companions, but none came. Of the twenty souls on board the pinnace, only these two were saved. Their quartette of little ones had passed on with the rest. With sad and dejected hearts they sought a resting place under a sheltering bank. Some provision and clothing came ashore, and also, fortunately, a "snapsack," in which was a steel and flint, and some dry gunpowder. They built a fire, and made themselves as comfortable as they could under the sorrowful circumstances. The question of subsistence arose and confronted them as soon as the storm was over and daylight came, and they discovered that they were upon an island. The waters slowly resumed their usual state, and the August sun shed its hopeful rays over the stretch of ocean. In three directions the sea and sky met in their limitless range, and on the west the main land stretched away. They had no chance of reaching it, and signs of distress could awaken no response, for none but the savage of the forest was there. What could they do! Day passed, and night came on with all its horrible memories. Another day dawned, but before it had worn away, they were discovered by the people on a passing vessel, and taken off, being carried to Marblehead. On leaving the island Mr. Thacher gave it his name, calling it "Thacher's Woe," and the next year it was granted to him by the General Court. It has since borne his name, and for a hundred and twenty years the lamp in the lighthouse there has shed its warning rays over the ocean billows.

Among the things brought away from the island by Mr. Thacher were a cradle and an embroidered scarlet broadcloth covering, which were saved from the wreck, and are still preserved by his descendants of the name in Yarmouth, Massachusetts.

The friends of Mr. Thacher, from time to time, gave him presents which largely compensated him for the loss of his property by the storm, and the vacant places in his household were afterward partially filled. He settled in Yarmouth, where he died in 1668, at about eighty years of age.

The story of this shipwreck was often told about the hearth-fires of the coast-dwellers in the long winter evenings of the years that followed. And the fishermen, with "grave and reverend faces," recalled the ancient tale, when they passed the fatal ledge and saw the white waves breaking over it.

Governor Bradford, who was a witness of the tempest, said that none then living, either English or Indian, ever saw a storm equal to it. It was universal, no part of the country being exempt from its injurious effects, which visibly remained for many years.

Chapter ii.

THE EARTHQUAKE OF 1638

The morning of Friday, June 1, 1638, was very pleasant. The sun shone brightly, and the wind came gently from the west. The month of roses never opened more auspiciously.

Noon came and passed, and the settlers proceeded to their various labors in the field. Between one and two o'clock acute ears heard a low murmur of distant sound, which grew louder and clearer until every one heard what seemed to be the rumble of thunder far away. In a minute or two it increased in volume and in sharpness until it resembled the rattling of many carriages fiercely driven over granite pavements. The people were startled by the noise and discontinued the work upon which they were engaged to discover whence the sound came, and what it was. A clear sky beamed down upon them. Not a cloud could be seen out of which the thunder tones could emanate. The more they thought of the matter, the greater grew their perplexity. Not many moments elapsed, however, before the earth began to tremble beneath their feet, and terrified they threw down their tools and ran reeling like drunken men, with ghastly countenances, to the first group of people they could find, for men like many animals will flock together when they are afraid. The shaking of the earth increased to such a violent extent that people could not stand erect without supporting themselves by taking hold of posts or palings and other fixtures. Not only the mainland, but the islands in the ocean were shaken violently, and the vessels that rode in the harbors and those sailing along the coast were acted upon as if a series of tidal waves had passed under them.

People in their houses were much alarmed, for not only did they hear the awful sound and feel the trembling of the earth, but the houses over them shook to their very foundations, and it seemed as if they must collapse. The chimneys of the first houses here were built on the outside at the ends of the houses, with the tops rising just above the roof. They were massive piles of rough and uneven stones, generally some six feet square, the sides being nearly perpendicular. Imperfectly built, without mortar except for filling, they readily yielded to the terrible shaking they received, and the tops of many of them fell off, striking on the house or on the ground. The noise of the falling stones outside accompanied the rattle of pewter platters and dishes and other things that stood upon shelves in the houses, which knocked against each other and fell down.

This first and greatest shock of the earthquake continued for about four minutes. It came from the western and uninhabited portion of the country and proceeded easterly into the Atlantic. It shook the whole country from the coast into the wilderness for many miles, the Indians reporting that they felt it far in the interior.

The first shock died away and the noise ceased. The people began to resume their several labors. Half an hour passed, when to their surprise and terror, the horrible rumbling of the thunderous sound, and the quaking of the earth were renewed. But it quickly passed, being less violent than the first shock. For twenty days the earth was in an unquiet condition.

Some of the people of Plymouth were about to remove to another place, and several of the principal persons of the town were gathered at a house for an hour of conference before their separation. While thus engaged, the terrible noise and shaking of the earth came upon them. The men were sitting in the house talking together, and some women and others were without the door. Those outside would have been thrown to the ground if they had not caught hold of the posts and pales near which they were standing.

At Newbury, a town meeting was in progress, and while the questions which arose for decision were being discussed, the sound of the on-coming earthquake burst upon their ears, as the historian says, like "a shrill clap of thunder." The building was violently shaken; and wonder and amazement and fear filled the minds of the people. After the tumult had ceased, before proceeding to further business, the assembly voted to record the fact of the earthquake, concluding their record thus, "wherefore taking notice of so great and strange a hand of God's providence, we were desirous of leaving it on record to the view of after ages to the intent that all might take notice of Almighty God and fear his name."

The summers for several years after the earthquake were cool and unseasonable for the ripening of corn and other crops, as compared with those of a number of years preceding it. They were also subject to unseasonable frosts, and on this account Indian corn seldom matured. Whether this was a change brought about by, or was a result of the earthquake is of course uncertain, though it does seem reasonable to suppose that the earth after its convulsions would be cooler than it was before.

Earthquakes are always fearful and impressive, but the people of the time when this one occurred must have had many doubts and fears in their minds. They were not only superstitious, but this was a new and unknown world, which but a few years before was pictured with the most awful terrors.

This, the greatest earthquake of the seventeenth century, marked an epoch in the lives of the settlers of New England, and for many years afterwards it was common for them to compute dates of incidents as "so long since the earthquake."

Chapter iii.

THE EARTHQUAKE OF 1663

The summer of 1662 was very dry, and the following winter was moderate, there being no frost in the ground until December 20, even as far north as Hampton.

On the evening of Monday, January 26, 1662–63, the people of New England were quietly sitting in the light of their hearth fires, telling stories, perhaps recurring to the earthquake of a quarter of a century before, which the older members of the families remembered so vividly, when suddenly outside the doors was heard a peculiar roaring sound, which grew louder and louder, until the fire places trembled and the flames from the burning sticks crinkled as they ascended the chimney. The trembling increased until the houses shook and rocked, and the tenons of the timbers moved in and out of their mortises. Many chimneys were broken, and others were thrown down. Lids of warming pans were flung up, and pewter dishes fell off the shelves. Persons who were standing when the shock came were compelled to either sit or fall down.

Boston was the only locality mentioned where much damage was done. There it wrought injury in various ways. In fact, the towns on the shore of Massachusetts Bay seemed to feel the shock more than other portions of New England.

Although New England was more or less shaken, the country on either side of it suffered more. It extended as far north as Canada, and south to Mexico, probably being felt farther in both directions.

Three distinctly separate shocks were felt, shaking in all more than a quarter of an hour. It would appear from the records that this earthquake exceeded in severity that of 1638.

Two days later there was another shock, and February 5 another, which was repeated at dark the same evening. Two days afterward, at nine o'clock in the morning, there was another shock. The earth did not cease to quake until the following July.

The people were again agitated, and became more pious than they had been, being fearful that they might be called before the Lord, the Righteous Judge, without notice and without preparation. A correspondent of a Massachusetts newspaper wrote the following lines on the morning of an earthquake in 1786, which are applicable to this earthquake: " When we consider the dreadful scenes that have been caused in the world by earthquakes, nothing is more truly alarming than the convulsions of the earth under us, threatening an instantaneous destruction. But let us be prepared for eternal happiness:

> Then if the frame of nature round us break,
> In hideous ruin and confusion hurled;
> We unconcerned may bear the mighty shock,
> And stand secure amidst the falling world.

Chapter iv.

THE COMET OF 1664

The first comet to appear in the heavens of New England, of which we have any account, blazed forth from Orion from the ninth to the twenty-second of December, 1652. It was large and had a long and beautiful tail. The people shuddered when they looked at it, for they thought its appearance was inevitably connected with some famine or plague. Another one appeared from February 3 to March 28, 1661. No calamity of any great consequence, certainly, happened in New England as the result of these celestial visits.

Now, in this mild winter of 1664–65, another had come to startle the settlers of New England. "The great and dreadful comet," as Josselyn called it, made its first appearance on the eighth of November. It came, not only as a visitor to New England's skies, but as a universal guest, being visible from all parts of the north temperate zone and probably from all settled portions of the globe. Night after night the whole winter through, "the great blazing starre" took its position in the southern sky as soon as the stars began to glint in the evening constellations.

Its size and extreme brilliancy greatly alarmed the people. Comets were generally believed to be omens of something to be dreaded, and the learned men of the times taught the people to fear their approach. Morton said to them that it was "no fiery meteor caused by exhalation but it appeared to be sent immediately by God to awake the secure world." By this sign they were, as they believed, forewarned of the judgment of Jehovah upon the people for their sins, but just what that judgment would be was a mystery. After a comet had disappeared, calamities which succeeded it within the space of a year or two were ascribed to its influence. In regard to the events which were believed to be foreshadowed by this comet, a writer of the time said, "The effects appeared much in England, in a great and dreadful plague that followed the next summer, in the dreadful war by sea with the Dutch, and the burning of London the second year following."

When we consider that after all the years astronomers have been telling us that comets are not dangerous, the great mass of mankind are still disturbed by the appearance of these heavenly messengers, we can understand how the people of the early period here, in their ignorance and superstition,

Comet. Undated woodcut. New York Historical Society.

must have been affected. The great meteoric ball and graceful curving tail of sparkling fire, many thousands, perhaps millions of miles in length, was to them frightful in two ways. First, as has already been stated, as the precursor of some dreadful event; and, second, as in itself an instrument capable of the direst consequences if a too close acquaintance was made with our little planet.

The end of the world must have been prominent in the minds of the people of early colonial days, for it has always been supposed by the general populace that the world would at last be destroyed by fire, and what messenger could perform this duty so quickly and so effectually? A comet had only to approach a little nearer, and with a whisk of its fiery tail it could consume everything combustible; or, a conjunction of the molten ball with the earth would annihilate the latter instantly.

So thoughts ran in the minds of the beholders of this fiery visitor of 1664, and as the evenings came and the unwelcome guest presented itself, fear and doubt and anxiety kept the people in an unhappy state of mind all through the long winter. Its disappearance was a welcome event.

Probably no one now living has seen such large and glaring comets as were visible here in the colonial and provincial days.

Chapter v.

STRANGE APPEARANCE IN THE HEAVENS IN 1667

The winter of 1666–67 was unseasonably warm. The ground was but slightly frozen, and very little snow fell in any portion of New England. It was one of those winters that gave the inhabitants the notion that the climate was changing, and that they would not again experience such severe seasons as they had passed through since the settlement of the country. Each mild winter has brought into men's minds the same thoughts, which would be dissipated when the succeeding winter with its cold and snow came upon them.

Toward the close of the month of February a singular and undefinable object appeared in the southwestern section of the sky. It sometimes resembled the tail of a comet without the star; and, again, in the imagination of the beholder, seemed like a spear, thicker in the middle than at either end. Its position was not perpendicular, but it leaned to the east, the lower end pointing to the place of the sun's exit. It was quite bright and of a whitish color. It appeared in the evening about an hour after darkness came on and slowly descended until it vanished beneath the horizon. It was seen only four or five nights in all and those successively.

Whether or not it was a lingering beam of the sun's rays we cannot of course tell. The people of that time believed it to be a sign of some impending calamity. Some writers have called it a comet, but it certainly was not. Morton calls it a sign and exclaimed after he had seen it, "God awaken us that we be not heedless spectators of his wonderful works." Those who thought it was a sign, and imagined that it resembled a spear, concluded that it gave warning of an impending massacre by the Indians, and that it had special reference to the war with King Philip in 1675 and 1676.

Several ministers and magistrates, who had been prominent in New England, died the following year, and Rev. Simon Bradstreet of New London, Connecticut, wrote in his diary kept at the time, that "Possibly the death of these precious servants of Christ might not be the least thing signified by that blaze or beam."

The strange visitor was not without its moral influence upon the people. A writer says, "it excited the magistrates to promote a reformation of manners;" though the Universal History observes that "the only thing of that kind that happened was a renewal of the persecution against the Baptists and Quakers."

Chapter vi.

THE STORM OF 1676 AND SHIPWRECK OF EPHRAIM HOWE

About the twentieth of September, 1676, a violent storm prevailed on the New England coast, causing vessels to be wrecked and otherwise doing much damage.

The most interesting portion of its history is the shipwreck of Ephraim Howe, a sea-captain of New Haven, Connecticut, who regularly sailed, in a vessel called a ketch, of about seventeen tons burden, between New Haven and Boston. On September 10, he set sail from the latter port, having on board two of his sons, who were able seamen, two passengers and a boy. Contrary winds detained them for several days and before they could double Cape Cod the storm came upon them. The ketch was driven upon the shoals and almost stranded. While endeavoring to keep afloat, the rudder was lost, from which time their control of the vessel was gone, and they were carried out to sea. Tossed to and fro and almost overwhelmed, the treacherous waters forced them farther and farther from the coast until the shore faded from their earnest gaze, and they were wanderers on the pathless, dangerous deep.

The father became sick from the exposure to wet and cold, but soon grew better. The oldest son suffered severely from the effects of the storm and eleven days only passed, after their last view of the sandy hills of Cape Cod, before he died and was entombed in the sea. Only a few more days elapsed when the other son, who had been unable to perform his duties for a short time, also fell a victim to exposure and died. The father felt their deaths severely at this trying time; but in speaking of the loss of his sons in after years said that their resignation and faith in Christ and their escape from a more terrible experience, which seemed certain to come, greatly consoled him.

Captain Howe was now sick himself in the cabin most of the time, and the vessel drifted at the pleasure of the winds and and waves. While in this hopeless state, one of the passengers died, also from the effects of exposure. Half of the company were now gone. Only Captain Howe, Mr. Augur, one of the passengers, and the lad were left.

Stranded Brig. Oil on canvas by Edwin W. Dickinson, Museum of Fine Arts, Springfield.

Their necessities and fears increased. Winter would soon be upon them. Something definite must be done! They must not be inactive longer. There seemed to be but two propositions to consider. They must either endeavor to reach the New England coast, or sail for the islands of the south. Divine guidance was sought, and after praying earnestly they drew lots to determine which course they should take. The lot fell upon New England and immediately, with a new rudder, which they had constructed, they turned their prow in the direction in which they supposed New England lay.

Storm after storm gathered about them and violently swept over them, threatening their destruction. Cold and penetrating winds rushed over the limitless waters, sometimes so forcibly that those stationed at the sail had to be fastened with ropes to enable them to stand in their places. Though in a state of bodily weakness, Captain Howe now stood at the helm for twenty-four hours, and sometimes even thirty-six hours, at a time, while the waves dashed over the deck so strongly that he had to be lashed fast to the helm to escape being washed overboard.

A month had passed since they set out for New England, when they again lost their rudder. Their courage was now so far gone that they did not think it worth while to try to make another. Hope had left them. In their despair the craft was permitted to drift wheresoever it would for a fortnight. All this time Captain Howe's clothes had rarely been dry, and none of the three had consumed any warm food more than three times while they had been in their lamentable condition.

About three months had elapsed since they had seen land, and it was nearly seven weeks since they determined to strive to reach their native coast. A strong wind was one day driving the vessel before it amid the white-capped waves, when to their surprise the sound of breakers was heard, and a peculiar motion was felt about the ketch. Upon examining into their situation, they found themselves aground on a reef, with the sea breaking violently around them. It was afterward ascertained that they were on a sunken island off the coast at Cape Sable, Nova Scotia, the tops of whose ledges were scarcely beneath the surface of the water, causing the waves to break above them, They looked away from the foaming breakers leeward and saw dreary rocks rising from the water, the spray flying over them. If the vessel had not caught on these hidden rocks, it would probably have been driven ashore and dashed to pieces on the relentless ledges. They immediately dropped an anchor and got out the boat, which they still had. Much to their relief the wind ceased its violence, and the waters grew less turbulent. They put a few things into the boat, but under the excitement of the occasion took much less than they afterward wished. The shore was reached successfully, and they landed.

The violent wind which had driven them on the reef had come from the east, bringing in its wake a storm which after the short lull, burst upon them. The vessel was stove to pieces, and from it floated ashore a cask of powder, a barrel of wine and several other things.

Ignorant of the place where they found themselves, their attention was now turned to an examination of the country. To their dismay they soon learned that it was a desolate island, with neither man nor beast upon it, and their great hopes of succor were dashed. Perishing of hunger here seemed hardly preferable to drowning in the sea, or starving in their vessel. But being on land was at least a change which was welcomed after their three months' voyage on the boisterous ocean.

With some things which they had brought from the vessel they made a sort of tent to shelter them from the storms and extreme cold of the region at this season. After the structure had become dilapidated, a cave was made which afterward served as their abode.

The only inhabitants of the island beside themselves were birds, consisting of gulls and crows. It has been already stated that a cask of powder had floated ashore. A gun or two also came with the wreck of the ketch. The guns and ammunition seemed to be their only means of obtaining sustenance, but the birds were so scarce that rarely more than one could be shot during a single excursion for that purpose. Consequently, the food was necessarily sparingly eaten, ofttimes only half a bird, with the liquor, sufficing for a meal for all three. At one time they had no food at all for five days; but they had become so accustomed to abstinence that the stomach forgot its cravings which seemed to them a special blessing.

The days dragged drearily away. Their time was spent in watching for the appearance of some vessel, in gunning for birds, and in meditation upon their hopeless condition. They knew not where they were, and it seemed to matter little except they could have wished the spot to have been in a warmer climate. They not only suffered from cold and exposure, for spring was not yet come, but also from unwholesome food,[1] one or more of them being sick most of the time. After twelve weeks had been spent on the island, death relieved Mr. Augur from further suffering. The youth also died in April, only a few days after Mr. Augur had left them.

Captain Howe was now alone on this forlorn island. If the days had passed wearily while his companions were alive, how great his lonesomeness now must have been. No hermit was ever more solitary. His was, indeed, the reflection of Alexander Selkirk, which Cowper supposes him to have had during his abode on the island of Juan Fernandez.

> *O solitude! where are the charms*
> *That sages have seen in thy face?*
> *Better dwell in the midst of alarms,*
> *Than reign in this horrible place.*
>
> *I am out of humanity's reach,*
> *I must finish my journey alone,*
> *Never hear the sweet music of speech,*
> *I start at the sound of my own.*

---

1. One account says that only Captain Howe's sons died at sea, the passengers and the lad dying on the island.

Ye winds that have made me your sport,
Convey to this desolate shore
Some cordial endearing report
Of a land I shall visit no more.

When I think of my own native land,
In a moment I seem to be there;
But, alas! recollection at hand
Soon hurries me back to despair.

Captain Howe was supplied with his daily food by the ravens, Elijah-like, for months after the winter was over. The weather became milder as spring came on, and he was more comfortable.

Fishing vessels, on their way to and from the Grand Banks, now frequently sailed within view of the island. He used all the means that his great need could suggest to attract their attention that they might come to his relief. But nothing availed; either they did not see his signals, or seeing them supposed that they proceeded from some band of hostile Indians, for this was at the time of King Philip's War, when all the savages within the regions of New England were arrayed on one side or the other in the last national struggle against the white settlers.

Captain Howe had now been alone nearly three months. He had spent much of the time in meditation and, being a Christian, in prayer, beseeching God to provide some way for his escape. At last, a new thought struck him, as it did Selkirk, that

There's mercy in every place,
And mercy, encouraging thought!
Gives even affliction a grace,
And reconciles man to his lot.

In spite of all the misery that surrounded him and while believing that death must soon relieve him from his sufferings, he fasted and prayed, repenting of the sins which were worthy of the calamities that had befallen him. Turning from his mendicant position, he could now see so much mercy that had been shown to him that he was sorry for his forgetfulness and selfishness and determined to acknowledge it in some solemn way of thanksgiving. He set apart a day for that purpose. A few days later, in answer to his prayers, as he believed, a passing vessel sailed much nearer the island than others had done. He eagerly adopted means to attract the attention of the people on board and make known to them the presence of a shipwrecked mariner. The vessel belonged to Salem, Massachusetts. His signal was seen, and a boat was sent to the island. With a heart overflowing with emotion he boarded the boat and was welcomed on the vessel which immediately proceeded on its homeward way. Joy and thanksgiving filled his breast. He arrived in Salem on July 8, 1677, a few days after his rescue, ten months having elapsed since he left Boston on his disastrous trip. He returned to his family and friends at New Haven, where he was hardly recognized, his sickness and suffering from exposure, cold and hunger having had their due effects upon him.

Chapter vii.

THE COMET OF 1680

Great notice was taken of all comets in the colonial days. Several have already been mentioned, but the Newtonian comet of 1680, as it was called, should not be passed unnoticed. It was first seen at Boston at five o'clock on the morning of November 14, 1680, appearing in the southeastern sky near fourteen degrees in Libra and one degree and three minutes southward of the ecliptic. The sky being clear, the comet at first appeared plainly, but in a few moments became faint, and vanished away as day began to break. The tail appeared to be about thirty degrees in length. Some writers have said that it reached from the zenith nearly to the horizon.

It appeared earlier and earlier in the morning until about December 8, when it began to be seen in the evening. It continued to be visible till February 10, when it failed to come within the view of the naked eye, though it could be discerned for some time longer with the aid of a telescope. Astronomers fix the time of its next visit to our planet in the year 2225, five hundred and forty-five years being necessary to the completion of its circuit, which is a fact too stupendous for us to realize when we think of the great speed of these bodies.

The magnitude and brightness of this comet caused consternation in Europe and America, and, in fact, in those times people all over the globe were alarmed at the uncommon things that appeared in the heavens.

Increase Mather gave a lecture on the comet, saying, in his introduction, that "As for this blazing star, which hath occasioned this discourse, it was a terrible sight indeed, especially about the middle of December last, the stream of such a stupendous magnitude, as that few men now living ever beheld the like."

Not only were the common people of New England terrified at the appearance of their heavenly visitor, but the alarm reached all classes. The governor and council of the Massachusetts Bay Colony appointed a general fast, one reason assigned for it in the proclamation being "that awful, portentous, blazing star, usually foreboding some calamity to the beholders thereof." The greatest strictness was observed by the people in keeping the fast. Probably the terror arose chiefly from ignorance and superstition, but it was as real to them as if it had been demonstrated to be true by the best astronomers. The clergy throughout New England sought to make the most of this fear, some have said with hypocritical intentions, for the purpose of making converts to their religious views. We suppose that most of them did really believe with the laity that the alarm was well founded, and that the time was at hand when they might be suddenly called to meet their Creator. Therefore, feeling the responsibility of their position, they besought their congregations to turn unto God while yet there was time. The result was that many were brought into the fold, and the ordinances of the church were more carefully observed.

Chapter viii.

STRANGE APPEARANCE IN THE HEAVENS IN 1682

The apparitions described in this chapter are supposed to have been instances of the exhibition of mirage, produced by atmospheric refraction. Several incidents of a similar character are recorded in the annals of New England, as the phantom ship of New Haven. In instances of mirage, the objects are generally inverted, though if there occurs a double refraction they will appear higher in the air, but standing in their ordinary positions.

Though not now deemed worthy of being classed with unaccountable things, yet two hundred years ago, people were strong believers in the supernatural, and ascribed everything that seemed to be of that nature to such a cause. The first instance mentioned below is believed by many to have been simply the product of a lively imagination.

At Lynn, Massachusetts, one evening in 1682, after the sun had set, and darkness had begun to throw its pall over the land, a man by the name of Handford went out of doors to ascertain if the new moon had risen. In the western sky lay a black cloud of strange appearance, and after looking at it a short time he discovered that it contained the figure of a man completely armed, standing with his legs apart, and holding a pike in his hands across his breast. Mrs. Handford also came out and saw the apparition. After awhile the figure vanished, and in its place appeared a large ship, fully rigged and with all sails set, apparently in motion, though retaining the same position. It was seen as plainly as a ship was ever seen in the harbor, and was to their imagination, the handsomest craft that they ever saw. It had a high majestic bow, heading southwardly, with a black hull, white sails, and a long and beautiful streamer floating from the top of the mainmast. This was plainly visible for some time. After awhile the people went into their houses though the image still remained in the cloud. On coming out again after a short time it was not to be seen, the cloud had also gone and the sky was clear. Many reliable people in the town saw the apparition, and all agree that the above statement is true; but what it was, and how it can be accounted for is still unknown. We merely record the facts, believing we ought to do so whether we can account for the strange appearance or not.

This brings to the mind of the writer a tradition in his family of a similar, but more astounding exhibition in the clouds. There appeared in the heavens two magnificent men-of-war, which slowly and steadily approached until they came comparatively near each other when flames simultaneously burst from their port-holes, and the sound of cannon was heard. The bright flashes followed by sharp reports continued for several minutes, and the vessels vanished. We believe it was said that this battle in the clouds occurred just before one of the wars of this country, but which one we have forgotten. The incident might be explained by the presence of heat or flash lightning accompanied by distant thunder and clouds containing forms like ships.

Chapter ix

THE DARK DAY OF 1716

The list of dark days in New England must begin with that of Sunday, October 21, 1716. The people were gathered in their respective houses of worship, when about eleven o'clock in the forenoon, the outlines of things about them lost their distinctness. It soon became so dark that the members of the congregations could not recognize each other across the small meeting houses of those days, and shortly after the forms of the people could not be seen except by looking at them toward a window. A writer says that "one could not recognize another four seats away, nor read a word in a psalm book." Some ministers sent to the neighboring houses for candles, unwilling that anything of this kind, preternatural though it might be, should interrupt the services. Others, believing it would soon pass away, sat down and waited. Some were ready to believe that the darkness of the last day was settling like a pall over nature before its dissolution. In fact, all people were in a state of more or less excitement.

The darkness continued about half an hour, and when it grew light enough the waiting clergymen rose and finished the services. The people gathered at the close of the meeting, and discussed the probable cause and meaning of what seemed to be a supernatural occurrence. The air had been more or less murky for several days, being, as a writer of that time said, "very full of smoke." It descended near the earth constantly, when the wind was from the southwest. On this Sunday dark clouds of smoke had passed over; and it was thought that the wind, which had changed to the eastward, had brought the smoke back again in a dense body, thus darkening the land. That was the explanation accepted at the time by many of the people, while others believed to the end of their lives that it could not be explained. Mather deemed the occurrence of sufficient importance to send an account of it to the Royal Philosophical Society in England, which soon after published it in its Transactions. This dark day was probably surpassed only by the famous May day of 1780, of which we have very full accounts. When we consider how much more superstitious the people were seventy years before, we can in some degree imagine their thoughts and feelings. Darkness always produces a peculiar feeling, probably from its dampness, and the mystery which seems to be involved in it. Unnatural darkness, or what seems to be such, certainly produces a weird and gloomy feeling, which would turn a superstitious mind into channels of fear and alarm.

Chapter x.

THE WINTER OF 1716–17

In December, 1716, snow fell to the depth of five feet, rendering travelling very difficult, and almost impossible except on snow shoes. The temperature throughout the winter was moderate, but the amount of snow that fell that season has never been equalled in New England during the three centuries of her history.

Snow fell in considerable quantities several times during the month of January, and on February 6 it lay in drifts in some places twenty-five feet deep, and in the woods a yard or more on the level. Cotton Mather said that the people were overwhelmed with snow.

The great storm began on February 18, and continued piling its flakes upon the already covered earth until the twenty-second; being repeated on the twenty-fourth so violently that all communication between houses and farms ceased. Down came the flakes of feathery lightness, until

> . . . *the whited air*
> *Hides hills and woods, the river and the heaven,*
> *And veils the farmhouse,*

within whose walls,

> . . . *all friends shut out, the housemates sit*
> *Around the radiant fireplace, enclosed*
> *In a tumultuous privacy of storm.*

Whittier, in his "Snow Bound," has pleasingly described the coming of the snow in the country. The east wind brought to the settlers the roar of the ocean rolling up on its frozen shore; as night came on, the chilly air and darkened sky gave signs of the coming storm; and soon the blinding snow filled the air.

Meanwhile we did our nightly chores,—
Brought in the wood from out of doors,
Littered the stalls, and from the mows
Raked down the herd's-grass for the cows;
Heard the horse whinnying for his corn;
And, sharply clashing horn on horn,
Impatient down the stanchion rows
The cattle shake their walnut bows;
While peering from his early perch
Upon the scaffold's pole of birch,
The cock; his crested helmet bent,
And down his querulous challenge sent.

Unwarmed by any sunset light,
The gray day darkened into night,
A night made hoary with the swarm
And whirl-dance of the blinding storm,
As zigzag wavering to and fro
Crossed and recrossed the winged snow;
And ere the early bedtime came
The white drift piled the window frame,
And through the glass the clothes-line posts
Looked in like tall and sheeted ghosts.

So all night long the storm roared on;
The morning broke without a sun;
In tiny spherule traced with lines
Of Nature's geometric signs,
In starry flake and pellicle,
All day the hoary meteor fell;
And, when the second morning shone,
We looked upon a world unknown,
On nothing we could call our own.
Around the glistening wonder bent
The blue walls of the firmament,
No cloud above, no earth below,—
A universe of sky and snow!
The old familiar sights of ours

Took marvellous shapes: strange domes and towers
Rose up where sty or corn-crib stood,
Or garden wall, or belt of wood;
A smooth white mound the brush pile showed,
A fenceless drift what once was road;
The bridge post an old man sat
With loose-flung coat and high cocked hat;
The well-curb had a Chinese roof,
And even the long sweep, high aloof,
In its slant splendor, seemed to tell,
Of Pisa's leaning miracle.

During the storm enough snow fell to bury the earth to the depth of from ten to fifteen feet on the level, and in some places for long distances it was twenty feet deep. The twenty-fourth was Sunday, and the storm was so fierce and the snow came in such quantities that no religious meetings were held throughout New England.

No church-bell lent its Christian tone
To the savage air, no social smoke
Curled over woods of snow-hung oak.
A solitude made more intense
By dreary voicéd elements,
The shrieking of the mindless wind,
The moaning tree-tops swaying blind,
And on the glass the unmeaning beat
Of ghostly finger-tips of sleet.
Beyond the circle of our hearth
No welcome sound of toil or mirth
Unbound the spell, and testified
Of human life and thought outside.
We minded that the sharpest ear
The buried brooklet could not hear,
The music of whose liquid lip
Had been to us companionship,
And, in our lonely life had grown
To have an almost human tone.

Indians, who were almost a hundred years old, said that they had never heard their fathers tell of any storm that equalled this.

Many cattle were buried in the snow, where they were smothered or starved to death. Some were found dead weeks after the snow had melted, yet standing and with all the appearance of life. The eyes of many were so glazed with ice that being near the sea they wandered into the water and were drowned. On the farms of one gentleman upwards of eleven hundred sheep were lost in the snow. Twenty-eight days after the storm, while the search for them was still in progress, more than a hundred were found huddled together, apparently having found a sheltered place on the lee side of a drift, where they were slowly buried as the storm raged on, being covered with snow until they lay sixteen feet beneath the surface. Two of the sheep were alive, having subsisted during the four weeks of their entombment by feeding on the wool of their companions. When rescued they shed their fleeces, but the wool grew again and they were brought back to a good degree of flesh. An instance of a similar nature occurred the present winter (1890–91) in Pennsylvania, where during a snow storm three sheep were buried in a hollow twenty feet under a drift. After twelve days had elapsed, they were discovered, and shoveled out, all being alive. They had not a particle of wool on them, hunger having driven them to eat it entirely off each others' backs. With proper care they were restored to their usual condition.

Other animals also lived during several weeks' imprisonment under the snow. A couple of hogs were lost, and all hope of finding them alive was gone, when on the twenty-seventh day after the storm they worked their way out of the snow bank in which they had been buried, having subsisted on a little tansy, which they had found under the snow. Poultry also survived several days' burial, hens being found alive after seven days, and turkeys from five to twenty. These were buried in the snow some distance above the ground, so that they could obtain no food whatever.

The wild animals which were common in the forests of New England at this period were robbed of their means of subsistence, and they became desperate in their cravings of hunger. Browsing for deer was scarce, the succulent shrubs being buried beneath the snow; and when evening came on, those in the forests near the sea-coast started for the shore, where instinct had taught them that they would be likely to find more food. Another, and a greater reason, perhaps, was that there were other starving animals in the woods beside themselves of which they were afraid. Bears and wolves were numerous then, and as soon as night fell, in their ravenous state they followed the deer in droves into the clearings, at length pouncing upon them. In this way vast numbers of these valuable animals were killed, torn in pieces, and devoured by their fierce enemies. It was estimated that nineteen out of every twenty deer were thus destroyed. They were so scarce after this time that officers called deer-reeves were chosen in each town to attend to their preservation. These officers were annually elected until the country had become so densely populated that the deer had disappeared and there was nothing for them to do.

Bears, wolves and foxes were nightly visitors to the sheep pens of the farmers. Cotton Mather states that many ewes, which were about to give birth to young, were so frightened at the assaults of these animals that most of the lambs born the next spring were of the color of foxes, the dams being either white or black. Vast multitudes of sparrows also came into the settlements after the storm was over, but remained only a short time, returning to the woods as soon as they were able to find food there.

The sea was greatly disturbed, and the marine animal life was in a state of considerable excitement. After the storm ceased, vast quantities of small sea shells were washed on shore in places where they had never been found before; and in the harbors great numbers of porpoises were seen playing together in the water.

The carriers of the mails, who were in that period called "post boys," were greatly hindered in the performance of their duties by the deep snow. Leading out from Boston there were three post roads, and as late as March 4 there was no travelling, the ways being still impassable, and the mail was not expected, though it was then a week late. March 25 the "post" was travelling on snow shoes, the carrier between Salem, Massachusetts, and Portsmouth, New Hampshire, being nine days in making his trip to Portsmouth and eight days in returning, the two towns being about forty miles apart. In the woods he found the snow five feet deep, and in places it measured from six to fourteen feet.

Much damage was done to orchards, the snow being above the tops of many of the trees, and when it froze forming a crust around the boughs, it broke most of them to pieces. The crust was so hard and strong that cattle walked hither and thither upon it, and browsed the tender twigs of the trees, injuring them severely.

Many a one-story house was entirely covered by the snow, and even the chimneys in some instances could not be seen. Paths were dug under the snow from house to barn, to enable the farmers to care for their animals, and tunnels also led from house to house among the neighbors if not too far apart. Snow shoes were of course brought into requisition, and many trips were made by their aid. Stepping out of a chamber window some of the people ventured over the hills of snow. "Love laughs at locksmiths," and of course, says Coffin, in his History of Newbury, Massachusetts, will disregard a snow-drift. A young man of that town by the name of Abraham Adams was paying his attention to Miss Abigail Pierce, a young lady of the same place, who lived three miles away. A week had elapsed since the storm, and the swain concluded that he must visit his lady. Mounting his snowshoes he made his way out of the house through a chamber window, and proceeded on his trip over the deep, snow-packed valley and huge drifts among the hills beyond. He reached her residence, and entered it, as he had left his own, by way of a chamber window. Besides its own members, he was the first person the family had seen since the storm, and his visit was certainly much appreciated.

In the thinly settled portions of the country great privation and distress were caused by the imprisonment of many families, and the discontinuance of their communication with their neighbors. Among the inhabitants of Medford, Massachusetts, was a widow, with several children, who lived in a one-story house on the road to Charlestown. Her house was so deeply buried that it could not be found for several days. At length smoke was seen issuing from a snowbank, and by that means its location was ascertained. The neighbors came with shovels, and made a passage to a window, through which they could gain admission. They entered and found that the widow's small stock of fuel was exhausted, and that she had burned some of the furniture to keep her little ones from suffering with the cold. This was but one of many incidents that occurred of a similar character.

Chapter xi.

WRECK OF THE PIRATE SHIP *WHYDAH*

The winter of 1717–18 was acknowledged to be unusually cold, and the spring which followed was late, windy and uncomfortable. On Saturday, April 26, a violent easterly storm prevailed along the coast of Massachusetts. It was made memorable on account of the wreck of the notorious pirate ship *Whydah*. The commander of it was that infamous leader among freebooters, Samuel Bellamy, stories of whose brutal cruelty and daring exploits were often told about the firesides of the people here, a

century and a half ago. The *Whydah*
carried twenty-three guns and was
manned by one hundred and thirty
men.

The pirates had made a visit to
this section of the Atlantic coast, and
had succeeded in capturing seven vessels, to one of which Bellamy trans-
ferred seven of his crew to sail the
craft and guard the captive mariners
who were imprisoned on their own
vessel. The pirates in charge of the
prize became drunken, and being at
last overcome with drowsiness lay
down and went to sleep. The rightful
possessors of the ship, in the storm
which almost immediately followed,
permitted the vessel to be driven
ashore on the back of Cape Cod near
Truro. The pirates escaped when the
vessel touched the sand, the attention

Whydah's bell. Recovered by shipwreck
diver Barry Clifford. Photo courtesy, Bill
Galvin, *Cape Cod Chronicle*.

of the ship's crew being entirely taken up with securing their own safety; but
they were soon afterward apprehended, tried, convicted and executed.

Bellamy's own vessel was driven ashore near the tableland on the outside of Wellfleet, on Cape Cod, a few miles from Truro, and broken to
pieces by the waves. The wind was so strong and the waves were so great and
powerful that the sea forced its way across the Cape, which was very narrow
at this place, creating a channel so large that a whale boat passed through it
at the time.

Great numbers of the pirates were drowned; Captain Southack, who
was sent by the government to the scene of the disaster for that purpose,
finding and burying one hundred and two bodies that had washed ashore.
Several of the pirates escaped, but whether their captain reached the shore
in safety, or was drowned, is not known to the writer. Six of them were
arrested and tried by a special court of admiralty, and being convicted were
executed on the gallows at Boston on the fifteenth of November following.

Among the pirates that escaped were an Indian and an Englishman.
The latter disguised himself and visited the place of the shipwreck from
time to time for the purpose of replenishing his purse with money from the

wreck. This was currently reported and believed by the residents of the neighborhood. Within a few years, pennies, bearing inscriptions which show that they were struck off in the reign of William and Mary, have been picked up there, and the celebrated Thoreau and William DeCosta of the *Charlestown Advertiser,* frequenters of those haunts years ago, found some on the bar at very low tide.

As late as 1814, almost a century after the wreck occurred, portions of the vessel were seen reposing on the white sand at the bottom of the still and clear waters.

Uncle Jack Newcomb, as he was familiarly called, an oysterman of Wellfleet years ago, told Thoreau that he had seen the iron caboose of the ship on the bar at an extreme low run of tides. About 1863, the wreck was again disclosed by the action of the sea.

A story has come down by tradition, being to some extent identical with that of the Englishman, which is told as follows: A man of peculiar aspect, who was supposed to have been one of the pirates, often visited the vicinity of the wreck, the residents generally believing that he at least knew of some place there where treasure was hid, and that he came hither for supplies as his necessities demanded. While there the hospitality of a private family was extended to and accepted by him. When the Bible was to be read aloud or prayer offered, he excused himself from being present, seeming to be greatly troubled. In the stillness of night he would talk in his sleep, and utter boisterous and profane speeches, as though quarreling or contending with some foe. After a while he spent much of his time there, and his last days were wholly devoted to walking meditatively on the beach, seeming to have but little interest in common with the people about him. Considerable gold was said to have been carried in a money belt, which was found upon his body after death.

Chapter xii.

THE AURORA BOREALIS IN 1719

The northern lights, as they are called, first attracted the attention of the people of New England in March, 1718, and there was a general fear that dire calamities would result therefrom. May 15, 1719, the more beautiful and brilliant aurora borealis was first observed here as far as any record or tradition of that period informs us, and it is said that in England it was

Aurora Borealis. Oil on canvas by Frederic Edwin Church. Smithsonian American Art Museum.

first noticed only three years before this date. In December of the same year the aurora again appeared, and the people became greatly alarmed, not dreading it so much as a means of destruction but as a precursor of the fires of the last great day and a sign of coming dangers. Just before eight o'clock in the evening of Saturday, the eleventh[1] of the month, the moon being within one or two days of the full, the aurora flamed up in the northern heavens with remarkable brilliancy, until that entire section of the firmament seemed to be on fire. Stephen Jaques of Newbury, Massachusetts, wrote in his journal at the time that a white " rainbow" appeared in the northern sky, reaching from the northwest to the northeast, and nearly straight in the middle, the curve being imperfect. It was apparently about eight feet wide, Jaques continues, and resembled a cloud. Then there appeared in the north very red clouds, which seemed to fly up almost to the zenith, as if driven by a swift wind. They then parted toward the east and vanished. The bow remained an hour or two, the people distinctly hearing the coruscation, which, in the language of a writer of that time, "rustled like a silken banner." Later, in the same evening, between ten and eleven o'clock, from the northwest came a cloud resembling a mist, through which the stars

1. Lewis, in his *History of Lynn, Massachusetts*, says that it occurred on the seventeenth.

could be seen, its color being deep crimson. The next year other luminous appearances in the evening sky occurred.

Though at first the people were fearful for the consequences of such sights, the feeling wore off as they became more frequent and it was found that they were without any apparent effect upon the world.

They have now become sights of curiosity merely to most people, who, while they cannot fully explain them, know that they portend no evil; though many have ever since those early times been more or less concerned when any strange cloud appears.

Dr. Edward A. Holyoke of Salem, Massachusetts, wrote the following in his diary under date of December 29, 1736: "The first aurora borealis I ever saw. The northern sky appeared suffused with a dark blood-red colored vapor, without any variety of different colored rays. I have never seen the like." The appearance of which he wrote was that which was supposed to have reference to the terrible throat distemper which carried off so many hundreds of children throughout New England at that period. Just before our war with Mexico occurred the red aurora appeared in its deepest color, and many that looked upon it still believe that it was a forerunner of the bloody conflict.

Chapter xiii.

THE STORM OF FEBRUARY 24, 1722–23

On Sunday, February 24, 1722–23, occurred a great storm, which brought in the tide so high that it has been rarely if ever equalled in New England. The wind was strong and from the northeast, which blowing at the time of a very high tide was probably the cause of this flood, which was at Dorchester, Massachusetts, only excelled by that of April, 1852. It was most severe in those parts where the coast lines ran north and south as on the Massachusetts and New Hampshire shores, though in Rhode Island several wharves were broken to pieces and carried away, cellars and warehouses inundated, and more damage done than had occurred from a similar cause for nineteen years. At Boston some hail accompanied the rain.

Cape Cod felt the storm very severely. On the southeast side, at Chatham, a fine harbor had some years before been made by a storm, banks of sand being thrown up as a protection. Over these ridges of sand, the wind now forced the waters, the marshes became overflowed, and a great many stacks of hay were lifted by the water from the staddles on which they stood, and floated away, much fodder for cattle being thus destroyed. A great many acres of marsh were damaged, and much of it ruined for future production of grass by being plowed and torn by the raging waters, or covered with sand from the beach.

On the inside of the Cape, the tide rose four feet, and outside, it was said, from ten to twelve feet higher than was ever known before. At Plymouth, it was from three to four feet above the highest watermarks then known there.

The *News-Letter* of that time said that the inundation in Boston "looked very dreadful." Damage had resulted from extremely high tides there in former years, but this one rose until it was twenty inches higher than any had been known to rise before. In the morning of the day of the storm the tide had risen even with the tops of the wharves, and slowly came above the timbers, but not anticipating a serious result, people went to the morning services in their several churches. While the preachers were dwelling on the sixteenthlies and seventeenthlies of their sermons the water came higher and higher above the wharves, flowing into the streets and cellars, and covering the floors of the lower rooms of the dwellings and warehouses along the more exposed streets of the town. Meanwhile the people in the churches—and most of the inhabitants attended church in those days—were listening to the words of their respective pastors, being wholly unconscious of the inundation and the great damage that was being done to many of their houses and to their furniture and provisions, and of the loss of goods in their stores and warehouses. A great deal of fault was justly found with people who knew of the condition of things because they did not give due notice of it to the owners of the property which was being injured or lost by the flood. In the middle of Union Street the water rose as far as the site of the house in which Mr. Hunt lived. It came two or three feet above Long Wharf, and flowed into the nearest streets to such a height that a boat could be sailed from the south battery to the more elevated part of King Street, as it was then called, and from thence to the hill on which the North Church stood. The loss and damage done in Boston was very great.

In the vicinity of Salem, the tide flowed back in places for several miles, and instances occurred in which people were compelled to seek safety in trees.

At Gloucester it was unusually high, and the storm was so violent that the wind and water forced the sand into the "cut," again filling it up.

At Hampton, New Hampshire, the storm caused the great waves of the full sea to break over its natural banks for miles together, and the ocean continued to pour its waters over them for several hours.

The tide was also very high at Piscataqua and Falmouth, doing much damage to wharves and to articles stored in cellars and warehouses.

Chapter xix.

EARTHQUAKE OF 1727

The greatest earthquake that New England has probably experienced since its settlement by the English occurred October 29, 1727. The people had suffered much in various ways through the summer and early autumn. A drought continued from the middle of June to the middle of September, the month of July and the first week in August being exceedingly hot. No rain fell in April after the first week, and but twice in May, only one or two slight showers occurring during the sultry, parching heat of the summer. The earth dried to a great depth, and many wells and springs, which had never failed before were now dry. There was much lightning and thunder, but very little rain. On the evening of August 1, at the close of a scorching day, the heavens burst out into a blaze of flame and a roar of thunder, the terrific display continuing for two or three hours. The flashes occurred so frequently that the sky was continually alight with them, and a writer of that time said it seemed "as if the heavens being on fire were dissolving and passing away with a great noise, and the earth also with its works was to be burned up."

After the drought was broken a violent northeast storm came on, doing much damage among the vessels along the coast, and the trees on shore. This occurred September 16. It caused a high tide which carried away about two hundred loads of hay from the marshes at Newbury, Massachusetts, and drove eight or nine vessels ashore at Salem and thirty-five at Marblehead.

After the lightning, thunder, and tempest the country was visited by a tremendous earthquake. October 24, 1727, the weather was very cold; three days later, snow fell, and on the 28th the temperature was still exceedingly low for the season. Sunday, the 28th, was fair and pleasant, and in the evening the moon shone brightly, the air was calm, and no noise disturbed the peacefulness of nature. People retired at their usual hour, and were fast asleep, when at twenty minutes before eleven o'clock a terrible noise followed by a roar and a rush suddenly woke them, and in about half a minute, before they had time to become conscious of what was taking place around them, there came a pounce as if gigantic cannons had rolled against each other from opposite directions. Latches leaped up and doors flew open, houses rocked and trembled as though they would collapse, timbers worked in and out of mortises, hearth-stones grated against each other, windows rattled, tops of chimneys pitched and tumbled down, cellar walls fell in, beds shook, pewter fell off shelves, lids of warming pans jumped up and fell back with a clang, and all movable things, especially in the upper rooms, tossed about.

Most people got up in a moment, and many of them ran out of doors in their night clothes, being so frightened that they knew not what to do. The earth shook so much that they could not stand, and were compelled to sit or recline on the ground.

People that were awake when the earthquake came said that a flash of light preceded it. It was seen as it passed the windows, and a blaze seemed to run along the ground, dogs that saw it giving a sudden bark as if frightened. Before they had time to consider the source or cause of the light a sound like a gentle murmur floated to them on the still evening air, followed by a slight ruffling wind. Then came a rumbling as of distant thunder, which approached nearer and nearer and grew louder and louder till it sounded as if innumerable heavy carriages were being rapidly driven over pavements, or like the roaring of a great furnace, but incomparably fiercer and more terrible, having a hollow sound as if it came from under the earth. Then the shock came suddenly and severely and the houses were felt to totter and reel with the trembling and heaving of the ground.

The noise and shake came from the northwest, and went in a southeasterly direction. The whole disturbance occurred within the space of two minutes of time.

The cattle ran bellowing about the fields, being thoroughly frightened at this sudden and fearful commotion in the still hours of night. They acted as though suffering from the greatest distress.

At eleven o'clock another shock came, less effective and quieter than the first, but heavy enough to keep the people in a state of fear. At a quarter before twelve another came, and many of the people would not return to their beds, but dressed, and prepared to stay up the remainder of the night, being very uncertain as to what might occur before morning came, and apprehending destruction. At Londonderry, New Hampshire, when the pastor of the town, Rev. Mr. MacGregor, became aware of what was occurring around him, his Scottish heart being full of sympathy for the people of his charge, he at once arose, dressed, and started out. He was met by someone with the reminder that his family would need his presence. "Oh!" said he, "I have a still greater family which I must care for." He hastened toward their houses, but had not gone far before he met large numbers of them flocking to his own dwelling, seeking advice and comfort in the trying and dreadful hour. At Salem, Massachusetts, the people sat up nearly all night; and at Rowley they flocked to the house of Rev. Edward Payson, the minister of the town, as if he were able to succor them from pending harm; but the house being too small to hold so large a number, the meeting house was opened at that midnight hour, and there the remainder of the night was spent in prayer and supplication. Rev. Benjamin Colman of Boston wrote the next day that he and his family arose, and did not retire until two o'clock in the morning, spending the time in humble cries to God for themselves and their neighbors and in fervent praises to him for their preservation.

The shocks were repeated at three and five o'clock, but with abated force, and in due time the sun slowly rose in the eastern sky, greeting with a complacent face the disconsolate and fearful inhabitants. It was a night never to be forgotten by those who experienced it.

In the towns along the Merrimack River the earthquake was felt more severely than in any other section of New England. A vast deal of stone wall was thrown down in addition to those injuries which occurred generally in New England. The geological formation that forms the bed of the river is of the primary order, which would naturally be affected more by an internal shock than if it were of a later origin.

An incident worthy of record occurred on the island of Newcastle, near Portsmouth, New Hampshire. At the hour of midnight, on the very quiet night of the earthquake, when the people were trembling with fear, the silvery voice of the bell of the old church there pealed forth from the belfry. This heightened the feelings of the people, and to the ignorant it seemed to be a knell rung forth by mystic hands. To the more phlegmatic citizens it was but the result of the shaking of the church by natural means; yet the surroundings, the time, and the dreadful commotion could not fail to impress them with a solemn dread.

At Cape Cod this shock was felt much more than that of 1638. At Dorchester, Massachusetts, the noise seemed to come from the Blue Mountains, which some people, who were out of doors when the shock came, supposed to have suddenly sunk. At Rowley, tops of many chimneys were thrown down; at Portsmouth, New Hampshire, several were cracked and others shattered, and the greater portion of Newbury, Massachusetts, suffered in the same manner. In the latter place the chimneys of Mr. Knight and Mr. Toppan are particularly mentioned as having fallen, and the door-stone of Benjamin Plummer fell into the cellar.

Brick houses were much cracked and in many places considerably shattered. But the principal damage consisted in the breaking of dishes and injuries to tops of chimneys, in many cases a few bricks only being knocked off, though in others the chimneys were so shaken as to make it necessary to rebuild them. Not a wooden house was broken nor a person or animal injured.

The islands off the coast were shaken as much as the mainland, and the water of the ocean was in a state of great commotion, its roar being much louder than usual. Mr. Carr, in his time a prominent boatbuilder of Nantucket, ran out of the house when the earthquake came, jumped into his boat, and rowed out on the boisterous waves, being afraid that the island would sink. Seamen who were upon the coast said that it seemed as if their vessels had suddenly struck upon a sand bar.

The earthquake had considerable effect upon the character of land, springs and wells. Some upland was changed into quagmire and in a few instances marsh land was raised up, being afterward too dry for its native grass to grow upon it. In the meadow near the house then owned and occupied by Samuel Bartlett at Newbury, Massachusetts, a new spring of water was opened. At Hampton, New Hampshire, a spring which had boiled over ever since it was first known, a period of eighty years, having never frozen, was so affected that the water failed to rise to the surface of the ground, and afterward froze in moderate weather. The water of some wells was improved in quality, while in others it was made permanently impure. Some became dry, and the temperature of several was greatly changed. There has been related an instance of a well thirty-six feet deep being affected by the earthquake. The water in it had always been very sweet and pure, but about three days before the shock the owner was surprised to find that it smelled so badly no use could be made of it; and that its odor so permeated the rooms into which it was brought that in a very few minutes' time it became unbearable. It was thought that some carrion had got into the well, but on a thorough examination it was found to be free from everything that was offensive, though the water was of a chalky color. It continued in this condition for seven days after the earthquake, and then commenced to change for the better, wholly resuming its original sweetness and appearance after the lapse of three more days.

Remembering that cities and other places had been swallowed by the action of earthquakes, some people in New England were alarmed lest they might be destined to such an end. There was indeed some foundation for such an idea, for chasms a foot or more in width were opened at some places, as at Newbury, Massachusetts, where there were more than ten in the low clay ground, fine white sand and ashes being forced up through them in varying quantities. In one place near Spring Island in that town were thrown up from sixteen to twenty loads of sand with some slight indications of sulphur. By throwing some of the sand on hot coals in a dark room blue sulphurous flames and a slight odor of brimstone were detected. In another place near the same island, about forty or fifty rods from the residence of Henry Sewall, the ground opened, and for several days water boiled out of the crevice like a spring. Within three weeks it became dry, and the earth closed.

The people of New England were affected by this earthquake as they had never been before, being fearful of divine judgments for their sins and lax responsiveness to the call to religious duties. The clergy taught them that it was "a loud call to the whole land to repent and fear and give glory to God." The next morning great numbers of the inhabitants of Boston gathered at the old North Church for prayer and other religious services. The fear of further immediate danger was somewhat dispelled in the pleasant sunlight, but as soon as the sun had set their fright returned, and in greater numbers than in the morning the people crowded to the old Brick Church, which could not hold them. The old South was then opened, and those who failed of admission to the Brick Church flocked thither, and that was also filled. Rev. Thomas Paine of Weymouth, Massachsetts, and some other ministers, tried to prove to their congregations that the earthquake had not a natural cause, but was a supernatural token of God's anger to the sinful world.

The selectmen of Medford, Massachusetts, appointed the next Wednesday as a day to be observed by fasting and prayer on account of the earthquake; and Lieutenant-governor Dummer recommended that Thursday should be kept in the same way for the same purpose throughout the province. Many sermons delivered on the latter and other days were printed and are still extant. In Salem, Massachusetts, a meeting was held on Saturday at the upper meeting house (then so called) which was attended by the largest congregation that was ever in that edifice.

The clergy improved the opportunity of leading the public mind toward the choice of a better portion than this earth can afford. The people were willing to be taught, and ready to believe, for the event they had just passed through convinced them of the uncertainty of temporal things, and a needed preparation for the life to come. Many who had before cared nothing for a religious life became penitent and devout. Seriousness was the expression on the faces of most of the people, and in some towns, large numbers were added to the church. In the parish of Chebacco in Ipswich, Massachusetts, for instance, seventy-six persons became church members. The earthquake had its effect upon some licentious characters, who became truly reformed, and afterward led honorable and moral lives. But, in too many cases, when their fears were gone, the religious thoughts and habits of the people lost their hold upon them.

Shocks of the earthquake continued at intervals through the following week, and from time to time during November and December, growing less and less in force. The great one was felt in New York and Pennsylvania, and it extended all along the coast to the Gulf of Mexico, doing considerable damage in the West India islands.

This, unlike the earthquake of 1755, was not preceded by great convulsions in other portions of the globe; and up to that time it was the severest one ever known in New England.

Chapter XV.

THE WINTER OF 1740–41

The summer of 1740 was cool and wet. An early frost injured much of the corn crop, and the long season of rain which followed hindered its ripening. One-third of it was cut when green, and the rest was so wet that it very soon molded. There was, therefore, very little seed corn in New England for the next spring's planting, and the amount of dry corn for the winter's consumption was also small. The rain of the summer and fall flooded the lowlands of the country everywhere.

The rivers of Salem, Massachusetts, were frozen over as early as October, and November 4th the weather became very cold. In that year the thirteenth of November was observed as Thanksgiving day. It was then

Ships in Ice off Ten Pound Island. Oil on canvas by Fitz Hugh Lane. Museum of Fine Arts, Boston.

severely cold, and all that day snow fell, continuing until the fifteenth, when in Essex County, Massachusetts, it measured a foot in depth.

The weather remained cold until about the twenty-second, when its rigor relaxed, and a thaw, accompanied by rain, came on. The rain continued to fall for nearly three weeks, during the day only, the stars shining brightly each evening, but the morning following, rain would be falling again as energetically as ever. The snow melted, and a freshet occurred in the Merrimack River, nothing like it having been experienced there for seventy years. At Haverhill, the stream rose fifteen feet, and many houses were floated off. In that part of Newbury, which was afterwards incorporated as West Newbury, was a piece of lowland at Turkey Hill, known as Rawson's Meadow, which was covered with water to the depth of twelve feet. In another part of Newbury between the mill and the residence of a Mr. Emery, a sloop could have sailed. The freshet carried away great quantities of wood, which was piled along the banks of the river, and from the shipyards located in that part of Newbury now included in the city of Newburyport considerable timber that was lying ready to be formed into vessels was also floated down the harbor, much of both wood and timber being lost. To save as much of it as possible, the dwellers on the shores of the river turned out, and for fourteen days worked from the banks and in boats, securing large piles which were scattered for miles on both sides of the river and the harbor. It was estimated that two thousand cords of wood were also saved at Plum Island.

The freshet was also very disastrous at Falmouth. On the twenty-first of the month the Rev. Thomas Smith of that town says, in his diary, that he rode to Saco, where he lodged with his father. He was there forced out of his lodgings "by vast quantities of ice, which jambed and raised the water eighteen inches higher" than his bedstead.

Plum Island River was frozen over on December twelfth, and remained so until the end of March. The Merrimack River was also closed by the extreme cold, which continued so severe that the ice very soon became thick enough to support teams, and before the end of the month the river became a great thoroughfare. Loaded sleds drawn by two, three or four yoke of oxen came from the towns up the river, and landed below the upper long wharf near where the ferry was then located in Newbury. From twenty to forty such teams passed down the river daily from Amesbury and Haverhill, and people travelled down the harbor as far as half-tide rock. On February 28, for the purpose of ascertaining the thickness of the ice in the Merrimack, Wells Chase cut a hole through it at Deer Island where the current ran swiftest and found it to measure thirty inches, although people had con- stantly sledded over it for two months. No one then living had ever heard of the river freezing so hard before.

As far south as New York, the harbors were so frozen that vessels could not come into them, and those already in were compelled to remain until a thaw should come to their release. The sea was also very much frozen, and people travelled out long distances. In Boston Harbor, a beaten road through the snow was kept open on the ice as far out as Castle William. Over this course horses and sleighs, and people on foot continually passed up and down, and on the way two tents for the sale of refreshments stood invitingly open. Loads of hay on sleds were drawn nearly straight from Spectacle Island to the town.

The ice formed so solidly around some mills that they could not be operated, as at Byfield parish in Newbury, where Pearson's mill was stopped from February 3 to March 31, and the people of Newbury had to go to Salisbury to get their meagre grists of corn ground.

The reign of cold seemed to be broken on January 10, when the weather moderated and a thaw began; but it continued only three days, and the low temperature was resumed.

Not only was the winter severe in temperature, but great snows came until, in the estimation of the people then living, taking it as a whole, it was the most rigorous season that had been experienced here since the first settlement. There were twenty-seven snow storms in all, most of them of good size. February 3, nearly a foot of snow fell, and about a week later there were two more storms, which filled the roads in Newbury, Massachusetts, and vicinity to the tops of the fences, and in some places the snow lay to the depth of from eight to ten feet. On April 4, the fences were still covered, and three days later another foot of snow fell. In the woods it was then four feet deep on the level; and there were drifts on the islands off Dorchester, Massachusetts, not quite melted on May 3. The snow remained so long that the spring was very backward; and when the ground was ready for planting, the farmers were almost discouraged, thinking of the failure of the corn crop the year before.

Chapter xvi.

THE EARTHQUAKE OF 1744

At a quarter past ten o'clock on Sunday morning, June 3, 1744, just after services at the churches had begun, there was a terrific earthquake, which reached about one hundred miles, being thought by some to have been nearly equal to that of 1727. During the preceding month there had been two slight shocks, both occurring in the morning. This shock was ushered by a loud rumbling noise, which put people in remembrance of the great earthquake of 1727, and great consternation was caused.

Many people, who were assembled in the churches at Boston for divine services, ran out into the streets, fearing the buildings would fall upon them. At Newbury, Massachusetts, in that part of the town which was afterward incorporated as Newburyport, the rector and many of the congregation ran out of the Episcopal Church. At the parish in Ipswich, Massachusetts, called the Hamlet, since incorporated as the town of Hamilton, the shock came while Rev. Mr. Wigglesworth, the pastor, was preaching, and the congregation was exceedingly alarmed; but he endeavored to calm them, remarking that, "There can be no better place for us to die in than the house of God."

In Boston and other towns, large numbers of bricks were shaken from the tops of chimneys; and much stone wall in several places in the country was tumbled down by it. It was felt severely at Falmouth, in Maine.

At about five o'clock in the afternoon, another and lesser shock was felt at Salem, Massachusetts, and adjacent towns, and the people, being surprised, screamed, and ran out of doors. Three or more smaller shocks were perceived that night and the next morning. On the twentieth of the month, another shock came, causing people to run out of meeting at Salem. Eight days later there was another. May, June and July were all dry months, but whether that fact had any connection with the earthquake, or not, we cannot tell.

During the two and three-fourths centuries of New England's history, there have been several hundred earthquakes, the great majority of them being but just noticeable, while a considerable number of them have resulted in damage. The people here have often expressed their satisfaction at living in a land free from the terrible convulsions that the warmer sections of the globe have experienced. But history shows us that we are not entirely exempt from the awful shakings and rumblings and dangers that are supposed to belong almost exclusively to other lands. Nearly every year the territory of New England is disturbed by these internal movements.

Chapter xvii.

THE WINTER OF 1747–48

The old people of to-day think that we do not have as severe winters as they had when they were in their youth, and they certainly have good reasons for such considerations. The winter of 1747–48 was one of the memorable winters that used to be talked about by our grandfathers when the snow whirled above deep drifts around their half-buried houses. There were about thirty snow storms, and they came storm after storm until the snow lay four or five feet deep on the level, making travelling exceedingly difficult. On the twenty-second of February, snow in the woods measured four and one-half feet; and on the twenty-ninth there was no getting about except on snow shoes.

There seems to have been more snow in Essex County, Massachusetts, than in other parts of New England, and it came there very early in the season. On December 14, it had become so deep, and the wind blew it so fiercely that John Bowles was smothered to death on the Neck at Salem.

There is an incident connected with this winter's weather which will fix it in the minds of readers. In the west parish of Newbury, on majestic Crane Neck Hill, lived a family by the name of Dole, their little son, but six years old, lay sick with a fever as the storms of December raged, and on the twenty-second of the month he died.

> Their kindred slept a mile or two away,
> The snow lay deep in drifts upon the ground,
> The roads unbroken no one could discern,
> 'Twas hill and vale of deep untrodden snow.
> 'Where should the little boy be laid to rest?'
> Was asked by anxious hearts. "He must lie there,
> Where generations gone beneath the sod
> Repose in peace, beneath the hallowed ground,"
> Was answered by the father.
>
> Across the fields
> And pastures, down through the vale they started
> The saddest Christmas morn they yet had known.
> They soon stopped, the horses wallowing deep
> Were fastened in the snow. Now on again
> They move, but in a moment more they stop,
> They start and stop, and start and stop again,
> And fail to gain upon their funeral way.
> Discouraged in his vain attempt to reach
> The sacred burial-place so far away,
> The father said, "We cannot further go;
> Let us bury our dead here where we are,"
> And there beneath the deep snow they laid him
> Alone upon the valley's broad expanse,
> Then turned their faces back to their lone home,
> From which the light had gone, no more to shine
> At least on earth.
>
> Around the little grave
> Others laid their dead, till in that lowland

Scores lay buried. To-day it is a place
Where antiquarians love to wander;
And hunting round for the oldest gravestone
They find this one of Micah Dole's, whose date
Is seventeen hundred forty-seven,
And looking farther down they read that he
Was first of all to lie upon that lea.

Chapter xviii.

THE HURRICANE AT PEPPERELL, MASSACHUSETTS, IN 1748

On Thursday, July 28, 1748, occurred a disastrous hurricane at Pepperell, Massachusetts. The people of the parish had finished eating their dinner, and were going to their work in the hay fields, it being about one o'clock, when the sound of thunder was heard. It came nearer and grew louder until it was deafening, and the wind came rushing across the fields and through the woods, increasing in force until it seemed to be irresistible, and developing a rotary motion. Its course was from the southwest to the northeast, though it slightly varied, blowing sometimes to the right and again to the left. It continued for fifteen minutes with such terrific power that the air was filled with hay, leaves, limbs of trees and pieces of lumber. The wind swept through the centre of the parish, not abating its force until it reached the New Hampshire line, a short distance away.

In the track of the hurricane much damage was done. Fences and stone walls were blown down, and the stalks of Indian corn were bent over and broken off near the ground. Hay in the fields was suddenly whisked up, and scattered over adjoining territory for a mile away, being lost. As the wind increased in force many large apple and other kinds of trees were torn up by the roots; in some instances enclosing animals in such a manner that they could not get away by their efforts alone, though they were not injured. A large portion of the roof of the church, and boards from the roofs and sides of several other buildings were carried away. Several dwelling houses were shattered, and two or three buildings were entirely destroyed. In the space covered by the wind was a house, with a wing which was garrisoned. The whirlwind swept down upon the garrison with such violence that it was instantly demolished, three of its sides falling to the ground, and the other being dashed against the main part of the house, the roof of which had been carried away. Some things that had been in the chamber of the house were found more than a mile distant. A woman and her three small children were in the body of the house at the time, and when the power of the wind became manifest, the woman took the children to flee to another building which stood near, in which she thought they would be safer. But before they could get out the garrison had fallen against the door, through which they had intended to pass out, and they were compelled to remain where they were, expecting every moment that the rest of the house would be demolished, and they be killed and buried beneath falling debris. With the exception of the roof, however, the house remained intact, and the inmates escaped injury. After the wind had spent its force the woman looked out, and saw that where the building to which she had intended to go for safety had stood only the underpinning remained to mark the spot; so thorough had been the work of its demolition that not even the sills were in their places. She felt grateful for the providence that had frustrated her plans by barring the door through which she had thought to escape, as otherwise she would probably have been killed and her children also.

Though much property was destroyed, one man losing corn, hay, fences, apple trees and buildings, in all amounting to more than five hundred pounds in value, no life of man or beast was taken, nor was anyone seriously injured.

Chapter six.

THE DROUGHT OF 1749

The spring of 1749 was uncommonly dry, and by the end of May pastures yielded but little feed for the cattle, the grass being so scorched and burned by the sun that the ground looked white, and shortly afterward several pastures in Dorchester, Massachusetts, and vicinity took fire and burned over like tinder. As the season advanced there was less and less for the cattle to live upon; after eating the dried up grass till they could get no more, they suffered greatly for the want of food, a writer of that time alleging that they strongly appealed to their owners for relief by the expression on their faces. Water was also scarce, for the drought had its effect on the brooks and springs, and even some small rivers were dried up. Many wells that had never been known to fail before now became dry, and the water was so shallow and so warm that many fish died in streams and ponds. The earth

was as the finest dust to a considerable depth, and in many places the
ground cracked open. The heat was so severe and everything so intensely
dry, that where fragments of broken glass lay on the ground the combustible
material lying near it caught on fire.

The grain was shrunken and sapless, and Indian corn rolled up and
became badly wilted. There were also great quantities of caterpillars and
similar insects throughout New England, which was another source of
destruction. The drought probably continued longer, and therefore was felt
more severely than any one the people had before experienced.

It seemed as if rain was hardly sufficient to revive vegetation which was
so thoroughly parched and lifeless; and the only ray of hope was in the coming of immediate showers. Consequently the government here ordered that
June 9 be a day of public fasting and prayer on account of the drought.
About three weeks later the weather changed, and rain began to fall, at first
only a very little at a time, but by the sixth of July there were plenteous
showers, which greatly changed the face of nature. The grass sprang up, and
the season took on the appearance of spring. The Indian corn also revived,
and a good crop was harvested. The fields yielded a considerable second
growth of grass, but not more than one-tenth of an ordinary crop of hay was
cut. The salt marsh failed as much as the fresh meadow, though it had the
benefit of tide water. The fields of barley and oats yielded but little more
than sufficient grain for seed with which to plant them again the next season; and many farmers cut their grain for fodder while it was green. Flax
and herbs of all kinds were also a failure. August 14 was appointed by the
government as a day of public thanksgiving for the rain and its consequent
good.

Rather than go to the great expense of keeping all their cattle through
the winter, the farmers killed many of them in the autumn. This made meat
very cheap at that season, but there were so few animals left, butter sold in
the spring as high as seven shillings sixpence per pound, and in the following May beef and mutton were also very dear.

Only a small number of cattle died during the winter for want of sustenance, for some of the farmers purchased hay which was imported from
Pennsylvania and England, paying for it as high as three pounds ten
shillings per hundredweight. The practice of browsing cattle in the woods
also greatly helped out their maintenance. The people were carried comfortably through the winter, suffering but little for the lack of many things
that they had been accustomed to have in plenty.

Chapter xx.

THE GREAT EARTHQUAKE OF 1755

On November 1, 1755, the city of Lisbon, in Portugal, with its convents, fine churches and royal palaces, was almost totally destroyed by a terrible earthquake, sixty thousand persons being killed by the falling buildings.

Seventeen days later, at a quarter past four o'clock in the morning of Tuesday, November 18, occurred the most destructive and awful earthquake that was ever known in New England. The heavens were clear, the air calm, a Sabbath-like stillness pervaded the region, and at the time of the shock the moon shone brightly, being about two hours high. It was a beautiful night, and nothing uncommon occurred except that the ocean was roaring along its shores louder than usual. The earthquakes in New England have come without announcement as this one did, in all seasons of the year, in all kinds of weather, and at all hours of the day and night.

Earthquakes are of two kinds: one begins with a gentle oscillation, the other comes suddenly, and in a moment templed cities are leveled with the plain. The earthquake of 1727 was of the first kind, while this one was of the latter. It came suddenly like gigantic pulsations of the earth and tossed everything about. This was followed for about a minute's duration with a peculiar tremulous motion of the earth, which some people thought was the resultant motion of the first shock and the gradual lessening of its force. But it was followed instantly by a quick vibration and several jerks, much more terrible than the first had been. Dr. Edward A. Holyoke, of Salem, Massachusetts, wrote in his diary that he "thought of nothing less than being buried instantly in the ruins of the house." It continued longer than that of 1727, occupying from two and a half to three minutes. Its direction was supposed to be from northwest to southeast.

People were in a state of extreme fright, thinking that the earth was in process of dissolution, and a writer of that time said, "I walked out about sunrise, and every face looked ghastly. In fine, some of our solid and pious gentlemen had such an awe and gloom spread over their countenances as would have checked the gay airs of the most intrepid." It is said that in those regions where earthquakes are very common and to be expected, the people are terrorized by them, no familiarity with them removing the awful feeling. No danger or alarm so disturbs a person, and no thought is so terrible

Night Earthquake. Undated woodcut. American Antiquarian Society.

as that of the earth crumbling to pieces beneath our feet. "What is safe,"
exclaimed the wise Seneca, "if the solid earth itself cannot be relied upon?"
This feeling disturbed the people of New England more than it would the
inhabitants of tropical regions. Animals were also alarmed at the mysteri-
ous and awful motions of the ground, and the oxen and cows lowed and hastened to the barns, the only source of protection that they knew, or ran
about the fields when no place of refuge offered. Dogs went to their masters' doors and howled, not knowing what else to do; and birds left their
perches, and flew into the air, fluttering there a long time, afraid to again
alight on the earth. The ocean along the coast was affected as perceptibly as
the land, and ships in the harbor at Portsmouth, New Hampshire, were
shaken so fiercely that the sailors who were asleep in their berths were
rudely awakened, their first thought being that they had struck upon a rock.
The river there was also in a similar state of agitation.

At New Haven, Connecticut, the ground moved with an undulating
motion like the waves of the sea; and the houses shook and cracked as if
about to fall. Mather Byles said, "It was a terrible night, the most so, perhaps, that ever New England saw."

The damage done by this earthquake was far greater than that caused by
any other that has been experienced here. The vibratory motion of the earth
was so great and sudden that pewter dishes were thrown from the dressers,
many clocks were stopped, and the vane-rod on Faneuil Hall in Boston,
and those on some of the churches, were bent. Much stone wall throughout

the country was thrown down, and the shaking of the earth caused a change in the subterranean streams, in consequence of which many wells dried up. The principal damage consisted of the destruction of chimneys, no portion of New England being free from it. In Boston, alone, about one hundred were leveled with the roofs of the houses, and in all about fifteen hundred were shattered and partly thrown down, the streets in some places being almost covered with the fallen bricks. The chimneys were dislocated in all sorts of ways, some being broken several feet from the top, and partly turned as though there had been a swivel at the place. Others fell on the roofs, the sections broken off remaining intact, and having slipped down to the eaves jutted over, being just ready to fall. The roofs of some of the houses were broken in by the chimneys. The wooden buildings were much damaged by being racked, and many in Boston were thrown down. Brick buildings were injured most; and in Boston the gable ends of twelve or fifteen were knocked down to the eaves. In spite of the great danger and many narrow escapes, no person or animal was killed or seriously injured.

In the valley of the Merrimack River, this earthquake was not quite as severe as that of 1727; its noise was not as loud, and it did less damage. The towns along the sea-shore felt it most, and it gradually lessened in force as it progressed inland. It was felt from Nova Scotia to South Carolina, and in adjoining territories inland for a great distance, the great American lakes feeling it severely as shown by the agitation of their waters. Traces of it still exist in some places after the lapse of more than a century and a third.

About an hour after the first shock of the earthquake, as day broke in the eastern sky, the ground again shook, but with abated force. For four days slight shocks occurred daily, and on Saturday evening the twenty-second of the month, many persons were again alarmed with what proved to be a slight shock only. Again, after the people had retired for the night on the evening of December 19, there were two or three more shocks. Dull and calm weather, with a heavy atmosphere, succeeded the severe shaking of the earth.

Religious services and fasts were held immediately after the first and greatest shock and appeals to God for preservation were made, the people being in a state of almost frenzied excitement. It is impossible to realize the perturbed state of the human mind. In Boston, a meeting was held at eleven o'clock on the same morning, and Rev. Dr. Sewall preached from the text: "Lest coming suddenly he find you sleeping."[1] The next day was kept there as a fast. December 24, Lieutenant-governor Phips ordered a fast, saying

---

1. Mark xiii:36.

in his proclamation therefor that, "It having pleased Almighty God, in a most awful and surprising manner to manifest his righteous anger against the provoking sins of men by terrible and destructive earthquakes and inundations in divers parts of Europe and by a late severe shock of an earthquake on this continent and in this province in particular, which has been succeeded by several others, although less violent than the first." The pastors of Gloucester, Massachusetts, kept a fast on account of the earthquake January 1, 1756, preaching forenoon and afternoon. Educated and ignorant people alike were greatly frightened; and it is said that Rev. Mr. Richardson, then minister at Wells, Maine, died from fear at this time.

The prospect of death turned the minds of the people toward those things that cannot be shaken, and the clergymen improved the opportunity to make a religious impression upon them. Many were led to reflect on the lives they had led, and to seek reconciliation with their Maker, the church membership being considerably increased.

Chapter xxi.

HURRICANE AT LEICESTER, MASSACHUSETTS, IN 1759

At Leicester, Massachusetts, in 1759, occurred a terrific hurricane, which passed over the westerly part of the town, its direction being from southwest to northeast. It seemed to make a dash toward the earth at the farm then belonging to Samuel Lynde, situated on the north side of what was then called the great post-road, and then rose from the earth higher and higher, until it was no longer perceptible. Its movement resembled a mammoth scoop or the swoop of a hawk, which makes a sudden and powerful evolution to snatch up some prey, and then as suddenly and quickly ascends.

The buildings on the farm of Mr. Lynde consisted of a house, barn and corn barn, and the wind struck them all. In the house at the time were ten or twelve persons, and both building and people were removed to a considerable distance, the house being torn into fragments. It was said that some of the nails with which the boards had been fastened were found driven into trees by the wind so firmly that they could not be withdrawn without a hammer. The people in the house suffered various experiences. One of them, a Negro man, who was standing at the door when the wind came, was carried nearly ten rods and dashed upon the ground with such violence that he was killed, several of his ribs being broken. A little girl was standing at the door by the Negro's side. She was carried forty rods, and had one of her arms broken. Four women were found in the cellar, having been very much bruised, but they did not know how they came there. A little boy was rescued from under a mass of broken timbers and fragments of boards. The rest of the people escaped probably, as history does not mention them. In a spot whose distance from the scene of the disaster was more than a mile was found a watch that was hanging in the house when the hurricane came upon it; and other articles were found in the town of Holden, ten miles away. The barn and corn-barn which stood near the house were also entirely demolished, and a horse that was in the barn was killed. Near the buildings was a pile of boards, measuring seven thousand feet, which were taken into the air, where most of them were reduced to kindling wood. The trees and fences standing in the track of the wind were leveled, and all the wooden structures belonging to this farm were entirely blotted out, while the rest of the neighborhood remained unharmed.

Chapter xxii.

THE DROUGHT OF 1762

In eastern Massachusetts, there was a distressing drought in the summer of 1762. There was scarcely any rain from April 9 to August 18, and in some places, as at Danvers, until September 22. The month of April was cold, and the season was accordingly late. There was a slight drizzling rain at Boston May 7, but the next did not come till June 3. It was also showery there June 18. Nearly all the wells became drained, and grass was dried up, all sorts of vegetation being scorched by the burning rays of the sun. Everything appeared to have been burned. On the seventh of July a fast was held at Falmouth, in Maine, on account of the drought, but the services were scantily attended, as the men were busy in putting out the numerous fires that prevailed all through the locality, because of the dryness of the earth and vegetation. On the same day, and also on the thirteenth of the month, fasts and prayer-meetings were held in the towns around Milton, and the fifteenth was observed as a day of fasting and prayer in that town, the public meeting taking place at Rev. Mr. Robbins' church. On the twenty-fourth, there was a shower with terrific thunder and lightning at Dorchester, but it was confined to a very limited territory; and it was thought that more water fell at this time than had descended since the first of April. On the twenty-eighth, the people, being fearful that a famine would ensue, kept a public fast at Boston, Newbury and Falmouth, and probably at other places, to beseech God to avert the dreadful evil. But the earth became dryer daily, and vegetation seemed to die. Fires continued to break out in the woods, some of them burning over extensive territory. By the first of August it was thought that the crops would be an utter failure. The heavens continued to withhold their rain, the parched earth became more parched, and still there were no refreshing showers, except at and around Falmouth, in Maine, where bounteous rain had gladdened the earth on July 30 and August 13 and 16. August 18, rain descended in great quantities throughout the country. From that time forth there was no reason for complaint on account of lack of rain, except in a few small localities that had not received their full share of the supply.

Crops were very light, hay being so scarce the next winter that it was sold for four times its ordinary price. The farmers could not afford to keep their cattle until spring, and for this reason they slaughtered many of the animals, consuming the meat with the meagre supply of bread, which the failure of the corn crop yielded them, some of the people being reduced to suffering for want of meal.

Chapter xxiii.

SHOWERS WITH THUNDER AND LIGHTNING IN 1768

Cotton Mather thought that New England suffered as much as any other portion of the world from lightning, or, as he termed it, thunder, it being in his day generally supposed that thunder and not lightning caused the damage. Lightning had struck buildings, trees, animals and people from the time of the earliest settlement, but it does not appear to have caused very much damage in any one season until 1768. The scattered buildings and people had but slight chance of being injured by lightning on account of their small number and wide separation.

The summer of 1768 is particularly noticeable on account of the very large number of showers accompanied with thunder and lightning, although they did not commence until the month of August. On the morning of the first day, which was Monday, during a shower the lightning destroyed a num-

Rising of a Thunderstorm at Sea. Oil on canvas by Washington Allston. Museum of Fine Arts, Boston.

ber of trees in the towns around Boston; in the afternoon another shower came up, during which the lightning struck the residence of the then well-known victualler, Mr. Shirley, at Roxbury. The lightning struck one end of the house in the gable, and entered it through a window which was destroyed together with its frame. The house of Dr. Sprague on Winter Street in Boston was also struck on the chimney down the outside of which the lightning came and entered a closet in one of the chambers where were some curtain rods which it was thought conducted the electricity to a clock directly under them in the room below. In the closet was a considerable amount of china, which was not injured, with the exception of a small saucer that was broken. A black smooch was left on some of the plates, which probably marked the track of the lightning. The clock case was knocked about the room in fragments, and the works were thrown on a couch uninjured. A large glass which covered some wax-work was also broken; and the partitions and doors of the house were much injured, the lightning evidently passing down into the bottom of the cellar. Another house in Boston, the residence of Mr. Davis, a barber, situated on Water Street, was also struck on the top of the chimney; the electric fluid came down its side, knocking out some of the tiles, and entering a closet, where were some curtain rods, tore it to pieces. The boards and also some articles of clothing which were hanging in the closet were thrown into the room. The lightning then entered another closet, where it partly melted some weights made of lead, and also the heads of several nails from which the boards had been torn, and then departed by way of the cellar. In a chamber in the house two children were stunned by the shock, but soon regained consciousness. Another house struck in Boston was that of Mr. Bacon, a carpenter residing on Temple Street. Here the lightning came down the chimney, broke one of the tiles in the hearth of the lower room, where it melted a pewter plate and broke the glass in a picture-frame and in one of the windows. No one was injured, and the damage was slight. On the same afternoon, in Hartford, Connecticut, the rain fell in torrents, and the vivid lightning struck a tree in the west part of the town under which were two cows belonging to Caleb Bull, which were instantly killed. A barn in Norwalk, Connecticut, owned by the widow Benedict was also struck, being set on fire and wholly consumed with the hay and grain which were in it. This shower was very slight in Salem, Massachusetts, but the people there were greatly interested in the grandeur of the movements and aspects of the forces contending together in the clouds toward Boston, and one of the citizens was led to pen the following lines, which were published in the *Essex Gazette* a few days later.

> *Hark!*
> *What grumbling Noise comes thro' the yielding Air!*
> *Is it the Cannon's Roar! The Din of War?*
> *No!—'Tis the Voice of God; he Thunder rolls,*
> *And flashes Lightnings to the distant Polls.*
>
> *The Clouds impregnate with electric Ire,*
> *Join and disjoin, and fold the Skies in Fire:*
> *At which the Thunders burst with dreadful Roar,*
> *Sweep through the Skies, and grumble on the Shore!*
>
> *But still the Sound augments: while through the Air*
> *Surprising Lightnings gleam with frightful Glare!*
>
> *See!—from the West the gloomy Tempest rise:*
> *Successive Flashes fire the burning Skies!—*
>
> *Such is the Noise, and such the Lightnings shine.*
> *They both proclaim the Author is DIVINE!—*

Are such his Terrors, when his kind Command
Bids pregnant Clouds water the thirsty Land!
What firy Vengeance will he then display,
In that great, awful and consummate Day;
When down the Skies to Judgment he descends;
To crush his Foes; and to reward his Friends!
When round his shining Throne (no more of Grace)
Shall stand a numerous Hoft, the human Race!
Angels and Devils! When the sov'reign Lord
Shall judge the whole, and give a just Reward!—

Amazing Thought!

On Wednesday evening, September 7, at Wrentham, Massachusetts, a shower occurred in which lightning tore a large oak tree to pieces. Some of the large sections were thrown from three to four rods, and a few of the pieces were carried more than ten rods. Only the trunk remained standing, and the top of that was completely broomed.

On the next evening, at about eight o'clock, during another shower, lightning struck the tavern of Daniel Mann. At the time, a number of ladies and gentlemen were sitting around the tea table, the room being lighted by a candle, and a flash of lightning came into the room, being followed by an explosion, apparently as loud as the discharge of a cannon. Large sparks were seen, and the air in the room smelled as if impregnated with sulphur. The explosion having extinguished the candle, another was obtained, and the premises examined. A pane of glass in one of the windows was found to be broken, and a large clock in one corner of the room was much injured, a steel spring that held the pendulum being melted. The ceiling and doors of the room were much damaged; and two of the floor boards were raised and split. A gentleman, who was sitting near the clock felt a violent shock on the top of his head, and the coat of another was scorched on the right shoulder. The last named man suffered some pain in the same shoulder, but he was the only one of the twenty-seven persons in the house that was injured. Some damage was also done in other parts of the house, and all the inmates were filled with terror. A man, upon coming into the room, was so affected by the sulphurous air that his head ached for some time. A tree near the house was also struck. A boy at Rehoboth, Massachusetts, ten years old, was instantly killed by lightning in the same shower. At Mendon, Massachusetts, it was very severe, and great quantities of rain fell, continuing from eight o'clock in the evening until four the next morning, with but brief intervals of relaxation. At about one o'clock, the barn of Dr. William Jennison was struck and set on fire by lightning, and in a few minutes it was consumed with the contents, being full at this harvest season with hay, flax and grain. The house of Joseph Reed of Uxbridge, Massachusetts, was also struck, the lightning coming down the chimney. The hearth and part of the floor were torn up, and Mr. Reed with several members of his family, who were standing near the fireplace were temporarily stunned. This shower was not as local as thunder showers generally are, but it extended over a large territory, and the lightning was sharper and more frequent and disastrous than it was remembered to have been before in many parts of the region.

As late as the afternoon of Wednesday, November 2, there was very heavy thunder at Boston. At Charlestown, the bakehouse of Thomas Rayner was struck by lightning, and considerably damaged on the roof, one side of it being torn to pieces. A lad at the bolting mill was knocked down, but soon recovered, the bolting cloth was burned and the mill broken.

Chapter xxix.

THE GALE OF DECEMBER 4, 1768

On Sunday, December 4, 1768, occurred a southeast rain storm, accompanied by a violent gale. The day before nine West-Indiamen sailed out of the port of New London, Connecticut. The gale came on fresh the next morning and one of them put back, but as far as the writer has learned the others sailed into the face of the wind and braved it through away from the coast.

At New Haven, Connecticut, the storm came on in the evening, and the wind blew terrifically till twelve o'clock. Four or five vessels at Long Wharf parted their cables, and two of them were driven ashore, but were got off without much trouble when it was high tide.

At Guilford, a ship commanded by Captain Landon, which had arrived but a short time before from Liverpool, went ashore, having parted its cables.

As far as we have learned, there were no vessels driven on the bars off the coast of Cape Cod during the gale.

On the night of the storm a brigantine belonging to the port of Boston, Thomas Morton, master, being inward bound from the West Indies, was driven on the rocks near the lighthouse in Boston Harbor, and instantly dashed to pieces. The cargo consisted of sugar and molasses, and was large and valuable. Everything was lost, including several hundred dollars in money which was in the captain's chest. The people on board were saved with much difficulty, some of them being severely bruised.

Another vessel of the same build and rig, Thomas Thomas, master, bound from the West Indies to Newburyport, with a cargo of molasses, was cast away near Cape Ann, and both vessel and cargo were entirely lost. The crew were saved, with the exception of the mate, who was drowned.

A coaster commanded by Captain Patterson had been sailed for several years between Boston and the Kennebec River, and on Thursday, three days before the storm, sailed from the last named place, having on board a number of passengers belonging to Pownalborough, Maine, who had been up the Kennebec to procure the winter's supply of provisions for their families, and were now returning with their purchases. They were Capt. Thomas Allen, Ralph Chapman, John Barker, Mr. Perry, John Pierce, Mr. Hersey, Mrs. Jonas Fitch and Mrs. Stilfin, a Dutch woman. The crew consisted of Captain Patterson, Mr. Rogers, Mr. Kinney and a Negro man belonging to the captain. In the darkness of the night and the terrific gale, they were cast away before they had reached Pownalborough, and the vessel with its freight and every person on board were lost. Mr. Chapman left a widow and seven children, and Mrs. Fitch five children. Only a few things of any value washed ashore, among them being several chests that were dashed to pieces before they could be secured, except the captain's which was strapped with iron.

At Fox Island, situated farther down on the Maine coast, was soon afterward discovered the wreck of a vessel, apparently of about one hundred tons burden, which was probably cast ashore in this storm. There were found several sections of the vessel, some wearing apparel, a feather bed, a Holland shirt marked with the letters "T. P.," and some other articles which had washed ashore.

Other vessels, according to the newspaper reports of that time, were said to have been wrecked in that vicinity. How many vessels and lives were lost in this storm will never be known; and when we think of the great number of vessels that have gone down in the tempest and the darkness and for a century have been lying so unconcernedly at the bottom of the sea or buried in the sand off the beaches we entertain a thought similar to that of Hiram Rich:

> O fleet that silent tarries
> Along our listening land,
> No night to come dismays thee,
> No bar and tempest strand.

Chapter XXV.

THE SUMMER OF 1769

The summer of 1769 opened with hot weather, the thermometer at Salem, Massachusetts, May 10, registering eighty-four and a half degrees above zero out of doors in the shade. The next day it rapidly grew colder, and in the evening there came on a snow storm, which continued twelve hours, the snow falling to the depth of six inches. For several succeeding weeks the weather continued cloudy, closing abruptly with a severe frost on June 2. The next day was very fair and pleasant, especially at Boston, and afforded a fine opportunity for viewing the rare transit of Venus which then occurred. The next day it was extremely hot again, and toward the end of the month near Boston the thermometer in open air and deep shade at three o'clock in the afternoon showed the temperature to be ninety-nine and one-half degrees above zero, which was three degrees higher than the same glass had ever indicated before at that place, though it had been in use for several years. That was the hottest day that had been known for a long period.

A week later, on the afternoon and evening of Wednesday, July 5, at Northampton, Massachusetts, occurred the severest shower of rain with thunder and lightning that had visited that place for a long period. For several hours it rained so hard that the meadows were covered with water to the depth of from three to four feet. A great deal of hay was carried off by the flood. The lightning also did some damage. It struck the chimney of the residence of Deacon Hunt, and ran down to the lower floor, where two of his children, one about fourteen and the other about seven years old, were standing. Both of them were instantly killed, but the house was only slightly damaged.

At about six minutes before seven o'clock on the evening of July 13 there was a slight earthquake, and on the evening of the nineteenth the northern lights were very beautiful, being more extensive and brighter than usual.

On Monday forenoon, July 31, there was a terrible shower of hail and rain, with thunder and lightning, which extended over a wide territory in Massachusetts, Rhode Island and Connecticut. The hail was of large size, and in some parts of Scituate, Massachusetts, it lay on the ground for thirty hours, being the next day at noon nearly a foot deep in several places. It broke nearly all the windows that were exposed to the wind, and did much damage to fruit orchards, grass, tobacco, corn, rye, etc., one man in West Greenwich, Rhode Island, having twenty acres of Indian corn totally destroyed. At Newport, Rhode Island, the hail-stones were said to have been as large as musket balls, at West Greenwich, the size of pullets' eggs; and some of those that fell at Scituate, Massachusetts, as large as goose eggs. The shower evidently began in the neighborhood of Danvers, Massachusetts, and proceeded in a southerly direction. At that place, the lightning struck a tree, and killed an ox and a cow that were standing near it; and in another part of the town a child was knocked down, but was not much injured. Proceeding to Charlestown, the lightning struck and slightly damaged three houses, one of which belonged to Richard Cary, Esq. The kitchen chimney was struck, and the electric fluid came down into the kitchen, knocking a Negro woman from the hearth to the middle of the room where she found herself when her senses returned a short time afterward. The lightning divided and took different courses through several rooms, proceeding upward and going out at a chamber window. In Boston, the kitchen chimney of the house of Capt. Job Prince at the west end of the town was struck by the lightning, which came down as far as the cross bar, and exploded, knocking a Negro woman down. She remained senseless for half an hour and then recovered. Two vessels lying at Hancock's Wharf were struck, each of them having a mast so split that it had to be replaced by a new one. Three men at work in the hold of one of the vessels were stunned, and it was some time before they recovered. The shower next proceeded in a southwest direction to the parish of Brookline, where the hail shattered many windows, among them those in the house of Rev. Mr. Whitney. At Wrentham, sixteen sheep were killed by the lightning. The shower then took a course nearly east, and was next heard from at Scituate, where much damage was done by the hail. The shower was about three-fourths of a mile wide as it passed over the town, in a southerly direction. At Abington, a barn was struck and burned together with a quantity of hay. At Middleboro, eight trees within eighty rods of each other were struck. The shower then continued in a southwesterly direction, and we hear no more from it until it had crossed the line into Rhode Island, at Middletown, where the lightning killed a cow. The shower reached Newport just before ten o'clock, having travelled very fast through Massachusetts. Here, much damage was done by the hail. At Jamestown, a stack of hay was burned, having been set on fire by the lightning. The force of the shower seemed now to be nearly spent, and it wandered away in a northwesterly direction to West Greenwich. Early in the afternoon it crossed the Connecticut line, and was last heard from at Windham, where the lightning struck three horses, which were under a tree, one of them being killed. The electric current ran about four rods from the foot of the tree, and entered a house under a door, which was shut. All the damage it did was to burn the foot of a young woman, and also of a lad.

Another shower occurred on Sunday evening, August 6, at Taunton, Massachusetts, when the lightning struck the house of Ebenezer Dean, whom it killed. At Norton, four sheep were killed, and at Assonet, a man was killed in his house. His wife was milking a cow by the door, and both the cow and herself were considerably stunned by the same shock.

At Hartford, Connecticut, at about two o'clock in the afternoon of Tuesday, August 15, a very heavy shower came up, and the rain poured down in torrents, being attended with heavy and loud claps of thunder. During the shower the residence of Jacob Seymour was struck by lightning, but no person was hurt. The rain continued to pour for several hours, and low lands were flooded to such an extent that it was estimated that more than a hundred tons of hay were swept off by the water. An interesting and well-attested incident of this shower was that of finding in the street after it was over great numbers of living animals, two or three inches in length, resembling fish, but not like any variety known in that part of the country. The street had been dry and hard before the shower, and these little fish must have descended in the rain, but from what section they came, we believe, has never been learned. During the same shower a barn in Simsbury belonging to a Mr. Cass was struck by lightning, set on fire, and totally destroyed with its contents.

During this summer the barn of Samuel Plummer, situated in that part of Rowley which has since been incorporated as the town of Georgetown, was set on fire by lightning, and with its contents was wholly consumed.

In August and September, the appearance of a comet contrary to the calculations of astronomers troubled the people to some extent, and the newspapers of that time contained many articles relating to it.

On September 8, occurred a violent northeast rain-storm, which caused several vessels to be driven ashore in Massachusetts Bay.

Chapter xxvi.

THE GREAT FRESHET OF 1770

At about one o'clock in the morning of Sunday, January 7, 1770, commenced a rain storm, with the wind blowing from the southeast, which caused the greatest freshet perhaps that ever occurred in New England. The weather had been very cold and dry through the month of December, and ice had formed extremely thick and strong. The storm continued with violence all through Sunday and until the next day at noon, when the clouds rolled away, and the sun again appeared. A very high tide occurred at this time and the combination of storm, wind and tide produced a freshet which caused the water to rise in many places ten feet higher than usual, and to remain at that height for several days.

For fifteen years the Connecticut River had not risen so high. The ice was quickly broken up, and the stream overflowed its banks one-half of a mile on either side, doing great damage in many ways. At Hartford, the river was impassable for several days. In the Tunxis, or Farmington River, which flows into the Connecticut, the torrent was much swollen and very rapid. At Simsbury, the buildings at the iron works of Richard Smith were carried away, and the whole plant was entirely destroyed.

On the Androscoggin and Kennebec rivers the freshet was greatest and most injurious; at Bowdoinham the tide rose from thirty to forty, and some placed it as high as fifty feet above its usual height. On Monday evening, the river had not perceptibly risen, and people were passing back and forth on skates and with horses, the ice appearing solid and strong, and as smooth and clear as glass. At about eight o'clock the spectators heard an uncommonly heavy rumbling sound, which slowly increased in loudness till shortly after eleven o'clock, when it quickly became louder and heavier, until, in the opinion of the people who heard it, it resembled the sudden approach of an earthquake, or the roar of the ocean in a storm, beating its mighty billows against a bold and rocky bluff, or a crushing like the fall of lofty ruins, or the continuous reports of cannon, or frequent bursts of thunder; and the earth trembled with the movement of the great body of water which endeavored to burst the thick, strong ice that like iron bound the

Winter flood. Androscoggin River, March 2, 1896. Pejepscot Historical Society.

stream to its channel. The waters swelled in volume and force, and the ice trembled and groaned as probably no one now living ever heard it. The people could not understand what it all meant, and some were more frightened than they had been when the earthquake of 1755 came upon them with its fearful noises and terrible commotion, being apprehensive that something dreadful was in store. The otherwise quiet and weird hour of midnight was at hand. The noise constantly grew louder, and the trembling of the earth increased, until with a last gigantic throb the seething water burst the icy shackles that bound it and spread itself over its banks, tossing the cakes of ice high above its angry billows as though they had been shavings, and carrying destruction in all directions. Ironhearted oaks and pines two feet in diameter, that had withstood the storms of nearly a century, were ground off by the ice or broken, and went down in the boiling flood. The inhabitants never forgot the horror of that night.

Morning dawned at last, and presented to the beholders a scene of ruin and desolation that cannot be described. Ice had again blocked the way of the current of the river, and nothing could be seen but a mass of ice, some of it consisting of vast floes of various shapes. Other sections rose like large pillars above the general level to the height of ten or twelve feet, while the great mass of it was crumbled into small pieces, most of them being the size of pebbles. In the bright sunlight of the morning, the colors of the prism showed beautifully from each angle of the infinite cakes and particles of ice, and by reflection caused such a variety of designs and an intermixture of colors and shades that it was one of the most beautiful sights that mortals ever witnessed. But the people had no eyes for beauty that morning. Desolation had come upon them, and the stream was now simply gathering strength to continue its work of destruction, rising four feet in fifteen minutes. No trace of the underlying water could be seen through the compact body of ice, though it was then surging and throbbing and striving to be free again. Along the banks and in upon the land, huge cakes of ice weighing several tons each had been driven, and the bushes and trees had been torn away and buried beneath the deluge.

The great quantity of ice dammed the river until nine o'clock in the morning, when the force of the accumulated water became strong enough to push it away, and for two hours it rushed down with terrific rage. Men and women stood awe stricken at the sight and sound, and the stoutest heart was moved to the uttermost. Huge cakes of ice rose high into the air and tumbled one over another, and great masses were tossed up, while many tons of fragments were violently forced in on the land. In the moving mass were also whole trees, immense logs, timbers, boards, shingles, clapboards, canoes, boats, gondolas, barns, houses and small buildings, crushing and grinding against one another, and rushing, tumbling down the thundering torrent. Before twelve o'clock the ice again stopped, and the river fell two feet, continuing at that height until night.

Swan Island causes the river to divide into two channels, and the ice and other debris which came down with the flood formed gigantic dams across both of them, about halfway down the island. These caused the water to flow over the land on both sides of the river. At one place, behind the point on the road to Richmond, the water ran in a stream as wide as the eastern river, and ten feet deep, sweeping away the trees and everything else before it. The water also swept around Cushing's Point, and left Judge Cushing's house standing on an island. This stream carried large quantities of ice, trees and timber, as it went dashing and foaming over the flats into the eastern river. Nothing could equal its fury as it swept away the ice below in an instant.

The Cobbessecontee stream was but slightly swollen; but in the Androscoggin River, which empties into the Kennebec, the freshet was most destructive. At the Brunswick falls, all the mills consisting of two double saw-mills and one grist-mill, and two other saw-mills a little farther up the stream were entirely destroyed, the monstrous dam at the falls also being partly carried away. Vast quantities of logs cut from the forests farther up the river were annually floated down to Brunswick to be converted into lumber. At the time of the freshet there were several thousand there, and when the dam gave way they swept down with the raging torrent. The damage at the falls was estimated at thirty thousand dollars (or, at that time, ten thousand pounds old tenor). After the river had resumed its usual height, the ridge of ice along its banks was measured below the falls and found to be sixty feet high perpendicularly above the water. Nearly a month afterward the site of the falls could not be distinguished, because the river was filled with ice forty feet thick, the great mass consisting of huge cakes lying one upon another as they were tossed by the torrent.

Many buildings were carried away. One of these, a large store at Cobbessecontee belonging to Dr. Gardiner of Boston, was swept down the river a little below Richmond, and lodged at the Narrows on the back of Swan Island. His potash house was removed to the rear of the Glidden, which was afterward known as the Smith house, and his chimneys were also demolished. His grist-mill, however, remained on its foundation though the water came almost to its roof. Henry McCausland's house was carried down and left upon the great sands. Several barns, in which were hay and grain and sheep and other animals were swept away in the flood.

The Brunswick falls are situated at the head of tidewater, and large vessels have been built there. At the time of this freshet several vessels in various stages of construction were upon the stocks, and the water floated them upon the high land, where it left them. Nearly all the gondolas, of which there was a large number, and the boats and canoes along the Androscoggin and the Kennebec were destroyed. Almost every family at Pownalborough that lived near the river suffered more or less damage. Martin Hayley's old house, which was filled with hay, was carried into the woods. The sheep belonging to the Nantucket people were drowned and their fences destroyed.

Six loads of hay were carried off from Bluff-head, and all the timber, boards, canoes and the gondola of Major Goodwin were swept down with the flood. Besides his hay, Mr. Ridley lost twenty thousand shingles. Mr. Lovejoy's wharf was shattered to pieces, his warehouse moved from its foundation, the stores being much damaged, his cellar and kitchen filled with water, and his blacksmith shop demolished.

It must have been thought before reading thus far that a flood of such great dimensions, which came so suddenly and at midnight, involved more or less personal danger. The people were indeed distressed, some of them being taken out of their beds and rescued in canoes. Henry Smith resided a short distance from the river, and his large house was filled with water to the chamber floor, he narrowly escaping out of a chamber window. Frederick Jacqueen and Merrick also barely escaped being drowned, and their families were obliged to be out in the open air all through the cold night. Deacon Chase's house and barn were both filled with water, his family being compelled to leave, and the torrent rushed with such violence over Call's point that old Mr. Call and his wife were saved with great difficulty.

The road from Deacon Chase's house to Bowman's was impassable for ten days after the freshet, the bridges having been carried away and the causeways covered several feet deep with ice and parts of trees. At this time, also, the cakes of ice were so piled one above another all along the shore that it was almost impossible to climb over them. In some places they seemed like mountains, and in others rose like magnificent towers with perpendicular walls. One of these ice hills situated on a point was forty rods in length, twenty feet being under water and twenty-five above. At a distance it resembled huge craggy boulders tumbled promiscuously upon one another. A great number of caverns were formed among the floes, some of which were of great length, and others so high studded that a man could walk upright, with a firm shelter overhead.

For a month, the Kennebec River, especially below where the Androscoggin joins it, was nearly filled with ice, trees, logs, ruins of buildings, boards, shingles, hay, canoes and debris.

Chapter xxvi.

THE SUMMER OF 1770

It was said centuries ago that lightning strikes churches oftener than residences. In reference to this saying Cotton Mather wrote in the seventeenth century: "New England can say so. Our meeting houses and our ministers' houses have had a singular share in the strokes of thunders." This summer of 1770 seemed to prove these assertions, and if Mather had then been alive he would doubtless have mentioned this evidence in support of his claim. The principal showers during the summer occurred as follows.

About eleven o'clock in the forenoon of Tuesday, May 29, during a shower a barn belonging to Capt. Enoch Angell in North Providence, Rhode Island, was struck by lightning, and burned to the ground. A house was also damaged from the same cause at Voluntown, Rhode Island, and two persons were much hurt, one of whom it was then thought would not recover.

During the second week in June, a similar shower occurred in Danvers, Massachusetts, during which a tree was struck by lightning, and four sheep standing near it were killed by the shock.

About July 10, in the midst of a drought at Natick, Massachusetts, there was a shower, during which the barn of Capt. John Coolidge was struck by lightning, a spar being knocked out, and the building otherwise damaged to a considerable extent. The lightning also struck three trees within a circumference of seventy rods; and under one of them was a cow belonging to Lt. John Bacon, which was instantly killed. A large oak tree that stood in the line of a fence near Chilewet Pond was also struck, the tree being torn to pieces and the rails of the fence split for three lengths. Hail also fell, damaging the corn and other cultivated crops.

The drought continued, and the earth became so dry that the crops were in a precarious condition. On this account, Thursday, July 19, was observed as a day of fasting and prayer by the people of several towns in the southeastern section of New Hampshire; and before the day closed a plentiful and refreshing shower fell throughout that region. At Rochester, it was accompanied with a violent tornado, which blew down several houses and barns, many trees, much of the fences, and a great deal of corn. The church and several other buildings were much racked and shattered, the hail smashed many windows, and left deep dents on the sides of the houses, which evidenced the great force with which it came. Thirteen sheep there were killed by the lightning, and a cow by the falling of a tree. During the same shower, in the west parish of Newbury, Massachusetts, Benjamin Poor's barn was struck by lightning and consumed.

At Bedford, Massachusetts, on the next day, the house of Hugh Maxwell was considerably damaged by lightning, which exploded in a room where there were eight persons, and melted two plates, out of which his children were eating, but they all escaped uninjured.

On Sunday, the twenty-second, the steeple of Rev. Mr. Thayer's church at Hampton, New Hampshire, was shattered to pieces by lightning while the people were coming out of the church, the services being over, but no one was injured.

As the month drew toward its close, the weather became very hot, and showers accompanied with thunder and lightning, occurred with great frequency. On Wednesday, July 25, two houses at Plymouth, Massachusetts, were struck and greatly damaged by lightning.

On Wednesday, August 1, the heat was very extraordinary, the temperature being a hundred degrees above zero in deep shade, four degrees higher than "blood-heat." This was at Sharon, Connecticut. The next day, the temperature was two degrees lower, and about five o'clock on that afternoon a thunder cloud arose in the southwest, and travelled toward the northeast. Before it was overhead, while the sun was shining brightly the thunder pealed violently and loudly, and out of the head of the cloud shot forth a stream of lightning which struck the steeple of the church at Sharon, and would doubtless have torn it into fragments, but for the lightning rod which had been placed upon it for protection. The rod carried off the current, and left the steeple uninjured. The same effort of the lightning was repeated ten or fifteen minutes later, with the same results. This is the earliest lightning rod the writer has found mentioned in New England. The newspapers of that date contain long dissertations on the usefulness of lightning rods, referring to this instance as evidence in support of their theory. In the same shower a house at East Greenwich, Rhode Island, was struck and much shattered, and at another part of Narraganset the lightning killed five hogs in one yard.

On the next day at five o'clock in the afternoon, at Waltham, Massachusetts, the steeple of the "new meeting-house" was struck by lightning in a shower, and set on fire, being considerably burned before the flames could be extinguished. On the same night, it rained a great deal in Falmouth, Maine.

On Sunday night, August 5, the lightning struck a large barn at Epping, New Hampshire, and burned it with its contents, there being in it at the time about twenty tons of hay. In the same shower at Newbury, Massachusetts, a barn belonging to Moses Newell was struck and entirely consumed with a large quantity of hay and a valuable horse, which were therein. Mr. Newell's loss was estimated at about three thousand dollars.

On the forenoon of Saturday, the eighteenth of the month, there was a violent shower, accompanied with thunder and lightning, during which the rain poured down in torrents. A whirlwind or hurricane was created by it at Salem, Massachusetts, which moved with impetuous fury from west to east over the lower end of the town. The wind blew but a few minutes, and its

track was only a few rods in width. No persons were injured, but the damage done was considerable, trees and chimneys being blown down and barns
unroofed.

The last shower of the season of which we have any record occurred on
Monday, August 20, when a man was killed by the lightning at Sudbury,
Massachusetts, while he was at work in a field.

Chapter xxviii.

THE STORM OF OCTOBER 20, 1770

One of the most violent and destructive storms of wind and rain that
ever occurred on the New England coast prevailed on Saturday,
October 20, 1770. It began Friday night and continued most of the following day, the wind blowing from the north-northeast.

At noon the tides rose to an extraordinary height, being greater than
any that had occurred since the famous tide of 1723, and within a foot as
high as that. The tide floated off vast quantities of salt hay from the
marshes of Lynn and towns south of Boston, also lumber, wood, and many
other things from wharves, and by wetting spoiled valuable stores of salt and
sugar. The wind blew down stores, barns and sheds, unroofed houses, and
tore up fences and trees. Along the coast it caused a large number of vessels to be wrecked and many lives to be lost. The principal damage was of
course done along those shores that lay most exposed to the sweep of the
wind. The coasts of Maine and Connecticut were so sheltered that but little if any injury was done in those parts.

Off the Isles of Shoals, fourteen schooners were engaged in fishing
when the storm came on. One of these, a small vessel, belonging to the
Shoals, Richard Randall, skipper, with four men on board, was anchored as
soon as the gale was upon them, but the wind blew and the waves beat so
furiously that the only way of escape that seemed open to them was to lessen
as much as possible the surface upon which the wind could exert its force.
The mainmast was thereupon cut away, but before this could be done the
anchor had been lost, and the vessel was driven through the merciless sea
until the wind abated and the storm was past. They were soon afterward
overtaken by a sloop from Maine which towed them into the harbor of
Salem, Massachusetts. Two of the schooners off the Shoals were driven

ashore at Cape Ann, and the men saved. Another, belonging to Kittery, Benjamin Parsons, skipper, was staved to pieces on the rocks near Thacher's Island, and the captain and one of the men were drowned. Still another was driven on the eastern point of Duck Island, and dashed to pieces. The skipper was drowned, but the rest of the men got ashore to safety, though their legs, arms and other parts of their bodies were very much bruised. Several vessels were riding at anchor in the Shoals road, and they were sunk at their moorings. Three or four other small schooners were lost off the Shoals in the same storm.

In the bay at Portsmouth, New Hampshire, two schooners from Rye were out fishing, and were seen about sunset Friday night, but were never again heard from. On one of the vessels were six men, John Sanders and his son John, John Yeaton, William Thomas and two others and two boys; and on the other were Samuel Sanders, Joshua Foss, Samuel Sanders Jr., and two boys. Six of the men left wives and a number of children. How many wives were made widows and children orphans by this storm is not known, but the number must have been large. In the joy and glow of youth and the strength of manhood, the men sailed out from the town, and the widows and the fatherless day after day eagerly watched the offing hoping against hope to witness the approach of the vessels on which their loved ones had gone out; but all in vain.

At Piscataqua, some goods in the warehouses were damaged and at Portsmouth much salt was dissolved by the great tide, which floated lumber and wood from off the wharves. The gale blew down several buildings and much fence in that and adjoining towns. At Newbury and Gloucester, Massachusetts, goods in storehouses were also damaged.

A new ship, Captain Dunlap, master, left Newburyport as the storm came on, and was driven on Plum Island. While pursuing its wayward course it struck a sloop belonging to Newbury, and stove it to pieces.

At Salem, Massachusetts, the wind prostrated fences, tore up trees, and injured bridges. On the south shore of North River, for a distance of a mile or more, firewood, timber, all sorts of lumber, as boards, shingles and plank, also staves, barrels, hogsheads, canoes, boats, and other articles belonging to many different persons were so promiscuously thrown together that the owners could not ascertain which of them were each one's particular property. About fifty cords of wood and fifteen or sixteen hundred bushels of sand for scrubbing floors were carried off from Mr. Barr's wharf at the North Bridge. At the south side of the town, where most of the business was then done, the confusion and destruction were much greater, vast quantities of lumber of various kinds and many boats being violently driven to the opposite shore. All the wharves were overflowed, and salt, sugar, and other perishable articles in the storehouses, of which there was a great amount, were destroyed by the water. The bridges over Forest River, one being on the same site as the present bridge, at the lead mills, and the other farther up the stream, were so much damaged that they were impassable. A large bridge at Danversport was also totally ruined. At Salem much damage was done to the vessels in the harbor and at the wharves. A schooner of large size broke away from her mooring, and dashed up against North Bridge, being kept off the top of it with difficulty. The bridge was considerably injured. Another schooner, which was fastened at a wharf farther down the stream, also broke her cables and drove over a small sandy beach up on the grassy upland. Still another schooner of nearly eighty tons burden, that had lately arrived from the West Indies, broke away from the wharf and was driven in a similar manner up on the land to so great a height that it lay with its keel considerably above the usual high-water mark. In the southern section of the harbor were anchored a ship, a snow,[1] a brig, and nine other vessels. They were driven from their anchorage, and forced up Forest River toward Captain Gardner's mills, which then occupied the site of the lead mills. Several of these vessels were laden, and ready to sail for the Straits and the West Indies. The brig, which was commanded by Captain Warren, and a schooner by Captain Wather were much damaged. Another schooner, commanded by Captain Motley, was driven so far on the land that it seemed impossible for the waves and wind to have performed the feat. The schooner of Capt. Samuel Webb was forced from its wharf across the harbor, and some distance up on the land of the opposite shore. With great difficulty the other vessels were prevented from leaving the wharves. Only one ship in the harbor out-rode the storm successfully, and that was the   which was commanded by Captain Putnam.

In the harbor of Marblehead, twenty-one brigs, schooners and sloops were cast ashore, but none of them were very much injured.

At Boston, most of the wharves were overflowed, much lumber was floated away, and quantities of sugar, salt, and other stores were destroyed. The water came up King Street (now State Street), as far as the head-tavern of Admiral Vernon, into Dock Square, about the drawbridge, and into the streets nearest the seaside at the northern and southern portions of the town, so far that it ran not only into the cellars, but into the shops and

---

1. A snow is a kind of sailing vessel which was common in the revolutionary era.

rooms of dwelling houses, compelling several families to retire into their chambers. Some of the stores on the wharves were almost filled with water. Fifteen or sixteen vessels were cast ashore on the several islands in the harbor, but few of them were materially injured. A schooner, with no one on board, was driven on Deer Island, it being supposed that it had drifted from Lynn or Marblehead. The men-of-war and other shipping in the harbor received little or no damage. A day or two after the storm was over, a chest was found floating in the bay. It was brought to shore, and found to contain a number of papers, among them being private accounts with Hezakiah Blanchard of Boston in 1759, and copies of several orders from Secretary Addington to a committee of the General Court bearing dates 1706, 1707 and 1708, for printing some bills of credit for the Province. The chest was carried to Cape Cod. Where it came from, and to whom it had belonged, was a mystery.

A ship from Glasgow, but last from Newbury, commanded by Captain Dun, was lying at anchor in Nantasket road when the storm began. The cable that held it parted and it was driven upon the flats in Braintree Bay, but the masts being cut away it was prevented from driving farther ashore.

All the small vessels at Hingham were carried on shore, and one or two of about forty-five tons burden were floated upon a wharf, which common high tides never covered.

Between Nantasket and Hingham a small fishing boat was sunk. The pump which it carried, a mast that had been cut away, and a boat or canoe came ashore, the other mast that the craft carried, holding to the rigging of the boat. The body of a fisherman washed ashore on the beach, but it was not identified. He was of large size, about six feet in height, wearing thick boots and an under and outer jacket. In his trousers' pocket was found a fish-hook, and a small knife with two letters cut in the handle.

At Nantasket, Captain Higgins, commanding a sloop bound to Connecticut, was obliged to cut away his mast and bowsprit; and the captain of another sloop was forced to do the same. A ship bound to Africa, commanded by Captain Bennet, was the only vessel at Nantasket that successfully rode out the gale.

The day before the storm a small fishing schooner sailed from Salem, Massachusetts, and was cast away in the storm at Scituate, the five persons on board being saved.

At Plymouth, Massachusetts, many of the stores were blown down, and considerable other damage was done by the wind. Sixty-one vessels were driven ashore there, and from forty to fifty lives were lost. One of the vessels was bound from Rhode Island to Boston, commanded by Captain Ellis. Another was a new schooner of about twenty or thirty tons burden, built wholly of black birch, cast away at Monument Point, and the vessel, with the men and everything on board was lost, bodies of two of the men being found on the sand near the wreck, probably having washed ashore. In a pocket of the jacket on one of them was found a small leather pocket-book, which contained some papers, very much torn,—one being a bill of sale of the schooner *Defiance* from Lemuel Lattimore to Damon Lattimore of Mount Desert, and another a letter, dated at Mount Desert October 8, 1770, signed by Lemuel Lattimore and Lucretia Lattimore, and directed to their mother at New London, whose Christian name (that being the only one discovered) was Ruth.

At the back side of Eastham, on Cape Cod, a vessel, commanded by Captain Scott, and bound from Turk's Island to Boston, being laden with salt, was driven ashore. A Rhode Island sloop, which was homeward bound from a whaling trip, was wrecked at nearly the same place. Another sloop, belonging to Plymouth, was driven ashore at Race Point. The people that were on these vessels were all saved. A whaling schooner, which belonged in Wareham, was beaten to pieces on a sand bar at the entrance to the harbor at Chatham, the crew and oil being saved.

At Tarpaulin Cove, on Martha's Vineyard, a brig belonging in Providence, Rhode Island, and a schooner in Newport, both returning from whaling, were also cast away.

As far inland as Providence, Rhode Island, the storm did some damage to the small vessels, and history relates the wreck at Fisher's Island of a sloop commanded by Captain Vredenburg, that had come up from Newport, the greater part of the cargo being lost.

At Newport, Rhode Island, the spindle on the tower of Trinity Church was broken off a little below the upper ball, but was prevented from falling by the lightning rods on the building. Though the town was not much exposed to the storm, two or three stores and stables were blown down, and several vessels were driven ashore, some of them receiving considerable injury, but none were lost,

This storm was more disastrous to the commerce on our coast than any other had been up to this date. Many valuable cargoes went to the bottom of the sea, more than a hundred vessels were wrecked, and a hundred lives lost.

THE SUMMER OF 1771

The summer of 1771 was the last of four consecutive summers, in which showers with thunder and lightning had been uncommonly frequent. During this summer a considerable number of lives were lost, and a great amount of property was destroyed.

In the month of April, quite a number of horses and cattle were killed by lightning at Danvers, Massachusetts.

At Stonington, Connecticut, on Wednesday night, May 8, during a shower, lightning killed a horse and seven sheep, and also struck a stack of straw and about twenty trees in different parts of the town.

A week from that day at noon, there was a severe shower at Warwick, Rhode Island, during which the lightning struck a large tree near the anchor shop of Nathaniel Green and Company, and split it in pieces. The electric current then ran along the roots through a stone wall into the shop, where it struck the pole which worked the bellows, and knocked down two men and a boy that were at work there, who soon recovered. Some of the bricks in the chimney were forced out, and thrown against the opposite side of the shop with such violence that they were nearly pulverized. A man near Swansicut Pond, about the same time, had his face scorched by a flash of lightning.

At Durham, New Hampshire, on Sunday afternoon, June 2, there was a severe shower with thunder and lightning, although the morning before there had been a heavy and injurious frost at Chester. Several posts were split to pieces by the lightning which descended during this shower, the damage being slight.

On Thursday, the sixth, at Danvers, Massachusetts, occurred a heavy shower, during which the lightning shattered several trees, and killed three oxen and a horse. A woman was also stunned by the shock, but soon after recovered.

At North Haven, Connecticut, on the afternoon of the following Sunday, a house belonging to a Mr. Ives was struck by lightning, which tore the clapboards off one end of the house, broke the windows, and stunned several members of the family who were in it.

The next day, two houses at Kensington, New Hampshire, were stuck by lightning, and a person was much hurt, but finally recovered.

At Boston, there was a shower with thunder and lightning on the afternoon of Friday, June 21. The ship called the *Blaze-Castle* of Bristol, commanded by Captain Smith, was lying at the wharf of John Hancock, Esq. The main-topmast was struck by the lightning, which shivered it to pieces, and then came down on the mainmast, which it gouged in several places. When nearly down to the deck, the electric current divided, and one branch of it descended to the steerage, where were ten persons, all of whom were knocked down and stunned. The current then went down the companion-way, where it broke a window and did some other slight damage; then entered the cabin, where it melted the gilding and painting in several places, and returning up the companion was heard of no more. There were three persons sitting in the cabin, all of whom were unharmed.

On the following Monday, during a shower at Petersham, Massachusetts, a cow and an ox belonging to Rev. Mr. Whitney, that were lying under a tree in a pasture, were killed by lightning.

On Saturday of the same week, a young woman was stunned by lightning at Abington, Massachusetts. During the month of June there were more showers with thunder and lightning at Newport, Rhode Island, than for many years.

On Wednesday, July 10, at Hopkinton, Massachusetts, a young man of twenty-two years, named Daniel Parmeter, was stacking hay in a field when a shower came up, and while it rained, he sheltered himself on one side of the stack. When the rain was apparently over, he went to a tree near by to get some of his outer clothing that he had left there, and as he was stooping to take up a bottle containing some beer, lightning struck the tree and killed him instantly.

More damage was done, and more people were killed and injured by lightning on Sunday, July 28, than ever before in New England during a single day. At Stratford, a parish in the town of Fairfield, Connecticut, a shower came up between eleven and twelve o'clock in the forenoon, while religious services were being conducted in the church. The flashes of lightning were incessant, and thunder was continually crashing through the air. Suddenly the church seemed to be filled with dazzling flames of white fire and a crash followed, compared with which all others were slight. The spire of the steeple had been struck, and dead and wounded men were lying on the floor, groans of sufferers indicating the intense pain that lightning sometimes effects. The spire had been erected the preceding autumn, and was in an unfinished condition. Several of the rafters were shivered to atoms, and the great ball at their head was split into three pieces. The lightning, descending on all the rafters, entered the octagonal base of the spire, and threw the boards and trimmings on the north and south sides entirely off. It then ran down the four corner posts of the square base of the steeple, and ripped off nearly all the shingles. The current then continued down the front posts of the body of the church by the side of the entrance, and when within four feet of the bottom of them, it turned into the church. Directly opposite the place where it entered were the pews of two men, who were instantly killed. One of them, Capt. John Burr, was standing in his pew, leaning on his elbow upon the rail, his body being eighteen inches from the post. The lightning probably passed through his body into the rail of the pew, as a large piece was knocked out where his elbow rested. Passing by a person who stood a little out of its range, the electric fluid then entered the body of Mr. Burr's brother Ozias Burr, and ran down his side, tearing off his shoe, and rendering his leg useless. It then passed through the pew door to the aisle, where it tore up the floor for some distance, and then went into the ground. The other man that was killed was David Sherman, who was in a situation similar to that of Captain Burr in his pew at the other side of the door. The course of the lightning could not be traced farther than his body, though several persons were stunned in that and neighboring pews, and indeed in many other parts of the church. The religious services, as may be supposed, were discontinued; and many willing hands did what was necessary to bring the stunned people back to their senses, and care for the bodies of the dead. The double funeral was held on the following day, when the pastor, Rev. Mr. Hobart, preached an excellent and appropriate sermon to a large congregation.

On the afternoon of the same day the lightning caused serious injury to several persons in New Haven. At about half past one, out of the southwestern sky, came a very dense and dark cloud, from which terrible flashes of lightning, accompanied by heavy thunder, issued with unusual frequency. Ten minutes after the cloud was first observed, when it had come nearly overhead, out of it came three streams of lightning, accompanied by deafening thunder, one clap succeeding another almost without intermission. The last was much more awful than the others, being a stream of dazzling flame, which went apparently from the northwest to the southeast, passing so near the vane of the village church that it was driven around the spindle with great velocity. The lightning struck a tree about twenty-four rods from the church and instantly killed three horses and a colt that were under it.

From the tree the electricity entered a Sabbath-day[1] house belonging to Capt. Joseph Pierpont, the nearest corner of which was not more than five feet from the tree, though the lightning left no mark on the building to indicate its course. In the house were Captain Pierpont and several of the parishioners with their children. Captain Pierpont's wife Lydia, Abel Brocket and his wife, and Giles Pierpont and his wife were sitting on a bench, and all five were struck by the lightning at the same time. Mr. Brocket had several holes burned through his shirt, and his flesh was severely burned but much less than the others. The lightning ran down the underside of Mr. Pierpont's thigh and leg, singeing off the hair, and burning the flesh about his loins so badly that it was as red as scalding water could have made it. Upon the bodies of the ladies rose blisters of a vivid red color, like the flesh of Mr. Pierpont, they being burned much more than the men. The lightning caused them all, with the exception of Mr. Pierpont, to instantly rise up from the bench, and when the shock had passed they all fell together upon the seat. Mr. Pierpont remained fixed to his seat, and could not move without assistance. Their flesh burned as though they were in the midst of a fire, their blood seemed to have almost stopped circulating, and breathing distressed them. As soon as possible a physician bled them, and it was found that there was considerable separation between the serous and globular parts of the blood, which evidenced the intense shock that they received. Two children of Giles Pierpont were reclining on the arms of their parents or friends who were sitting on the bench, but they received no injury. A large number of people were in the house at the time, but none other besides the five already mentioned were injured.

During the severe thunder shower at Wallingford, Connecticut, on Friday, August 2, the clouds came from opposite directions, one from the southwest, the other from the northeast, and met over the town, producing as terrific a shower as had ever been known there. The lightning knocked down the weather-cock on the old church, and shattered the steeple considerably, making a large hole in its roof. This was the third time the

---

1. Most of the people in early days lived far from the church, and they remained during the intermission between the morning and afternoon services, bringing their lunches with them. The churches were not heated, and near them were erected small buildings with fireplaces, in which fires were kindled to furnish heat to the room and coals for the foot-stoves that were used in the church. The Sabbath-day houses, as they were called, were generally built by one or more persons, rarely if ever more than one being erected at a church, and they furnished a comfortable resort.

weather-cock and steeple had suffered a similar calamity. The first time it was struck was while it was being finished, and a young man was at work upon it. The shock threw him off, and he fell a distance of about eighty-six feet, living about three-quarters of an hour and suffering excruciating agony. The houses of Mr. Nott, Mr. Isaac and Hezekiah Johnson were struck, the first and last named houses being about four miles apart, one of them in the line of one shower as it came up, and the other in the course of the shower from the opposite direction. A Negro belonging to Mrs. Merriman was also struck, but he did not seem to notice it very much. On the same day the steeple of the South Church in Hartford was greatly damaged by lightning, probably in the shower which came from the northerly direction.

At about two o'clock on the afternoon of the next day the church at Westford, Massachusetts, was severely injured by lightning. On the same day, at the neck in Providence, Rhode Island, lightning set fire to a brush fence belonging to the estate of John Merrett, who had recently died, and seventy or eighty yards of it were burned. At Palmer's River, two cattle were killed within a few rods of the house of Deacon William Blanding.

During this week, a barn at Chebacco parish, in Ipswich, Massachusetts, and another at Andover, were set on fire by the lightning and consumed with the hay that was in them.

Tuesday, August 6, was the hottest day, except one other, that had been experienced in Salem, Massachusetts, for twenty-two years, the thermometer indicating ninety-one degrees above zero indoors at noon. The heat had been very oppressive for a long time, notwithstanding rain fell in such great quantities that cereal crops were injured by it.

The severest thunder shower that the people then living in Fairfield, Connecticut, remembered occurred on Monday, September 2. The whole sky seemed to be filled with lightning for nearly four hours, considerable damage being done by it. The concussions of the air were so powerful that the houses shook and rocked, and pewter dishes were jarred off the shelves on which they stood. The tavern of Abel Wheeler, situated near Black Rock Harbor, was struck by the lightning, which so thoroughly permeated it that traces of its course could be seen in every room. Mr. Wheeler and several members of his family were stunned, but no one was much injured. Evidently, the lightning struck the top of the chimney, which was entirely thrown down, and the post on which the tavern sign-board hung was shivered from top to bottom. At the western end of the town plot, a large barn belonging to David Barlow, filled with wheat, barley, oats and English hay, was set on fire by the lightning, and with its contents entirely consumed. The house of William Bennett Jr. was also struck and he was injured to a considerable extent. A few moments later another flash came and his shop, which stood on the opposite side of the street, was struck, six swine that were lying near it being killed. In Stratford, Connecticut, a man by the name of Curtis had an ox died in the same way. Many trees were struck, and large numbers of sheep, geese, etc., were killed in many localities. At New Haven, the thunder was very heavy, the lightning sharp, and rain fell in torrents for some time. The shower arrived there in the night, and continued with great severity for five or six hours, the lightning striking in several places near the town. After the shower was over the air was very oppressive, and the people generally complained of dull pains in the head, and of stupid feelings.

The next forenoon, New Haven suffered from another shower during which the lightning struck the masts of two sloops and a brig, that were lying in the harbor. The sloops were but slightly injured, but the masts of the brig were knocked into fragments. The people on board had gone below a few minutes before on account of the rain, so that none of them were injured.

Chapter xxx.

THE HURRICANE ON MERRIMACK RIVER IN 1773

One of the most disastrous tornadoes or hurricanes that has ever been experienced in New England occurred in Massachusetts along the Merrimack River, Saturday, August 14, 1773. It commenced its havoc a few rods above Deer Island, and took its course up the northern bank of the stream.

During the preceding night, which was one of intense darkness, there had been a hard rain, and a gentle breeze had come from the east all the morning. At a quarter before eight o'clock, there had been no perceptible increase of its strength, but a moment later, unannounced, the hurricane, terrible in its irresistible force, swept up the Merrimack. Its effect first appeared upon the water in the river, which rolled up its northern bank so furiously that the people near it were afraid that they would be washed away by a tidal wave. They had hardly glanced toward the stream, when the wind struck their houses, and they were struggling to free themselves in the cellars and amongst the ruins elsewhere. Such was the manner in which it burst upon Salisbury Point. In a moment more it had crossed the Powow, and laid low the village of Amesbury. Speeding up the river with almost the quickness of lightning it swept through Haverhill, causing destruction all along its path. There its force abated, and beyond it did no damage.

Its general course was westward following up the river, but in different localities it seemed to blow in other directions. This is accounted for by the tornado having the character of a cyclone, which is a revolving rather than a direct force. At Haverhill, a cloud which came up in the southwest was supposed by the people to have had some connections with the tornado. The wind blew about three minutes, at times whirling with surprising rapidity, and carried along with it not only lumber, fences, trees, and all sorts of movable things, but the frightened inhabitants themselves, who were let down upon the ground in safety after being carried some distance. The debris of some of the buildings was scattered in all directions for four or five rods.

The territory for one-fourth of a mile up the Powow River, which separated Salisbury and Amesbury, and for three-fourths of a mile below the Powow and the same distance above, on the northern shore of the Merrimack, were the portions of those two towns that suffered the most. At Haverhill, the wind continued near the river, over the hill which is now known as Mount Washington, and the principal part of the damage done in the town was in that section.

Only those who have seen the work of a cyclone have an adequate conception of what it is able to accomplish. It is difficult to form an idea of its force, and the way in which it acts. This instance of the display of its powers was said to be almost beyond description. Entire orchards and trees of all kinds and sizes were eradicated, stout oaks, strong walnuts and towering elms being twisted and broken, and some of them thrown into the middle of the Powow River. Fields of corn were levelled, many of the fence rails were shivered to atoms and scattered over the ground for a great distance, and buildings of every kind were more or less injured. In the middle of its path every movable thing was driven before it; and the air was filled with pieces of a great variety of articles which were hurled along with impetuosity against houses and people who were out of doors, so that many lives were in great danger. Much household property was destroyed, and some was never found. Large oak planks were taken from the stocks of the ship builders and hurled, almost with the velocity of cannon balls, through the roofs of houses; and more than one hundred and fifty buildings of all kinds were blown down or injured. In the buildings when they fell, there must have been more than two hundred persons. When the people perceived the houses falling over their heads, they sought the cellars for safety, or endeavored to get out of doors and run. Most of them escaped unhurt, others received slight wounds, and a few were dangerously injured. No life was lost, and on Salisbury Point, where the tornado displayed its greatest power, no bones were broken, nor any one dangerously wounded. This is something wonderful as the buildings and chimneys sometimes fell in such a manner that the people were fastened down, and in some instances were almost entirely buried, being afterward dug out by their neighbors.

At Salisbury Point eight dwelling houses belonging to Archelaus Adams, Joseph Adams, John Bartlett, Issachar Currier, Thomas Hackett, Joseph Hudson, Capt. Joseph Stockman, and John Webster, were completely levelled with the ground, fifteen others were unroofed, and twenty-six more were considerably damaged, amounting to forty-nine in all that were injured. Twelve barns were also blown to pieces, their fragments being strewn over the ground around their sites, and five more were greatly damaged. Four blacksmith shops were badly injured, three of them being blown down. Those that fell belonged to Joseph Adams, Ezra Merrill, and Lt. Joseph Page, and the other to Meletiah Merrill. Several persons were injured by the falling of these shops, though slightly. Two new carpenter shops were injured, and two warehouses were blown down. Issachar Currier's store was demolished; and in the store of Captain Hackett, salt, sugar, grain, fish, and other articles were damaged. In the fall of the barn of Jacob Stevens a chaise was crushed. Oliver Osgood's wife was wounded, and he and his son were buried by the falling chimney, being dug out unharmed save for a few bruises. His house was unroofed and wrecked, the chimneys falling with the roof. A small schooner that was owned by Mr. Osgood was also much damaged. Samuel Webster's house, which was almost new, was unroofed, and the floors forced down into the cellar by the falling of one of the chimneys. In one of the rooms was a bed, on which was lying a sick child, and the child, the bed, and everything but the walls of the house, were heaped together in the cellar, with tons of bricks on top. The child was so buried that it took willing hands more than half an hour to complete the rescue, and strange to say he was but slightly injured. The six other persons in the ruins of the house escaped unhurt.

Most of the buildings across the Powow, in Amesbury, were comparatively new, and the destruction of them was not quite as complete as in

Salisbury. The house of Theophilus Foot, however, was entirely blown down, eight more houses were unroofed, and twenty-two others were more or less injured. Sixteen barns were levelled with the ground, and five others considerably damaged. Three blacksmith shops belonging to David Blazedell, Richard Currier, and Eli Gale, were blown down, and another, belonging to Thomas Pearsons, was partly unroofed. Richard Currier's mill-house was also blown down, and the hatter shop of Moses Chase was partly unroofed. A cooper's and also a barber's shop were damaged, and Captain Bailey's workhouse and storehouse, each measuring forty by twenty feet, two stories in height, were both blown down. Eliphalet Swett's house was half unroofed, the barn moved down into a gully, and his workshop considerably blown apart. Among the incidents of the gale in Amesbury was the breaking of the bones of both legs of an aged lady who was struck by a large oak plank from one of the vessels on the stocks, as she was fleeing from her falling house. When the cyclone struck the village, Captain Smith, whose home was in Beverly, was sitting in a sail-maker's loft over Captain Bailey's warehouse, and in a moment the building was swept away as quickly and easily as if it had been a child's card house, and the fragments were scattered far and wide. Captain Smith was found lying by a piece of timber on the bank of the Powow River, ninety-four feet from the loft where he was sitting. One of his legs was broken, and his head and other parts of his person suffered severe contusions; yet he survived. A white oak post, measuring fourteen feet in length, twelve inches wide and ten inches thick, was carried one hundred and thirty-eight feet. A very large bundle of shingles was taken from the ground and thrown three hundred and thirty feet in a direction opposite to that in which the post was blown, and at right angles to that in which two vessels, then on the stocks and unfinished, were carried. These vessels were each of ninety tons burden, and were lifted from the blocks on which they rested, being carried sidewise through the air twenty-two feet.

In Haverhill, the cyclone attacked a large dwelling house, and wrenched away every board and rib from the roof, shaking the chimneys to their foundations. This was the residence of Mrs. Bradley, on Silver Hill, which was in modern times the home of Hon. Moses Wingate. The family were much frightened, and put in great consternation. Mrs. Bradley ran to the door, followed by the other members of the family that were in the house, to flee to the barn, which stood but a few rods away, thinking it would be a safe place to retreat, it being nearly new, and filled with about thirty tons of hay. Before she could get the door open, they were all thrown into the greatest confusion, and ran higher and thither amid the falling bricks, fragments of boards and timbers of various sizes and shapes, that had fallen from the roof of the house, and broken glass from the windows, every one of which had been rendered paneless. When they glanced in the direction of the barn-yard nothing but the yard was there, the barn, having been swept away, was lying in fragments in adjoining lots, some of the pieces having been carried three miles in a northeasterly direction. A valuable horse that was in the barn escaped unharmed, the large quantity of hay that was with him probably being the cause of his preservation. In the attic of the house was a bundle of wool, which was carried by the wind to Great Pond. No persons' limbs were broken in this town. Five barns were wholly destroyed, many houses, barns, and other buildings much damaged, and nearly five hundred apple trees torn from the orchards. The main force of the wind seemed to blow a little back from the immediate shore of the river, thus leaving the greater part of the buildings along the wharves uninjured.

If we could have cast a glance at the territory in Salisbury and Amesbury where the tornado did its most effective work, instead of seeing the pleasant luxuriant fields, and streets lined with commodious and well-kept residences, stores and workshops, and hearing the hum of business, the carpenter's hammer, the ringing anvil, and the ship-builder's mallet, we would have seen piles and rows of broken boards and timbers, parts of chimneys standing above their fire places, houses and barns without roofs, being rent and twisted, the roots of gigantic trees with rocks and earth still clinging to them, and would have heard the sound of falling timbers and cries for help from many a heap of ruins. We cannot form an adequate idea of what the wind did in this strip of territory, measuring a quarter of a mile wide, and a mile and a half long.

The people suffered greatly from the loss of their houses and furniture, their barns and the hay that was in them, their places of business, tools and property stored in warehouses, most of that upon which the force of the wind came being lost or destroyed. The people in the towns around sympathized with the sufferers, and made contributions for their assistance, the churches in Portsmouth, New Hampshire, and other places taking collections for their benefit.

Chapter xxxi.

THE STORM OF NOVEMBER 1774

The New England coast is probably the most perilous of any to be found on either shore of the United States. It is generally bold, "stern and rock-bound," and Cape Cod has extensive and dangerous sand bars that have been the scene of many a shipwreck. Storms have been frequent on our shores, and until the number of lighthouses were multiplied the loss of property and life continually increased with the growth of commerce. The government has now made known to the navigator each dangerous point and bar and hidden reef; but too late to change the history of the early storms.

On the night of Monday, November 21, 1774, occurred a violent rain storm, the wind blowing from the east-southeast with the force of a gale. Out on the ocean it was about as severe as any that had been known, and several vessels foundered. The brig *Polly*, belonging to Piscataqua, and commanded by Captain Jackson, arrived at Salem, Massachusetts, from St. Kitts, the day after the storm, and the master reported that the heaviest of the gale was at midnight, when he was off Cape Cod, the wind continuing to blow until five o'clock in the morning. The people on the vessel thought the wind was much stronger than any they had ever before known on the ocean, though some of them were old sailors and had followed the sea for more than a score of years. Their foresail, mainsail, main-topsail and close-reefed fore-topsail were split, and the sea broke in the vessel abaft, stove in her dead lights, which had been well secured, and entered the cabin in large streams, until it was filled. The seamen were much alarmed, and expected every moment that the vessel would go to the bottom with all on board; but she kept above the water, and arrived at the land in safety. The wind was so strong that Captain Jackson sailed under a close-reefed fore-topsail from Cape Cod to Baker's Island breakers in Salem Harbor, a distance of more than forty-five miles, in about six hours. Captain Chapman, in a schooner, lost his masts and rigging somewhere off the coast of New Hampshire, while coming from Newfoundland. He arrived at the harbor of Salem, Massachusetts, on the third day after the storm, having succeeded in doing so with extreme difficulty. He had got within ten or twelve miles of the shore when the storm drove him from his course.

Shipwreck Off a Rocky Coast. Oil by Thomas Birch, Kennedy Galleries, New York.

There were several wrecks on the coast of Massachusetts, between Cape Cod and Cape Ann. On the back of Cape Cod, a brig was wrecked and the life of only one seaman saved. Two vessels, a brig and a schooner, were seen bottom upward off Plymouth. At Marblehead, three or four vessels broke away from or dragged their anchors, and were driven on shore, receiving much damage. One of them a sloop, belonging to Colonel Lee, came from the eastward loaded with wood, and was bilged, the people being saved. In the harbor of Salem, a sloop that had come from Connecticut with a cargo of grain, was driven on shore and greatly damaged. A schooner, belonging to Thomas Russell, a merchant of Charlestown, lying at Blaney's Wharf, was driven with such violence against the wharf that her quarter deck was stove in, and one of her sides greatly damaged. Several other vessels were driven ashore near Stage Point, but the tide having begun to ebb, they were gotten off at the next tide without much injury. At Beverly, a brig belonging to Timothy Fitch, Esq., of Boston, was driven on the mussel bed near the old ferry-way, but was gotten off with little damage. Captain Perkins in a sloop, from the eastward, laden with wood, while crowding sail to clear the Salvages, off Cape Ann, was upset, and the vessel sank. The lives of the people were saved by their boat. A brig from Newfoundland and a sloop foundered on the back of Cape Ann, and all the people who were on board both vessels perished.

Chapter xxxii.

THE DARK DAY OF 1780

The date of Friday, May 19, 1780, is written in the annals of New England as that of "The Dark Day," when the light of the sun seemed to be almost taken away from the earth, and a strange darkness filled the hours that should have been brightest, bringing fear, anxiety and awe into the minds of the people, who generally believed that it was the darkening of the sun and moon preparatory to the day of the consummation of all things, some perhaps expecting the appearance in the clouds of the Son of Man. It was undoubtedly equal to the darkness that overspread Judea during the hours that our Savior was dying upon the cross.

From about the first of the month, great tracts of forest along Lake Champlain, extending down to the vicinity of Ticonderoga, were on fire. New settlements were being made in northern New Hampshire and in Canada near the New Hampshire line, and the settlers were burning over their forests preparatory to cultivation after the manner practiced by the later settlers of northern New England.[1]

In the autumn they would select the ground to be cleared, and blaze the trees along its border. The succeeding winter would then be spent in cutting every tree on the lot about half through and breast high, leaving them standing until they were all in the same condition.

The men then patiently waited for the strong winds of March to sweep through the woods, and blow down the half-cut trees; or, if for any reason it was desired to have them fall as soon as the lot was prepared, the choppers would cut a tree at one end of the lot entirely off, letting it fall against the next one, and that against the next, and in a minute or two rows of those immense timber trees would be falling to the earth with a grand and terrific crash. In a few moments the whole lot would be piled upon the earth in a mass of the most combustible material to the depth of twenty feet. As soon

---

1. The early settlers of the northern and northeastern portions of the New England states cleared their land by fire. They spent the winter in felling the giant pines, one falling above another as if a tornado had swept them down.

as the snow had gone and the limbs had become partially dry, in April or May, after proper precautions had been taken, fire would be placed under one end of the huge pile, and for a week it would burn until the boughs and the great logs were almost entirely converted into ashes. The land was not only cleared of wood by this process, but the ashes were an excellent fertilizer, and in them mixed with the little soil which was grubbed up between the logs and stumps, the corn was planted, strong large stalks springing up and bearing abundant crops of golden ears.

Pieces of burnt leaves were continually falling, and the rain water that fell during this period in southern New Hampshire was covered with a scum-like soot which, on the Piscataquog River, says the History of Weare, New Hampshire, was in some places six inches deep. The air had been very thick and heavy with smoke while these fires existed, and at Melrose, Massachusetts, a high hill only two miles away could not be seen from Monday till Thursday of the week in which the dark day occurred. Through this period the sun seemed unusually red, as it often does when the air is dense with smoke. In the vicinity of Boston, on the afternoon before the dark day, a breeze sprang up, driving all the smoke to the south, causing the air the next day to be free from dense clouds of smoke, fog and haze, and making it purer though the sky was none the less dark. At sunset, a very dark cloud-bank appeared in the south and west, where it remained all night. In southern New Hampshire on the same night the wind changed from the west to the east, and a dense fog was brought in from the ocean.

On the morning of the ever-memorable day, the wind came from the east, though there were other currents from various directions. The sun rose clear, continued to be seen for a short time, and was then overcast. The wind changed to the southwest, setting in motion the foliage of the trees, and bringing back the clouds. It soon became lowery, and from out the black clouds, that had arisen suddenly and quickly and were now overhead, lightning shot its livid tongues, thunder rolled and rain fell, though not in great quantity. The thunder and lightning occurred principally in southern New Hampshire, being hardly noticed in Massachusetts, but as far as we have learned no damage was caused by the shower. Considerable rain fell as far north and east as Berwick, in Maine, but very little south of New Hampshire.

Toward nine o'clock the clouds seemed to be breaking away, they grew thinner and gradually the sun threw more light upon the land. A peculiar yellow tinge was cast over everything. Some described it as of a brassy color, while others spoke of it as having a coppery appearance. Doubtless it resembled the "yellow day" which was experienced here in 1881, but that of 1780 was more intense. The earth, rocks, trees, buildings, and water were robed in this strange enchanting hue, which seemed to entirely change the aspect of all things. A few minutes after nine a dark dense cloud gradually rose out of the west and spread itself until the heavens were entirely covered, except at the horizon, where a narrow rim of light remained.

A few minutes later the sky was as dark as it usually is at nine o'clock on a summer evening, and at that hour in the morning ladies in Ipswich, Massachusetts, who were weaving were compelled to postpone their work for want of light.

At ten o'clock rain began to fall at Melrose, Massachusetts, and the heavens grew very dark, the light space that had been seen at the horizon all the morning having vanished. Women stood on their thresholds, looking out upon the dark landscape with anxious, curious expressions upon their faces, while the little ones stood at their sides, taking hold of their skirts, their little hearts filled with fear. Husbands and sons returned from the fields where they were engaged in planting, and saw the ubiquitous candle of the time sending its faint gleams into the brooding darkness. The carpenter left his tools, the blacksmith his forge, and the tradesman his counter. Schools were dismissed, and with pale faces and trembling hearts the children went home finding there no answer to their queries, and travellers put up at the nearest farmhouse until the wonderful darkness should be past. A common fear as well as joy unites human hearts. "What is it?" "What does it mean?" "What is coming?" queried every one of himself or of his neighbor. One of two things seemed certain to most minds, either a hurricane such as was never known before was about to strike, or it was the last day when the "elements shall melt with fervent heat, the earth also and the works that are therein shall be burned up."

Shortly after eleven o'clock the darkness had reached its height, and for hours New England was enveloped in this seemingly unnatural gloom. Candles were a necessity both indoors and out for the transaction of ordinary business, and dinner tables were lighted by them. At twelve it was as dark as evening, common print could not be read by the best of eyes, time could not be ascertained from clock or watch faces, and domestic work of the household had to be done by candle light, its aid being necessary even in going about the house.

Fires on the hearth shone as brightly as on a moonless evening in late autumn, and the candle or fire light threw distinct shadows on the walls. Objects could be distinguished but a short distance away, and everything bore the appearance and gloom of night. At Haverhill a person twenty rods away could not be seen, and one person could not be distinguished from another in a room with three large windows in it.

The effect on the animal kingdom was the same that the approach of night produces. Fowls retired to their roosts, mounted them, and tucked their heads under their wings, going to sleep as quietly and assuredly as if it had been sunset rather than noon. As the appearance of twilight prematurely came on, cattle lowed and gathered at the pasture bars, waiting to be let out that they might return to their barns and make ready for another night's repose, apparently forgetful of the short lapse of time since they had gone out to their daily feeding. Sheep huddled by the fences, or in the open fields in circles. Frogs peeped as they were accustomed to do as soon as the sun went down. The day birds sang their evening songs and then retired to their recesses, their places being taken by night birds. The whippoorwills appeared and sang their songs, as their evening habit was, woodcocks whistled, and bats came out of their hiding places and flew about. Near fences and buildings many birds were found dead, probably having flown against these objects in the darkness, and been killed by the contact.

The effect on human minds was very different. They knew that night had not come, and that the darkness was due to some cause, but whether natural or supernatural they could not ascertain. In Boston one of Rev. Dr. Byles' parishioners sent her servant to him when the darkness was grossest asking whether or not in his opinion it did not portend an earthquake, hurricane or some other elementary commotion. "Give my respectful compliments to your mistress," facetiously replied the Doctor, "and tell her I am as much in the dark as she is."

People knew of the prophecy of the darkening of the sun and the moon, and ignorant and learned alike were not certain that this was not at least a token of the dreadful day of universal destruction. Melancholy and awe filled most minds, many thinking that the sun of mercy had set, and the night of despair, of judgment, and the end of all things was at hand. People gazed upon each other in wonder and astonishment. It was popularly believed that the Revolutionary War, which for more than five years had been waged, was the fulfillment of that other prophecy that announces "wars and rumors of wars" as coming before "the great and dreadful day of the Lord." A sort of superstitious horror brooded over all the people. It influenced the minds of all classes, of the strong and learned as well as the weak and ignorant. At many a dinner table no food was eaten, and the family sat pale and silent. The more excitable persons ran about the streets, exclaiming, "The day of judgment is at hand!" while the more conservative were almost convinced that it was indeed true, though they did not express themselves. Many of those who had wronged their neighbors went to them and confessed, asking their forgiveness; others dropped on their knees in the fields and prayed, perhaps for the first and last time in their lives; and some sought to hide themselves thinking thus to escape the "great day of God's wrath." Astonishment, anxiety and fear were manifested in almost every countenance, though some tried to hide their feelings.

A party of sailors undismayed by the unaccountable gloom around them, and with bravado, went noisily through the streets of Salem, Massachusetts, crying to to ladies who passed them, "Now you may off your rolls and high caps."

An incident with a certain humorous tinge took place at Medford, Massachusetts. When the day was darkest, a Negro, named Pomp, who was very much frightened, went to his master and said, "Massa, the day of judgment has come: what shall I do?" "Why, Pomp, you'd better wash up clean, and put on your Sunday clothes." Perceiving that his master showed no signs of fear, Pomp began to draw his attention to evidence of his conviction. "Massa, it has come; for the hens are all going to roost." "Well, Pomp, they show their sense." "And the tide, Massa, in the river has stopped running." "Well, Pomp, it always does at high water." "But, Massa, it feels cold; and this darkness grows more and more." "So much the better, Pomp, for the day of judgment will be all fire and light." Pomp concluded that he would wait for something further to turn up before preparing for the great day.

The legislature of Connecticut was in session at Hartford on that day. The deepening gloom enwrapped the city, and the rooms of the state house grew dark. The journal of the House of Representatives reads, "None could see to read or write in the house, or even at a window, or distinguish persons at a small distance, or perceive any distinction of dress, etc., in the circle of attendants. Therefore, at eleven o'clock adjourned the house till two o'clock afternoon." The council was also in session, and several of its members exclaimed, "It is the Lord's great day." There was a motion to adjourn, but Col. Abraham Davenport, a member from Stamford, quickly arose and with great moral courage and reason said, "I am against the adjournment. Either the day of judgment is at hand or it is not. If it is not there is no cause for adjournment. If it is, I wish to be found in the line of my duty. I wish candles to be brought." Whittier has put the relation of this incident into a most befitting dress, and introduced it among the stories told in his "Tent on the Beach," as follows:—

In the old days (a custom laid aside
With breeches and cocked hats), the people sent
Their wisest men to make the public laws.
And so, from a brown homestead, where the sound
Drinks the small tribute of the Mianas,
Waved over by the woods of Rippowams,
And hallowed by pure lives and tranquil deaths,
Stamford sent up to the councils of the state
Wisdom and grace in Abraham Davenport.

'Twas on a May-day of the far old year
Seventeen hundred eighty, that there fell
Over the bloom and sweet life of the spring,
Over the fresh earth and the heaven of noon,
A horror of great darkness, like the night
In day of which the Norland sagas tell,
The twilight of the Gods. The low-hung sky
Was black with ominous clouds, save where its rim
Was fringed with a dull glow, like that which climbs
The crater's sides from the red hell below.

Birds ceased to sing, and all the barn-yard fowls
Roosted; the cattle at the pasture bars
Lowed, and looked homeward; bats on leathern wings
Flitted abroad; the sounds of labor died;
Men prayed and women wept; all ears grew sharp
To hear the doom-blast of the trumpet shatter
The black sky, that the dreadful face of Christ
Might look from the rent clouds, not as he looked
A loving guest at Bethany, but stern
As Justice and inexorable Law.

Meanwhile in the old state-house, dim as ghosts,
Sat the lawgivers of Connecticut,
Trembling beneath their legislative robes.
"It is the Lord's great day! Let us adjourn,"
Some said; and then as if with one accord,
All eyes were turned to Abraham Davenport.
He rose, slow clearing with his stately voice

The intolerable hush. "This well may be
The day of judgment which the world awaits;
But be it so, or not, I only know
My present duty, and my Lord's command
To occupy till he come. So at the post
Where he hath set me in his providence,
I choose, for one, to meet him face to face,—
No faithless servant frightened from my task,
But ready when the Lord of the harvest calls;
And therefore, with all reverence, I would say,
Let God do his work, we will see to ours.
Bring in the candles!" And they brought them in.
Then by the flaring lights the speaker read,
Albeit with husky voice and shaking hands,
An act to amend an act to regulate
The shad and alewive fisheries. Whereupon
Wisely and well spake Abraham Davenport,
Straight to the question, with no figures of speech,
Save the ten Arab signs, yet not without
The shrewd, dry humor natural to the man;
His awe-struck colleagues listening all the while,
Between the pauses of his argument,
To hear the thunder of the wrath of God
Break from the hollow trumpet of the cloud.

And there he stands in memory to this day,
Erect, self-poised, a rugged face half seen
Against the background of unnatural dark,
A witness to the ages as they pass,
That simple duty hath no place for fear.

At Salem, Massachusetts, Dr. Nathaniel Whitaker's congregation came together at their church, and he preached a sermon, in which he maintained that the darkness was divinely sent for the rebuke of the people for their sins. In many other towns church bells were rung to call people together for religious services, and crowds attended. Multitudes of individuals sought their pastors for some explanation of what seemed to them so thoroughly consonant with the fulfilment of the scriptural prophecy, and were almost invariably answered by reference to the following and other similar passages: "For the stars of heaven and the constellations thereof shall not give their light; the sun shall be darkened in his going forth, and the moon shall not cause her light to shine;"[1] "And when I shall put thee out, I will cover the heaven, and make the stars thereof dark; I will cover the sun with a cloud, and the moon shall not give her light. All the bright lights of heavens will I make dark over thee, and set darkness upon thy land, said the Lord God;"[2] "The sun shall be turned into darkness, and the moon into blood, before the great and terrible days of the Lord come;"[3] "Immediately after the tribulation of those days shall the sun be darkened, and the moon shall not give her light, and the stars shall fall from heaven, and the powers of the heavens shall be shaken: And then shall appear the sign of the Son of Man in heaven: and then shall all the tribes of the earth mourn, and they shall see the Son of Man coming in the clouds of heaven with power and great glory;"[4] "And I beheld when he had opened the sixth seal, and, lo, there was a great earthquake; and the sun became black as sackcloth of hair, and the moon became as blood."[5] The sermons also were founded upon such texts. In the middle of the day, with their families around them, devout fathers reverently read aloud from the sacred volume, and then knelt and prayed. Pious men were sought to by their neighbors for advice and consolation. The Lamb of God was pointed out to them as the only refuge at all times; and some of the more zealous Christians went with lighted lanterns, from house to house, delivering at each door the message of mercy and salvation.

About two o'clock in the afternoon, when a little rain fell at Norton, Massachusetts, the darkness had begun to abate, and the horizon to grow lighter. It still remained for some time as dark as a moonlit night, and housekeepers could not see how to perform their ordinary work without the aid of candles until later in the afternoon. As the sky grew lighter the yellow brassy appearance of the morning returned, and remained until an hour or two before sundown, when the sun was seen, shining through the murky air with a very red hue. When it began to grow light the cocks on their roosts were crowing all around as if a new day had dawned, and followed by the hens they soon appeared in the yards again.

After sundown the clouds again came overhead, and it grew dark very fast, the evening being as remarkable as the day. The moon had become full

---

1. Isaiah xiii:10.
2. Ezekiel xxxii:7, 8.
3. Joel ii:31.
4. Matthew xxiv:29, 30.
5. Revelation vi:12.

the preceding day, and this evening rose at nine o'clock; but in spite of that the night was the darkest that the people of New England have ever seen. It was as nearly total as could be imagined, and was almost palpable. A person could not see his hand when he held it up, nor a sheet of white paper held within a few inches of the eyes, and the sky could not be distinguished from the earth. Those who were away from home though well acquainted with the roads could only with extreme difficulty and great danger reach their own houses, and several persons lost their way in familiar places, some totally bewildered shouting for aid but a few rods from their own door. Horses could not be persuaded to leave their stables, and many of those upon the roads being unable to see where to step, refused to continue on their way, their riders being compelled to dismount and put up. The rising of the moon did not lessen the darkness, which continued as complete as before. About eleven o'clock a slight breeze sprang up from the north-northwest, and a faint glimmer of light pierced the sable pall. By midnight it had become considerably lighter.

With the night the gloom and fear passed away, and the people gratefully welcomed the sunlight of another morning, though the sky was obscured by clouds and unusually dark, the temperature low and a northeast wind blowing.

The darkness extended over the middle and southern portions of New England, but it varied in density in different localities, being grossest in Essex County, Massachusetts. It was noticed as far west as Albany, New York, north as far as Portsmouth, and out on the ocean for a score of miles.

The great question that has constantly arisen since that famous day has been, What was the cause of the extraordinary darkness? Some still hold the opinion that it was preternatural, but the great majority conclude that it was the effect of the conjunction of several natural causes. Without entering upon a scientific discussion of its solution, the general reader will be satisfied with a popular statement: The smoke that had come over the country and remained in this region for several weeks ascended under a dense stratum of cloud, and another thick stratum of vapor had been driven by a lower current blowing in an opposite direction under the stratum of smoke, beneath which smoke had arisen in such quantities that another stratum was formed, the whole being held there by the heavy fog that came in from the sea. All these strata made a curtain that was nearly impervious to the light of the sun, and counter currents held the clouds in place during the hours that the darkness continued. What seems to confirm this view is the fact, that where the darkness was grossest more ashes of burnt leaves, and soot and cinders were precipitated than in other sections.

Chapter xxxiii.

THE HURRICANE OF JUNE 23, 1782

In southern Vermont and vicinity, on Sunday, June 23, 1782, occurred a terrific wind, accompanied in some places by a thunder shower and by hail. It first appeared in the northwestern part of Massachusetts, in the town of Dalton, which was then known as Ashuelot-Equivalent, at about noon. As far as reports show the hurricane was unaccompanied by hail or rain. It pervaded the place, and tore up many trees by the roots, twisting off some that were a foot in diameter six or seven feet from the ground. A new house, measuring forty-seven by eighteen feet, two stories in height, the outside of which had just been finished, and a tan-house forty-two feet in length and twenty-two feet wide, both of the buildings being the property of Maj. Jeremiah Cady, were blown from their foundations, and both dashed to pieces, the tan-house being carried about twenty feet.

The tornado swept on to Manchester, in Vermont, where it arrived at about three o'clock in the afternoon. There it did great damage to grain and buildings. As it left Manchester it divided into three parts,—one taking a northwesterly direction to Pawlet, another proceeding northeasterly, and the third taking an easterly course. The northeast branch of the hurricane was accompanied by a terrible thunder shower during which the flashes of lightning were incessant, the whole heavens seeming to be one blaze of fire. The wind and the hail that accompanied the shower almost entirely destroyed the grain. It passed onward to Royalton, where the rain fell in such quantity that the water was knee deep in the houses, and many buildings were undermined and ruined. One house was thrown down and carried a considerable distance by the flood. Hail of extreme size fell here plentifully, and it was affirmed by credible people that some of the stones were six inches in length, and by estimation weighted a pound. The shower passed over the Connecticut River, but history gives no account of further damage in that direction.

The easterly branch of the tornado was about one-half of a mile in width, and passed through Weathersfield, then crossed the Connecticut

River into New Hampshire, where it proceeded through Claremont and Croydon. Its path was a scene of devastation. The wind tore up and twisted off many trees, and all the houses, barns and other buildings within its range were razed to their foundations or racked and torn in a terrific manner. At Claremont, a house belonging to a Mr. Spencer was blown down, the sills even being torn up and twisted like withes. Mr. Spencer caught his ten-year-old daughter up in his arms and attempted to escape with her, together with his wife, but it was too late, the house fell, and they were all buried in the ruins, the child being killed in her father's arms. Mr. and Mrs. Spencer were dug out soon after the storm was over, and he was found to have escaped with slight contusions, but she was almost fatally injured.

Whether the same shower continued as far as Newburyport, Massachusetts, or not, is uncertain; but on that afternoon Capt. Edward Burbeck was struck by lightning and instantly killed while standing near a clock in his chamber in that town.

Chapter xxxix.

THE GREAT FRESHET OF OCTOBER 1785

A considerable amount of rain fell in the month of September, 1785, and from time to time during October it continued to fall in usual quantities until Thursday, the twentieth. The rain descended through that day, and in the evening the wind shifted from west-northwest to the opposite direction, blowing hard through the night. The wind continued to blow from the east-southeast for two days, and during this time the rain steadily fell in extraordinary quantities. The storm cleared up at about ten o'clock on Saturday night, nine inches of water having fallen during the three days. It fell principally in southeastern New Hampshire and the adjoining country, and was the heaviest fall of rain on record that has occurred in New England in so short a space of time. It caused a great freshet in the region that it covered and proved exceedingly distressful to the inhabitants.

The Merrimack River rose higher at Haverhill, Massachusetts, than it had for very many years, and the Cocheco River, in New Hampshire, continued to rise until Sunday, when it attained its highest mark, being fifteen feet above its usual height. No other freshet in that river has been known to equal this. There were carried away seven mills and several hundred thousand feet of lumber, besides plank and timber from the landing. A valuable store belonging to Major Tibbets, with more than one thousand bushels of salt contained therein, was wholly destroyed; and another; the property of a Mr. Horne, was removed from its foundations and almost ruined. Two bridges over the river at Dover were also washed away. On the Salmon Falls branch of the Piscataqua River, the water continued to rise until the afternoon of Sunday, at which time the banks were overflowed and the houses of 'Squire Lord and a Mr. Marshall were filled with water to the depth of four or five feet. Every bridge on the river was carried away, and a saw-mill in Great Falls came floating down the stream. The freshet raised the river the whole distance to the sea, carrying off at Portsmouth several vessels that were upon the stocks, and in a greater or less state of completion, besides stores, mills, bridges, and great quantities of lumber.

Eastward of Portsmouth, many of the bridges were floated off, and on that account the post from Portland (which was then a part of Falmouth), was prevented from making his trip for several days, all travel through that region being greatly impeded until temporary bridges could be thrown across the numerous streams. All the bridges on the Presumpscut River were also carried away.

At Berwick, Maine, the freshet was most disastrous, almost every mill and bridge being wholly destroyed, and the inhabitants left without bridges, mills or logs. At this town, the river began to rise rapidly on Saturday, and in the evening the water rushed down the stream like a torrent, deep and wide. By ten o'clock Quamphegon Landing was overflowed, and the timber was adrift, the water being two or three feet deep in the houses. The fulling- and grist-mills belonging to Major-general Sullivan were carried off from Parker's Falls, and saw- and grist-mills and mill logs continually came over the falls at Berwick. These were the Quamphegon grist-mill, and also those of Andrew Horn, a Mr. Downes, Parson Hassey, and Captain Allen, Hoggen's new saw- and grist-mill, Wentworth's new saw-mill, and 'Squire Rolling's double saw-mill. Only two grist-mills were left on that river, and most of the mills for sawing lumber were either carried away or rendered useless. The lowest estimate of the loss in the town of Berwick alone was twenty thousand dollars. With their logs gone, and their mills destroyed, the people found it very slow work to build anew the bridges that they must have across the streams.

This freshet brought calamity upon the town of Kennebunk in Maine. The river Mousam overflowed, sweeping away the saw-mill, grist mill, lower iron-works, the bridge, and nearly every other structure on the stream. The iron-works were rebuilt, and the business prosecuted at the place for many years. The Kennebunk River was also greatly swollen, and at length became so flooded that it swept away the saw-mill there. The growth of the village was greatly checked by the damage caused by this freshet. Property was also destroyed at Wells. The losses of the people of that neighborhood were so great it was very difficult for them to pay the taxes next assessed upon them by the state, and application was made to the legislature for an abatement. Their petition was granted, ninety pounds being deducted from the tax of Wells, Kennebunk, and four adjoining towns.

The Saco River probably rose higher than the other streams in that region, as it receives the waters of the minor rivers and brooks of a wide extent of country on either side of it along its whole length from the Notch in the White Mountains to the sea, a distance of a hundred and sixty miles. Through the mountain region the river flows rapidly over a rough and rocky bed, and with a very variable course, now running east, now south and at places in other directions of the compass. These changes in its course have caused the formation of broad areas of level river land at several points along the course of the river. One of the largest and certainly the best known of these tracts of intervale is that at North Conway, New Hampshire, which is from fifty to two hundred and twenty rods in width, and fertile, producing abundant crops of corn and rye. The river here is from eight to twelve rods wide, and only from two to seven feet deep. This beautiful spot, nestled under the mountains, was early settled, and at the time of this freshet was populated by thriving farmers, who were enjoying the brilliant colors of the autumn foliage on the mountain sides, and the sweet perfume of wild flowers that came down on the gentle breezes of Indian summer, when the rain storm began on the twentieth of October, 1785, causing the river to rise until it overflowed the intervale, the channel of the stream being indistinguishable in the broad lake which was formed. Farms were entirely submerged, barns floated away, and grain, hay and other crops destroyed. The freshet produced greater damage at this place than in any other portion of New England. The river had never been known to rise so high before, and it was estimated that about three hundred and twenty-seven acres of mowing and ploughed land were totally spoiled. Two barns were carried away with all the grain and hay in them, and seven dwelling houses and four barns were so much damaged that they had to be rebuilt. The greater portion of the hay that had been cut that season was lost, and a large quantity of flax which was spread in the intervale, and the greater part of the corn in the fields were carried away. A large number of domestic animals were drowned,—ten oxen, twelve cows, eighty sheep, two horses, twenty swine, and probably others. One and a half tons of potash were also destroyed. Almost every rod of fence in the town was carried away, and every bridge, great or small, two of which had cost the town about one hundred pound, was floated off. The loss of cattle and the larger part of the season's produce, upon which the inhabitants depended solely for support, was very distressing, and the people became considerably disheartened. Newspapers of that time suggested that outside assistance should be given to the sufferers, and their distresses became so great that they at length petitioned the Assembly for relief.

One of the effects of this storm was the washing into the sea of a part of the venerated Cole's Hill Burying-ground at Plymouth, Massachusetts, and with it the bones of many of the pilgrim fathers.

An incident of the storm occurred on Friday night, when the wind blew a gale from the southeast, driving before it upon the sands of Plum Island a Dutch ship from Amsterdam, bound to New York. The storm had been so severe that the captain had lost his calculations and supposed that he was four hundred miles from land when the vessel struck. The lives of the men who composed the crew were all saved, but the ship and cargo were lost.

Chapter xxxv.

THE TORNADO OF 1786

About five o'clock in the afternoon of Wednesday, August 23, 1786, the people of Sturbridge and Southbridge, Massachusetts, and Woodstock, Pomfret and Killingly, Connecticut, saw rising in the northwestern sky a dark cloud, which whirled around and around, and with unusual velocity moved up to the zenith. It spread over all the sky that was visible to the people of that neighborhood in a few moments, and darkness, surpassing that of the dark day of 1780, settled over them. The people had not long to ponder on what was about to take place, as in a moment or two a whirlwind or hurricane struck across the towns named, and the wind had wrought its work and sped on and up. The sky quickly grew light again, and the clouds passed away to the eastward. So suddenly and so expeditiously was the entire destruction wrought, and the sky so quickly cleared again, it would have seemed like a dream but for the killed and wounded people and cattle, the levelled houses and barns and other evidences of the awful hurricane lying all about. Pen cannot describe the dreadful havoc and injury that can be accomplished in a moment's time by one of these unwelcome visitors, and this instance of the wind's power is accounted one of the most destructive in our history.

The tornado proceeded in a southeasterly direction from Sturbridge, passing over Southbridge, then crossing the Connecticut line, continued its course over the north parish of Woodstock and over Pomfret to Chestnut hill in Killingly, its track being about a quarter of a mile wide. At Sturbridge, considerable damage was done to trees, crops and buildings. A number of fences and even heavy stone walls were tossed about in a state of confusion, and an orchard was wholly destroyed. A house and a barn were also torn into fragments, one of the plates of the latter being carried to a great height, whence it fell endwise, striking the earth fifteen rods from the place where it was taken up and penetrating the ground so deeply that it was almost immovable. At Woodstock, some groves, a large number of timber trees, and the fruit trees on thousands of acres of orchard were levelled, many fields of corn and other grain being also devastated in the same manner. Several hundred stacks of hay were lifted up and blown to pieces, being scattered over a wide extent of country. More than a hundred buildings were either unroofed, partly torn to pieces or wholly destroyed, a number of barns being blown down, and many having their roofs taken off. Some of the farmers in the town lost several cattle, they being killed by falling timbers. A child was taken up by the wind, carried a long distance and dropped upon the earth, being much bruised. In Woodstock, only one human life was lost, and that fatality occurred in a very singular manner. Two large elm trees were torn out of the ground, carried by the wind above the roof of a house, upon which they were dropped, thereby crushing the entire dwelling and killing a woman who was in it. Among the incidents connected with this hurricane at Woodstock was the taking up of a wagon by the wind and placing it upon an apple-tree. At Pomfret, some damage was done, but at Killingly the wind was much more disastrous. A new house there, belonging to Othniel Brown, was blown entirely to pieces, and the boards and timbers, together with the household furniture and other articles were carried to a considerable distance. There were six persons in the house at the time, and they all escaped injury except Mrs. Brown, who was killed by being struck with a stick of timber.

In other places, a shower with thunder and lightning accompanied the tornado, doing considerable damage. At Providence, Rhode Island, it was as dark as it was in Connecticut, vivid lightning lit up the heavens from time to time, and some rain fell, but the air was still, though in this town and at

Rehoboth, in Massachusetts, a large quantity of leaves fell apparently from a great height indicating that a whirlwind had visited some place in the vicinity with its mighty power. Several places in Connecticut also suffered from the effects of the shower. At Canaan, a house was set on fire by the lightning and consumed. At East Haddam, a yoke of oxen had a very singular and narrow escape. They were standing yoked together, when the lightning struck the yoke staple, splitting the wood in such a manner that it released the animals from each other without injuring either. At East Hartford, four cows were killed under a tree; and at Wethersfield a woman was struck by the lightning and fatally injured. At Windham, the darkness was almost as gross as it was at Woodstock, and during the shower here a stack of hay was set on fire by the lightning and wholly consumed.

At New London, Connecticut, the thunder shower was very violent, continuing about three hours, and being attended with almost incessant and intensely vivid lightning. At about eight o'clock, the house of Jonathan Brooks was struck, the lightning entering a chimney, and descending it in various directions. Mr. Brooks' only daughter, a very promising girl of fifteen, who was in a chamber near the chimney, was instantly killed. She was struck on her right temple, and the lightning ran down her right side badly burning her body. Mr. Brooks was in the room beneath that in which she was killed and was knocked down. Three others of the family who were near him also escaped injury.

Chapter xxxvi.

THE SNOW STORMS OF DECEMBER 1786

The winter of 1786–87 set in very early. At Warren, in Maine, on the fourteenth of November the St. George's River was frozen so hard and thick that the ice bore horses and sleighs as far down as Watson's Point, and on the following day to the mouth of the stream. It did not break up until the latter part of the following March. The sloop *Warren*, lying at the wharf in Thomaston and loading with a cargo for the West Indies, was frozen in and compelled to remain there all through the winter. By the twentieth of November, the harbor of Salem, Massachusetts, was frozen over as far out as Naugus Head; and the Connecticut River was congealed so quickly that, at Middletown in that state, within twenty-four hours after boats passed

Snowbound in Connecticut. Litchfield Historical Society

over it the ice had become strong enough to bear heavy weights and people were driving on it with their horses and sleighs. Frozen into the river were between thirty and forty vessels that had been prepared for their voyages, the masters expecting to sail before the river was closed by ice. The month of December was unusually severe, and snow storms came frequently and terrifically, great quantities of snow covering the earth to a depth that impeded travel in all portions of the country. The remainder of the winter was also severe, and in the vicinity of Rockland, Maine, snow remained on the ground as late as April 10, so deep and hard-crusted that teams passed over the fences in every direction without obstruction.

The first storm in the month of December began about noon on Monday, the fourth. The weather was very cold, and during the forenoon a piercing northeast wind blew. About noon snow-flakes began to fall, and they increased in number so fast that soon a blinding snow storm was raging in all its fury. The strong wind brought in the tide, until it became one of the highest that was ever experienced on our coast. On the salt marshes, stacks of hay were lifted from the staddles and floated away, most of them never being recovered, while much that was saved was so wet that it was worthless as fodder. On the marshes of Rowley, Massachusetts, hundreds of tons of hay were floated across the river and marshes to the lee shore of Ipswich, most of it being lost. The storm continued all Monday night, through the next day and until another evening, without intermission, so much snow falling that it lay six feet deep in Boston. The newspapers of that time said that it was as severe a snow storm as had been experienced for several years.

The tide was so high on Tuesday that at Boston the water overflowed the "pier" to the depth of several inches and entered the stores on the lower part of it, greatly damaging the sugar, salt and other articles that were in them. The wharves generally were overflowed, and from them quantities of wood and lumber were floated away.

Several vessels were expected to arrive in Boston at the time of the storm, and their owners and the families of the crews were very anxious concerning them. They all, however, afterward came safely into port, with the exception of two or three that were wrecked. One of these was the brig *Lucretia,* Captain Powell, master, owned by Messrs. Bolling and Sharp of New Haven. She had come from St. Croix, had weathered the storm during Monday night and reached the entrance to Boston Harbor when, about nine o'clock on Tuesday morning, in the violent wind and blinding storm she ran on Point Shirley. There were eleven persons on board. When the vessel struck, Mr. Kilby the mate, two of the crew, a Mr. Sharp, who was a merchant, and a Negro jumped into the foam, at the risk of losing their lives in the terrible surf, and succeeded in reaching the shore. They travelled through the deep snow and endeavored to find one of the houses on the point; but being exhausted by their terrible struggle with the waves they were not able to battle with the storm, and they perished in the show. Captain Powell and the five men who remained on the brig continued there until the storm abated, when they made their way to the shore in safety. The vessel was so strained and racked that it was bilged, but the cargo was saved. Mr. Sharp's body was brought to Boston, and his funeral was held at the American Coffee House, on State Street, at four o'clock on the afternoon of Tuesday of the following week, it being attended by a large number of merchants of Boston and other people.

On Monday night, the sloop *Thomas,* from Baltimore, which was commanded by Jonathan Smith, was wrecked on Marshfield Beach, and the captain and mate were frozen to death before assistance could come to them. The cargo was saved, but the vessel was cracked so much that it was bilged.

A day or two before the storm a sloop, owned by Jacob Curtis, sailed from Arundel, on the coast of Maine, for Salem; and on Tuesday, in the violent snow storm, was driven on Plum Island and wrecked. There were only three persons on board, and two of them, Mr. Curtis and Benjamin

Jeffries, died from the effects of the cold. Mr. Curtis left a wife and eight children who deeply felt his loss of the husband and father of whom they were in so much need. Mr. Jeffries was about twenty-two years of age and unmarried. The survivor of the crew was severely frozen, but after good treatment and months of suffering he recovered. On the next day, the bodies of the lost mariners were found under a stack of hay and brought to Newburyport, where a jury held an inquest. The remains were properly interred on the following Friday afternoon.

Among the several incidents of this storm is one that is curious and interesting. Where the river which flows down through the marshes of Rowley, Massachusetts, empties into Plum Island sound, is a tract of upland known as Hog Island, on which at the time of this storm was a hut belonging to Samuel Pulsifer and Samuel Elwell, both of Rowley. They had gone down the river on Monday morning with the intention of spending the night there, a practice which has ever since been common among the people of the towns bordering on the marshes. Fresh, succulent clams constitute the principal food of such excursionists and these men had been digging their supply on the flats of the sound off the island during the forenoon. After obtaining the quantity they desired they returned to the house. The snow storm had already begun, and it increased so rapidly that they concluded to give up the idea of staying there in such a storm as appeared to be beginning and return to their homes. The tide was now low, and they started across the marshes and creeks, but soon lost their way in the blinding storm. Finding no landmarks to direct them across the level marshes that stretched away for miles, they wandered about for some time, bewildered and tired. At length they found a stack of dry hay in which they dug a hole, and concluded to encamp therein until the storm should be over in the morning. They passed the night as well as the circumstances and severe cold would permit. At length morning came, but the storm had not abated. It still raged as fiercely as when darkness closed in upon the marshes the night before. To their astonishment, the men found the tide had risen so high that it wet the hay around the place in the stack where they had spent the night, and they were obliged to go to the top of the stack to keep above the water. They began to consider the new dangers of their situation, which had become truly alarming. How much higher would the water rise, and would their weight be sufficient to keep the stack upon the staddles if the water rose much higher, were questions which arose in their minds, and they had but slight expectations that the result would be in their favor. The questions were soon answered. A huge cake of ice struck the stack, jarring it off the staddles, and it floated away with its human freight through the sea that was raging around them. The snow was falling so thickly and the clouds were so heavy and dark that they could see nothing but the water that covered the marshes. The points of the compass were entirely unascertainable, and they could not tell the course in which they were being driven. Around them only the turbulent waters could be seen. Sometimes they went directly forward, and at intervals the stack whirled around, threatening every time to go to pieces or throw them from it into the freezing waters where they would become benumbed and quickly perish by drowning. At length, with horror, they felt the stack suddenly disintegrate beneath them. But their hopelessness was turned to joy as another stack of hay, large and solid, came along so near to them that they leaped upon it. They were driven along on this new stack, exposed to the extreme cold, snow and wind, and the water which continually dashed upon them, for two hours longer. During their inactivity they became almost stupefied with the cold, and began to feel sleepy. In this semi-conscious condition they chanced to look about them and saw land only about four rods away. Toward this the wind had driven them. Between them and the land were cakes of ice, which hindered the stack from approaching nearer the shore. The place was Smith's Cove, so-called, at Little Neck, in Ipswich, situated between three and four miles from the place where the men were set adrift on the first stack. They made no exertion to get ashore, but lay there a considerable time. After a while, they discovered that they were being carried out to sea by the wind and tide. This brought them to their sense of self-preservation. Mr. Pulsifer immediately threw himself upon the ice and advised his companion to do the same. Mr. Elwell was so stupefied with the cold that it seemed impossible for him to ever reach the land; but after considerable endeavor he managed to get on a floating cake and reached the shore in safety. Mr. Pulsifer succeeded in getting near enough to the shore to touch the bottom with his feet; but his legs were so benumbed by the cold that he could not step. For a while it seemed that he must die though only a rod from the shore; but before it was too late he conceived the idea of moving his legs ahead one at a time by his hands, as if they had been sticks. By this means he reached land safely. Now they felt themselves saved, and the thought of their preservation invigorated their faculties. They ran a few rods to get warm and recover the full use of their limbs. But where were they? They had not given a thought to the location of the land where they were. The fact that it was the solid earth was enough to satisfy them for the first few moments they were upon it. Probably they had but a faint conception of the distance and direction they had been driven while on the stacks of hay. On looking about they found that they were on an uninhabited island, and though the mainland was not far away it was impossible to reach it. They must either freeze or starve to death if they remained where they were. They found a stack of dry hay and into that they crept for warmth. At length, they came out and went upon the highest part of the island and with what strength of voice they had they shouted for help, that being the only thing they could do. After a while a man was seen on the mainland by Mr. Pulsifer, and feeling that by him was a way of escape from their dangerous situation they made a vigorous demonstration; but in vain, the man unheeding passed out of sight. They now became utterly discouraged, and death seemed to be their inevitable lot. They had had nothing to eat for about two days, and the pangs of hunger intensified their hopelessness. Their hopes again revived, however, when three-quarters of an hour later Maj. Charles Smith of Ipswich, with his two sons, came within sight of the island in search of some stray sheep. One of the men stood upon the stack of hay, waved his hat, and hallooed for assistance. One of Major Smith's sons saw him and the father, who knew of a causeway leading to the island which was then covered with water about a yard deep, waded through it to the place where the men were. They were assisted to Major Smith's house, which was some little distance away, and he provided them with everything necessary to their comfort. On Thursday they returned to their homes, thankful that their lives which had several times seemed lost were preserved.

On the night of Friday of the same week another terrible snow storm with a furious northeast wind began. It continued through the next day, increasing as night came on, and abated Sunday morning. The snow was already very deep, and this storm so increased its depth that it was estimated at this time there was more snow on the ground than there was in the winter of the great snow, seventy years before. Travelling was extremely difficult and in many places it was totally stopped. In Boston, on the day following that on which the storm had cleared off, a number of people were employed in "levelling" the snow in the streets, and the next day the *Massachusetts Gazette* of the time said, "It is hoped they and many others will turn out this day for the same laudable and necessary purpose." Up to this period the roads and streets were not cleared of snow, except in a few unimportant instances, and they remained in the condition in which the storm left them, whether the snow came on a level or in drifts. And it would seem that even in Boston it was unusual for the people to remove, level or path the snow. The roads were completely filled from wall to wall throughout New England. The people could not get to the churches on Sunday on account of the great drifts, and so of course no religious services were held.

This was one of the most difficult storms to withstand that was ever experienced. Several persons who were out in it became lost and were smothered to death in the snow, or, becoming exhausted, sank down and perished with the cold. A man living near Portland, Maine, left that place for his home and was never again heard from, it being supposed that he died on the way.

On Saturday evening, Thomas Hooper and Valentine Tidder Jr. of Marblehead, Massachusetts, who had been in Salem during the afternoon, started in the storm on the return home about dark. They did not come, and it was supposed by their families and friends that they had forborne risking their lives in the cold and snow, remaining at Salem overnight and that when the storm abated and travelling became practicable they would return in safety. But before the storm had cleared, news came that the men had been seen in the evening on their way to Marblehead. Then their families knew that there was but little chance of their being alive, for if they had reached Marblehead they would have come home. A searching party, consisting of a large number of their townsmen, was formed and during Monday they searched the snow in the road over which the men would be most likely to travel on their way home; but night came, and they had not been found. The search was renewed on the following morning, and this time it was successful, the bodies being found in the fields at some distance from the road and apart, as if the men had become separated and wandered from each other. The funeral of one of them took place on Thursday and of the other on the Friday following. Mr. Hooper left a wife and a large number of children, and Mr. Tidder, who was considerably younger than Mr. Hooper, left parents and a wife and child. The bereaved were very deeply affected by the sad and sudden deaths.

A sadder case than the foregoing occurred on the same evening at Litchfield, Connecticut. The storm was very severe there, the snow came in great quantities, and the wind blew a gale. A man by the name of Elisha Birge lived in a house which was so old and decayed that his wife Mary, who was naturally timid, thought it could not withstand the tempest. She was afraid to remain in it through the night, and on this Saturday evening, in spite of her husband's persuasions, started out to go to a neighbor's to spend the night. She soon lost her way in the blinding storm and wandered about in the cold and whirling snow, floundering in the great drifts until she knew not where she was. She had not been gone long when her husband repented letting her go off on her hazardous journey alone and started after her. He soon overtook her, and together they tried to find the house she sought. But after wandering about for some time in their fruitless search, she sat down by the trunk of an ancient tree to rest. Mr. Birge suggested that they had mistaken the road and urged her to return. She made no reply, and looking at her he discovered that she had fallen asleep, cold and exhaustion having taken away her senses. He tried to arouse her from her stupor, but it was too late, and she expired in his arms.

The storm was very severe along the coast. In Long Island Sound, many vessels went ashore, and some were entirely lost. All the vessels at Stonington, Connecticut, were driven ashore, except a small schooner which was forced out to sea and never heard from. At Newport, Rhode Island, ten or twelve ships, brigs and other vessels of the larger build were driven from the wharves and forced on shore at Brenton's Neck, and a considerable number of small craft were dashed to pieces. A small schooner bound from Freetown to Newport foundered, and several people that were on board were drowned. Two sloops went ashore at Nantasket Beach, and a small schooner was cast away at or near Cape Ann, its crew perishing.

A sloop, engaged in coasting between Damariscotta and Boston, Capt. John Askins, master, was driven on Lovell's Island in Boston Harbor. There were thirteen persons[1] on board, twelve men and one woman, all of whom perished. Their bodies were found, and on the Thursday following brought up to town. Besides the captain, the persons lost were John Adams (or Adamson) of Medfield, two young men by the name of Cowell, a Mr. Grout of Sherburne, Samuel Ham of Durham, New Hampshire, Miss Sylvia Knapp of Mansfield, Henry Read of Boothbay, Joseph Robeshaw of Wrentham, two men by the name of Rockwood, Capt. Oliver Rouse and a sailor belonging in Nova Scotia, whose name is unknown. All the bodies were soon found except those of Captain Rouse and John Adams, which were not discovered until the second day of January, more than three weeks after the disaster, when they were dug out of the snow and brought up to the town. Adams was buried the same day, under the direction of the coroner. Captain Rouse had been an officer in the American army in the revolution, and his body was conveyed to the house of his friend John McLane, on Newbury Street, whence the interment took place on the evening of Sunday, the next day. The next year the Massachusetts Humane Society erected on

---

1. A later report said that there were fifteen, and that thirteen of them were lost, but failed to give the names of the other two.

this island a small house for the relief of shipwrecked mariners. It stood on the northwest side of the island, about sixty rods from the shore.

On Cape Cod, a schooner, belonging to Boston, Captain Godfrey, master, while on a trip from the eastward, was driven ashore, and all on board perished. On Sunday morning, the schooner *Nancy* of Salem, Massachusetts, Captain Fairfield, master, bound from Port-au-Prince to her home port, was also cast ashore there, about three miles from Provincetown. The storm was so terrific that the waves washed over the deck and filled the cabin and hold, and the men were obliged to leave the wreck at ten o'clock in the evening. In the deep snow they travelled all night in search of shelter, but in vain. Eastick Cook of Salem perished in the search with the cold, and the limbs of the rest were much frozen. In the morning the other men returned to the place of the wreck, and found several persons there, they having observed the vessel and come down to it to render what assistance they could to the needy mariners, if they were still alive. They treated them very humanely and furnished them with clothes from their own backs, affording them every assistance in their power. The vessel was wholly lost, but the cargo was saved.

A coasting sloop, Capt. Samuel Robbins, master, bound to Plymouth, sailed from Long Wharf, Boston Harbor, between one and two o'clock on Saturday morning, it being deemed that the impending storm would not be very severe. There were several passengers, who with the crew made the number on board sixteen, among whom was Rev. Mr. Robbins of Plymouth. When they started the wind was blowing from the northeast, but after they had sailed about six miles beyond the harbor light it veered to the east-northeast, the heavens suddenly grew dark, and a squall of snow set in. They concluded to return to the harbor, and endeavored to do so, but the compass being out of order they could not find the harbor light again in the blinding snow. After sailing in what they supposed to be the right direction for about half an hour it was thought to be very hazardous to proceed further toward land, and the sloop was again headed in the opposite direction. The storm increased until the wind blew with great violence, splitting the mainsail, and with extreme difficulty they kept off the shore until morning. They hoped that daylight would bring some one to their rescue, but such a hope had no fruition. They could not discover land. It seemed that the only probable means of saving any of their lives was to run the vessel ashore, and at about eight o'clock in the morning it was solemnly agreed to do so, though they knew not where they were. The reader can, perhaps, imagine the thoughts that now came into their minds. There was but slight hope of being saved, and death seemed to be certain. As one of them afterward said, "Heaven appeared for us!" The order was given to run ashore, and a solemn and awful interval of ten minutes elapsed before the vessel struck. Each one gave himself up for lost. They had reached the border line of time and must immediately appear before their Maker. They saw the terrible breakers on shore, and the faint-hearted among them grew pale and weak as they gazed at them— "dread harbingers of their approaching destiny." A shudder ran through their already chilled bodies and hearts when the helmsman (though mistaken) cried out, "Nothing but rocks! The Lord have mercy on us, not a single life to be saved." A minute later the sloop struck upon a sand-bar and was carried over to a point within two hundred feet of the shore. When the vessel stopped, her boom suddenly broke and fell upon the deck among the people, but fortunately only one person was injured, and that one but slightly. Thinking that the sloop would beat to pieces in a very short time, the boat belonging to it was immediately gotten out and by means of a long warp, one end fastened to the boat and the other to the vessel, the people reached the boat in safety. By making three trips, every person safely reached the shore. The success of the undertaking, considering its dangerous nature, the surf being heavy and the undertow exceedingly powerful, was almost wonderful. They found themselves on the beach at the northern end of the Gurnet peninsula, several miles from any human settlement. Though wet and cold, they travelled about to keep from freezing, being perfectly ignorant of the locality. The storm became more severe, and the cold seemed to be driven through their very vitals by the piercing wind. After all but two of them had been travelling about a mile in a northerly direction, as they thought, at about eleven o'clock in the forenoon they found a small hut that had been erected by some gunners as a temporary residence. In it they discovered a loaded gun, by means of which they made a fire; and but for this some of them at least must have perished. The others of the shipwrecked company upon landing took an opposite course in quest of shelter, and at length arrived at the Gurnet lighthouse. One of the assistants there was despatched to seek the other members of the company. He came to the hut, found them and told them where they were, offering to conduct them to the house. All but five, who spent the succeeding night in the hut, seeking rest before travelling so far, set out with him. They travelled the whole distance of nearly seven miles, in the violent snow storm, for five hours on the desolate beach, suffering from inexpressible fatigue and being wet, cold and hungry, some of them having eaten nothing for more than twenty hours. They all, finally, arrived at the friendly house of Mr. Burgiss on the Gurnet, where they received every attention and kindness that compassion and generous hospitality could afford, until means were obtained for their safe return home.

Chapter xxxvii.

THE CYCLONE OF AUGUST 1787

The difference between a cyclone and a tornado is that the former is a wind storm revolving about a centre of low barometer and absolute calm, the greatest force of the wind being at the outer edge of the circle; and a tornado is a local disturbance without regularity of movement. Cyclones blow generally in circles of from one hundred to seven hundred miles in diameter, while tornadoes are generally limited to tracks rarely more than a few hundred feet in length. The best specimen of a cyclone that we have discovered in the history of storms in this section of the world is that which occurred on Wednesday, August 15, 1787. The wind blew in a circle of about two hundred and fifty miles in diameter, which probably had its centre at or near Lake George, in New York. It first came near enough to the earth to do damage in the parish of New Britain, Connecticut, then proceeded in a northeasterly direction through the southern part of the parish of Newington, then over Wethersfield, East Windsor, Glastonbury, Bolton, Coventry, Thompson (which was then a parish of Killingly), Connecticut, then over Gloucester, Rhode Island, continuing its course over Mendon, Framingham, Southborough, Marlborough and Sudbury, Massachusetts, into New Hampshire, touching at Rochester, where it was last heard from.

If the reader will examine the map of New England, he will notice that the line of the cyclone was a curve, and not a straight course, like that in which tornadoes blow. A cloud carried along by the wind was observed about noon on that day in the northwest, the direction of Lake George. Between one and two o'clock it had arrived at the west of the point where it began to do its destructive work in New England; and this seems to be additional evidence that this was a cyclone.

During the day there had been at New Britain, Connecticut, quite a strong breeze from the south, and about noon a cloud somewhat similar to those accompanying violent thunder showers, unusually black, ranged along the horizon from the north to the west, reaching about one-third up to the zenith, and its upper edge being indented and forming irregular columns, like pyramids. It was different from the common thunder cloud, being one continuous sheet of vapor and not a collection of small clouds. This cloud was seen approaching the south between one and two o'clock. People on high hills had an excellent view of it as it came toward the place that was soon to be the scene of its desolation. They saw a column of black cloud, about thirty rods in diameter, reaching from the earth to the cloud above. It was so dense that the eye could not penetrate it, and it appeared luminous, peals of thunder coming from it, which grew louder as it advanced. It whirled along with great force and rapidity, and was productive of an awful roar, that caused feelings of terror to arise in all hearts. The cloud sped along in a majestic manner, as though sliding on an unseen plane, while from it the black column reached down its horrible arm and touched the earth. When it came quite near, the column instantly divided horizontally, at a short distance from the earth, as though a strong wind had dashed it asunder, the upper part of it appearing to rise, and the lower to spread itself to the extent of sixty or eighty rods. In a moment it would apparently burst from the ground like the thickest smoke, spread the above-named distance on its surface, then instantly whirl, contracting itself to the size of the column described, and lifting its head to the cloud, being charged with sections of fences, huge limbs of trees, boards, bricks, timbers, shingles, hay and similar articles, which were continually crashing against each other in the air, or falling to the ground. At intervals of different lengths, the column performed this movement. But seeming to disdain to stoop toward the earth the cloud itself sailed grandly along on its errand of desolation and death.

The cyclone passed over New England at about three o'clock in the afternoon. Its width varied from twenty to one hundred yards, being most violent at the narrower places. In some portions of its course the clouds appeared luminous, in others not, and sometimes thunder rolled in its midst. In Connecticut only a few large drops of water fell, but in Massachusetts rain descended in such quantities that large tracts of low land were inundated, causing great damage. It was probably not true rain but water that had been taken up bodily from the streams and ponds over which the cyclone had passed.

The wind destroyed all before it, houses, barns and other buildings being utterly shattered, fields of Indian corn and flax blown away, and all varieties of vegetables swept even with the ground. A great many stacks of hay were scattered over the country for miles, much of it being carried into the woods and left on the tops of trees. Apple orchards, whose trees were bending under a great quantity of ripening fruit, and peach and pear trees were torn out by the roots or twisted off near the ground, some of the largest apple trees being carried many rods. Forest, timber and shade trees were also torn up by the roots, or twisted off at the trunks, and carried long distances with cartloads of earth and rocks clinging to some of them, being dropped in field, meadow or street. Whole groves of fine young trees were utterly destroyed. The toughest saplings and closest pasture white oaks were twisted off and woven together, their smaller boughs looking as if they had been struck upon a rock many times. Fences and stone-walls were levelled in all parts of the cyclone's track, and many articles, such as stones and logs, weighing several hundred pounds were lifted into the air, and carried to other places. In some localities the column acted like a plow, tearing the sward off the ground to the depth of from four to six inches, as it did at Southborough, Massachusetts, in the pasture of Lieutenant Fay. Strips of the sward were torn off several yards in length and from two to four feet in breadth. There were no trees, bushes, nor brakes growing upon the sod upon which the wind could exert its strength in the ordinary manner, nor were any trees blown across the place that could plow the ground. The evidence clearly shows that the wind itself tore the turf from the underlying strata of gravel. Several men were standing in the vicinity of the pasture when the wind passed, and noticed that a heavy undulating sound, like thunder at a great distance, issued from the column.

By this cyclone, many a hard-working farmer was rendered homeless, and the crop on which he depended for the support of his family during a long winter and until another harvest season should come vanished in a moment.

At New Britain, Connecticut, where the cyclone first struck, the only injury it did was to unroof a barn belonging to Elnathan Smith.

In Wethersfield, probably more damage was done than in any other place. After upsetting a vessel in the river, the cyclone swept away the residence of Wait Robbins[1] in the southern part of the town, some of the timbers being carried three miles. When the cloud approached, it was watched by the family, but none of them had a thought that it would prove harmful to them until it had come quite near, and they had seen it take up a horse and toss it to some distance. Then they attempted to escape from the buildings, running into the street. In the house were Mrs. Robbins, four children, an infant five months' old, and an aged Negro woman, who was a servant in the family. Mr. Robbins' farm hand was in the barn near the house. Mrs.

---

1. One communication gives Mr. Robbins's Christian name as Ralph.

Robbins ran with her babe in her arms, followed by two little boys and the laborer. When about ten rods from the house, the latter passed the rest and had gone but a few paces beyond them when the wind overtook them. The laborer was thrown over a fence into a garden, and escaped with but little injury. Near the place where the man had passed Mrs. Robbins and the children, the two boys were found amidst the rubbish and timbers of the demolished buildings, they having run in the direction of the wind. The oldest boy, who was about ten years of age, was lifeless, and the other, aged about three years, was so badly wounded that for a while it was feared he would die. Mrs. Robbins was killed, being hurled half way back to where the house had stood. She had clung to her babe, however, through all her terrible experience, and only when death deprived her of her senses did she release her hold. The child was found lying about three rods from her mother, alive, but somewhat injured. The Negro woman, with the other two children, fled in a different direction, and they were saved, though not without receiving some wounds. The Negress was taken up by the wind, and much more bruised than the children. A part of the house remained standing, but so much shattered that it could not be repaired. Two silk dresses were taken from a drawer in an upper room of the house, carried over the Connecticut River, and dropped at the door of Mrs. Robbins' brother in Glastonbury, three miles away. The barn was large, and stored with grain, hay and flax, all of which were distributed over the country, together with the orchard of large trees that stood near the barn, every tree in it being torn up by the roots, or twisted off near the ground. Mr. Robbins' cider-mill, a building used for pressing hay, and a corn-barn were also levelled with the ground. In the corn-barn were three ox plows, two of which were not found, but the share of the third was carried a distance of forty rods. On the morning of this day, Mr. Robbins had set out on a journey to Dartmouth to make arrangements for his eldest son to enter a school there; but that night a messenger arrived and informed him of the terrible news concerning the fate of his family.

In the same town, the house of a Mr. Rockwell was unroofed, and his small barn was demolished. The havoc among the trees in this section of the town was very great. One large apple tree was torn up and carried almost half a mile. A swamp white oak, that was more than two feet in diameter, was also torn up and carried a distance of eight or ten rods, together with two or three tons' weight of earth and rocks that clung to the roots. Another large oak was twisted off and carried more than twenty rods without striking the ground, bounding on as much farther, the trunk of the tree plowing up the earth in its course. A lad on horseback was hurled from the horse,

receiving no material injury, but the animal had his legs broken. Several
cattle were also injured, some of them being killed. It was exceedingly fortunate for the town that the path of the cyclone was taken where it would
do the least injury. If it had gone half a mile either to the right or left it
would probably have been fatal to a large number of people, and a mile and
a half farther in either direction would have swept the centre of the town on
the north, or the centre of the parish on the south, and probably hundreds
would have been killed or wounded.

At East Windsor, the cyclone came within about half a mile of the church
of the First Society on its eastern side, and in its path twisted from their roots
several trees two and a half feet in diameter. John Stoughton's house there was
much damaged, the greater part of the roof being taken off and carried a considerable distance. Several articles of household furniture were taken out of
the chamber and carried away. A barn belonging to Capt. Noah Barber shared
the same fate, a large part of the roof being carried forty rods.

A barn belonging to William Moseley was destroyed in Glastonbury,
and also in the same town a barn and a large brick house were unroofed,
another barn was entirely demolished, and an old house was nearly
destroyed. These buildings were the property of Theodore Gale.[1]

The wind unroofed a barn in Eastbury, belonging to a Mr. Andrus, and
also did much damage in Bolton and Coventry.

At Gloucester, Rhode Island, the cyclone was more terrible in its effects
than anything of the kind that had ever been known there. Several houses
had their roofs taken off, and were otherwise much damaged. A large new
barn, full of hay, was levelled with the ground, and an old house and another
barn were torn to pieces. In the house were the family, who escaped injury
by fleeing to the cellar. A corn-crib was taken up, and carried about four
rods; and a woman was carried some distance, but escaped with a few
bruises. A chimney, that had been lately built to a new house, was twisted off
about eight feet from the top and turned around two inches.

In Southborough, Massachusetts, a number of buildings were attacked
with great violence, and rocks weighing several pounds were carried a number of yards.

At or near Framingham, a house was lifted from its underpinning,
whirled to some distance, and dashed to pieces. In it were two women, who
could not escape, and they were very dangerously injured. Some of their
household furniture, such as beds and bedding, etc., had not been found two

---

1. "Theodore Hale," one account says.

weeks after the cyclone; a pewter plate was blown half a mile. A yoke of oxen hitched to a cart which was loaded with hay, with a boy on top of it, the team and load weighing about two tons, were lifted from the ground, and carried six rods, the hay being scattered broadcast over the country. A grey oak, sound and green, whose trunk was more than eighteen inches in diameter, was broken off near the surface of the ground and tossed into the air, being moved along in a curved line. For a hundred rods it rose and fell, changing its course, as a writer of that time said, like a sporting eagle. Sometimes it appeared to be ten rods or more from the ground. At length it pitched from the cloud column to the earth about twenty rods to one side of the path of the wind, being left about a quarter of a mile from its stump.

In Marlborough, a barn was hurled from its foundations, and the timbers thrown various ways, much of its contents being carried a great distance, and lost. Some of the shingles in which the nails remained were found fixed on the trunks of trees, as if the nails had been driven into the trees with a hammer. The roof of one dwelling house was torn off, and much of the heavier portions of the debris blown many rods, pieces of boards, shingles, etc., being found three-fourths of a mile away. Several other buildings in the town were also much damaged.

At Rochester, New Hampshire, the cyclone lifted a house in which were eight persons, and carried both house and contents a considerable distance, when the building was demolished, the pieces being found the next day three miles from the spot where the house had stood. Two of the people in the house were bruised, but the others escaped uninjured. A barn was also carried off, and had not been found several days after the cyclone occurred.

Tornadoes also occurred in connection with the cyclone in several towns in Massachusetts and New Hampshire. In Oakham, Massachusetts, the house of James Hasset, situated in the southern portion of the town, had its roof taken off, and its main body much shattered. Mr. Hasset, his wife and two children were all considerably bruised and otherwise wounded by the whirling timbers and furniture. His barn, measuring thirty by forty feet, though nearly full of hay and grain, was entirely destroyed, not a timber being left whole. His corn-house was also torn to pieces. A large iron bar, about six feet long, and two other bars about four feet in length, were carried nearly ten rods, and pieces of board, shingles and timbers of all sizes were scattered for nearly two miles in an easterly direction.

At Rutland, the wind blew down a great number of large and deep-rooted white oak trees, clearing a wide path through the lot, twisted the sturdiest of the trees from their roots, and scattered them in every direction.

It also destroyed a considerable part of a field of corn. Seemingly gathering new fury, it continued down the side of a hill, struck a corner of Captain Bent's house, and lifted his barn into the air, knocking it to pieces, and throwing several large timbers a considerable distance. In the barn were four or five tons of hay, which was wholly lost. A blacksmith shop and part of a shed were also entirely carried away, together with nearly two hundred apple trees, and much of the walls and fences were demolished.

At Northborough, a little after three o'clock on the afternoon of the cyclone, several clouds running very fast and low were seen to meet over the town, and a black cloud resembling smoke or soot instantly arose from the point of meeting. The two clouds ascended side by side, as smoke rises when forced upward from a furnace chimney, with great rapidity. Their rise was watched by many people, who became very much interested in the outcome of the seeming contest, for the clouds appeared as though racing, each struggling with all its might to reach the zenith first. From all directions a variety of clouds flew to those that were ascending, which formed the common centre of attraction, and were immediately enwrapped by them. All the clouds were greatly agitated, and appeared, as a newspaper correspondent of that time said, "to be rallying to a war of the elements." The clouds from the east at length gave way, and the tornado dashed through the region. It was first felt at the eastern part of the town, but its violence very much increased as it approached the line between that town and Marlborough and Southborough, and then went through Framingham. Its path of devastation in Northborough was from thirty to forty rods wide, though much less in some places. In Boylston and Harvard, several houses and barns were unroofed, and several barns demolished. Fences, trees and fields of corn and grain were destroyed here as well as in the main path of the cyclone.

At Dunbarton and Concord, New Hampshire, tornadoes also appeared on the same afternoon. The owner of a new house in the former town, which as yet had no glass in the windows, was in it when the wind approached. All the family but himself went into the cellar while he attempted to put a board up at one of the windows to keep the wind out, but he was blown with the board across the room, and into another without material injury. The house and also his new barn were considerably damaged. In Concord, the tornado destroyed several houses, barns, fields of corn, orchards, etc. A cider-mill that stood at some distance from the Merrimack River was taken up and set adrift in the water. The stream was greatly agitated, and a ferry-boat passing at the time was taken up, and carried a considerable distance, being dropped on the water again.

Chapter xxxviii.

THE METEOR OF 1787

There are recorded several instances of meteors having been observed in New England very near the earth, and that which was seen on Thursday, August 30, 1787, was one of the most interesting that we have learned of. It passed over the country at about twenty minutes after four o'clock in the afternoon. It was first noticed at Stow, Massachusetts, and it then proceeded over Exeter and Portsmouth, New Hampshire, York, Portland and New Gloucester, Maine, being said to have been heard as far east as Frenchman's Bay.

The meteor appeared to be a ball of bright and glowing fire, apparently about six inches in diameter, and it proceeded with great velocity through the heavens in a northeasterly direction. It left behind a train of fire about twenty degrees in length, terminating in a point which appeared near the ball like a flame, and gradually lessened in brightness until it apparently turned to smoke. Behind it was left a cloud of smoke which settled down in the northeast, and was visible until after sunset. At New Gloucester, Maine, it seemed to be as large as a nine-pound cannon ball.

The day before had been cloudy and wet, and it had rained quite hard on the morning of the thirtieth, the wind being southeast. By nine o'clock the wind became more easterly and the rain abated, though it continued wet and misty all through the day. At night the wind came round to the northwest, and dispersed the fog. A fresh breeze was blowing all day, and the clouds flew high till toward night, when the sky was nearly clear.

At Stow, about eight or ten minutes after the meteor disappeared, a noise resembling heavy, distant thunder was heard, apparently much above the clouds. Several persons that heard it said that it was like the firing of field artillery two or three miles distant. The explosions were perfectly distinct, but without intermission, and continued for a minute, being uniform from beginning to end. The noise was preceded by a flash, though the spectators could discover no cloud from which thunder or lightning would issue, nor did the sound at all resemble thunder except in intensity. At Exeter, it shook a house slightly, but there was no unnatural motion of the earth. At Portsmouth, several persons, who were in their houses, observed a flash of light come into their windows about a minute before the explosions began; but at York several hundred people, who had just come out from a mid-week religious meeting, watched the cloud, but saw no light issue from it. The cloud was in the direction from which the sound came, and was seen some ten or fifteen minutes before the sound was heard. It attracted the people's attention from its very singular appearance. There were at the time a few small clouds moving across the sky toward the southeast. The motion of the meteor was in a different direction from that of the cloud, and it was soon generally believed that the cloud and the noise had no connection. At Portsmouth, the sound appeared to come from the cloud of smoke that the meteor left behind it, and the people in that town said that the explosions were repeated in very quick succession, growing less intense for the space of a minute, and resembling the report of Chinese firecrackers, or the scattering fire of an ill-trained company of soldiers. At every explosion the cloud threw out arms of smoke in every direction, which seemed to increase its size. At York, the meteor appeared much higher in the heavens than at other places, being only about twenty-five or thirty degrees from the zenith. Clouds apparently passed below the smoke, which continued to be visible for half an hour after the explosions ceased, and then gradually moved before the wind to the southeast. At New Gloucester, the explosions were like the discharge of several heavy cannon a short distance away, and in very quick succession, the smoke that followed the meteor seeming to be beyond the clouds in a southeasterly direction. At Portland, three reports like cannon were heard, followed by a rumbling noise like thunder, and the buildings were perceptibly shaken by the explosion.

The common people of the time believed that the noise was caused by the bursting of the meteor in the air, though they could not understand the reason of the repeated reports. Rev. Thomas Clapp, a former president of Yale College, who was an authority on meteoric bodies, gave his opinion of such meteors as this as follows: "They are solid bodies, half a mile in distance, revolving round the earth in long ellipses, their least distance being about twenty or thirty miles; by their friction upon the atmosphere they make a constant rumbling noise, and collect electrical fire, and when they come nearest the earth or a little after, being then overcharged, they make an explosion as loud as a large cannon."

A newspaper of that period said that the superstitious people of Maine regarded the meteor with awe, being convinced that the sounds accompanying it were a premonition of a bloody conflict among the citizens of Massachusetts on account of the separation of the province of Maine from

that state, to which it then belonged, which they prophesied would occur.[1]
The journal above referred to said: "The old women at the eastward plainly
heard the firing of cannon and musketry, with the regular beat of drums,
and saw the ensigns of war wave in the air, and are of the opinion, that it is
a prognostication of the Province of Maine being separated from the rest
part of the Commonwealth, and the other part fighting them!"

Chapter xxxix.

THE GALE OF 1788

A very disastrous gale was experienced in the western portion of New
England on the afternoon of Tuesday, August 19, 1788. New York also
suffered from its injurious effects.

During the forenoon the wind blew from the southeast, and the weather
was very changeable, rain and sunshine alternating. About noon the wind
changed to the south and became fresher, the sky darkened somewhat, and
the rain increased, apparently settling down for a long storm. At about one
o'clock, the wind suddenly changed, becoming more westerly, and the gale
burst upon certain portions of four of the New England states. For about
twenty minutes at a time the wind blew terribly. It continued with variable
force all through the afternoon, its direction also being very changeable. At
times it was extremely powerful, and as late as four o'clock it blew with great
force from the northwest, in the neighborhood of Pittsfield, Massachusetts.

The strong southerly wind brought in the tide at New Haven,
Connecticut, to such a height that the wind forced the waves against Long
Wharf so fiercely that considerable damage was done to it, and several vessels there snapped the ropes that held them, but did not receive any material injury.

A considerable number of houses, barns and other buildings were blown
down, and many more unroofed by the wind. Hundreds of acres of tall timber trees were broken off or torn up by the roots, apple-trees were destroyed,
and fruit was blown from the trees that remained. Fields of Indian corn
were levelled evenly with the ground, appearing in places as if they had been
mowed with a machine. Grain was also destroyed, and in some gardens cab-

---

1. The separation took place in 1820, thirty-three years after this prophecy was given.

bages even were torn out by the roots. Great damage was done to fences, pole fences even not escaping, and stacks of grain were swept away. Roads were so blocked with the fallen trees that they were rendered impassable for a number of days, and many cattle and horses, and several persons were killed or more or less injured by the trees as they fell.

New Haven, Connecticut, not only suffered from the tide and the wind in the harbor, but fields of corn, and orchards with the fruit still on the trees were destroyed.

In Massachusetts, the gale wrought havoc in many towns. At Springfield, it wholly destroyed a number of dwelling houses and other buildings, orchards, forest trees, and crops of various kinds, and many cattle were killed by falling trees. The loss suffered by the inhabitants of that town alone amounted to a considerable sum. At Northampton, the wind blew hardest at about three o'clock when the gale came from the southwest for some twenty minutes with almost irresistible force. Three barns and several small houses were levelled with the ground, and several barns were unroofed, much damage also being done to crops and trees, but no human lives were lost. A child was killed in Hatfield, and at Whately, Conway and Ashfield several buildings were blown down, many horses and cattle being killed. It was the most terrific wind remembered by the people of Pittsfield, where several houses and barns were demolished, one of the barns belonging to the tavernkeeper, Mr. Wood. Across the street from the inn stood the barn of Dr. Foot, which was partly unroofed. Boards, shingles, and other fragments of the buildings that were destroyed mingled with branches of trees in the air, and were carried a considerable distance. No persons lost their lives there, but several head of cattle were killed by the falling trees. The wind was even more severe at Lanesborough than at Pittsfield. Many acres of fine timber trees were laid level with the ground, and a cow and horse were killed. In Petersham, Westminster, and the surrounding towns the gale was very disastrous, and at Deerfield and the towns northwest of it the wind was exceedingly strong.

Vermont also suffered considerably from the gale, buildings, fences, trees and crops being destroyed. At Dummerston, a young child, while fleeing through the woods to the house of the nearest neighbor, was killed by a falling tree. The trees also fell upon many cattle, which died from their injuries, while others were killed outright. Many buildings were unroofed, and some blown down. In some places acres of strong large oaks were swept away, root, trunk, and branch. The town of Putney also suffered severe losses, a number of barns being unroofed, and several cattle killed by falling trees. Scarcely a town in that vicinity escaped the fury of the gale.

In the state of New Hampshire, the wind was strong, and effective of much injury in many towns. At Sanbornton, several barns were unroofed, and nearly every shed was taken up and blown to pieces, one eighty feet in length being carried half a mile. Acres of strong oaks and great rock maples, two feet in diameter, were torn away by the roots, or broken off only a few feet from the ground, and carried along by the wind for many yards. Several young and finely growing apple orchards yielded to the fury of the wind, and were destroyed. A large number of cattle were killed by the trees in the woods, but no person was materially injured. In Hanover, the gale was said to have been beyond description. A new house belonging to Captain M'Clure and several other buildings were demolished. A sad result of the wind in that town was the destruction of a shed, in which were two men and fourteen horses, the men and animals being so badly bruised and otherwise injured that all of them soon after died. In one of the adjoining towns a number of great timber trees came crashing down upon several persons who were travelling through the woods injuring them fatally. Meredith, New Hampton, and towns around them had a large part of their crops, trees and fences destroyed by the wind, which was as furious there as in the other places named.

Chapter xl.

THE WHIRLWIND OF JUNE 19, 1794

The most terrible wind that had been experienced in western Connecticut since its first settlement passed over a portion of the country at about five o'clock on the afternoon of Thursday, June 19, 1794. Its general direction was from the northwest to the southeast. It first appeared in Poughkeepsie, New York, where it blew down several buildings, and destroyed other property. In Connecticut, it passed through the towns of New Milford, Newtown, Watertown, Waterbury, Northford and Branford.

Before anything unusual appeared in the heavens a peculiar sound was heard in a westerly direction. After the noise had continued for several minutes a dense, dark cloud appeared over the hills. As it approached it seemed like an immense body of smoke or fog, and at length it was discovered to be in a state of extreme agitation, wreathing in and out and whirling in the most furious manner. The foremost part of the cloud had the appearance of a common thunder cloud, being thick and heavy, but not very dark. Its height and width were about an eighth of a mile either way. We have said its width, but diameter would be more correct as the cloud was round. It whirled along like a cylinder revolving perpendicularly. Those who saw it directly in front, and only six or eight rods away, said the innumerable streaks of fire ran across it in every direction, and at a distance the cloud seemed to lighten up now and then. It was supposed by some people at the time that the light was due to friction caused by the articles that were revolving with great rapidity in the vortex of the cloud, among which were the herbage of the field, parts of fences, leaves, boughs and trunks of trees, boards, doors, barrels, clothing, live geese and other fowls and birds. The centre of the cloud was clear air. At Northford it seemed to divide into several smaller whirlwinds, yet forming one complete cylinder of air and cloud. The vortex contracted and increased in diameter at several periods of its progress. When it contracted its force seemed to lessen, and as it grew larger it became correspondingly more frightful and disastrous.

Its course was irregular, and it travelled with great rapidity and in the wildest confusion. Its path, though well defined, greatly varied in width. It was very narrow on the highlands, but when the cylinder of cloud and whirling wind descended a hill it seemed to spread out like a flood of waters rushing down with a velocity that constantly increased, and became quite wide when it reached the valley. As it approached, the noise became louder until it rumbled like the roar of an earthquake. Those persons who were carried up by the wind into the cloud and yet escaped with their lives said that it was as dark as night during the three or four minutes they were in it, and that the noise was deafening and awful. Those who were quite near it, and yet escaped said that it appeared to them most fearful and sublime. After the column of wind had passed by, a little rain fell from the rear end of the cloud, accompanied by a small amount of hail.

The destruction occasioned by the wind was most disastrous, many houses, barns, and other buildings being blown to pieces, a number of cattle killed, and several human lives lost. Orchards and forests yielded to its irresistible power, and strong oaks, sturdy maples and elastic walnuts were torn up by the roots or twisted off leaving stumps from three to fifteen feet in height. Every fence and stone wall in its course was demolished.

On either side of the path of the whirlwind the air was calm. An incident showing this is thus related. A gentleman was quietly sitting in the stoop of his house, unconscious that such a terrible messenger of destruction was so near him, when without feeling the force of the wind in the least, he was amazed to see his barn, which stood but about four rods from his house, lifted up and moved off its foundations.

At New Milford, the whirlwind came into the town on the northwest side and passed through in a southeasterly direction. Fortunately its course lay just outside the village, as it there encountered few dwelling houses and other buildings. It made broad paths through extensive tracts of woodland, that were visible as far as the eye could reach. Timber trees of various kinds and sizes and of great strength were prostrated, being broken down or town out of the ground by the roots. A few cattle were killed by falling trees and timbers from demolished barns. Three houses were wholly destroyed, and twelve were unroofed and much shattered. Eight barns were snatched from their foundations and torn to pieces.

Benjamin Stone Jr. saw the cloud approaching, and being aware of its terrible import, he took his four children (his wife being away from home) and hurried to his new, strong barn, which he thought would withstand the wind. The building was but a few rods away, and they had time to reach the bay in it before the whirlwind struck the place. But Mr. Stone was wrong in his estimate of the wind's force, the barn tipped over, and he and the children were carried under the sills into the yard, amid timbers and fragments of trees that were moving hither and thither in great confusion. They escaped, however, with only slight wounds. Mr. Stone's house was stripped of all its shingles, clapboards, boards and windows, leaving the frame bare, and several of the timbers were also scattered about. All the contents of the house above the lower floor—furniture, clothing, and provisions—were carried away, scarcely anything being found that was still whole, and many of the articles were never seen again. A purse containing sixteen dollars, that was kept in a case of drawers was found eight or ten rods away. The residence of Thaddeus Cole was torn into fragments. When the whirlwind struck the house there were in it Mrs. Cole and her infant child, and a Mr. Tucker, who were all buried in the ruins. The neighbors discovered their condition, and with willing hands they hurried to relieve them, but an hour elapsed before they could be extricated. The child was found dead, having been killed in its mother's arms, Mrs. Cole was greatly bruised, and Mr. Tucker was so severely injured that for a long time it was supposed he could not recover.

John Carpenter was in a field with five or six hired men and two of his sons, one of whom was eleven years old, and they were suddenly overtaken by the whirlwind. They immediately fell on their faces, and, grasping the

herbage of the field, clung to it while the furious wind repeatedly raised
their bodies up and let them fall upon the ground, bruising them considerably. Fence rails and parts of trees fell thickly about them. Mr. Carpenter
was wounded in his back by a rail, and his younger son had his head beaten
two inches into the ground, almost mortally wounding him. Mr. Carpenter's
horse was whirled into the air, being carried twelve rods up a steep hill,
where he struck with so much force that his body indented the ground to
the depth of five or six inches. He was then whirled back, nearly the same
distance, being found dead at about the same place where he was first
attacked by the terrible wind. Another horse, that was hitched to a post, was
carried over a stone wall into a field of wheat, a distance of forty to fifty
rods. A new ox-cart was completely broken into pieces, which were scattered in all directions. One of the wheels was carried two or three rods farther, being forced some distance into the ground. The body of the cart was
found four or five rods farther away and an iron washer that had belonged
to it had been carried a rod or two beyond. The water in a large brook was
also taken up and distributed over an adjoining field. Several large trees
were carried from thirty to sixty rods. A hackmatack, or tamarac, tree was
taken up by the roots, and carried along in its natural position. At times it
would descend nearly to the earth, then rise with great rapidity to the height
of some three hundred feet. Appearing to play around it were two or three
large objects that were supposed by the people who witnessed the scene to be
barn doors. They attended the tree in all its evolutions until it disappeared
from sight. One barn door was found eight or ten miles from the place
where it was snatched up by the wind. A heavy oak log, fifty feet long, and
nine inches in diameter at the small end, was lying on the lower side of a
road which ran along the slope of a steep hill, and smaller log lay on one
end of it. The two logs were taken up by the wind and carried to the other
side of the road. At Newtown, several houses and barns were blown down,
and its effects were also severely felt in Watertown and Waterbury. In
Northford, the whirlwind providentially passed over a portion of the town
that had but a scattering population, and therefore did not destroy many
buildings or injure any persons in its course. Several buildings were however
removed from their foundations, and some were torn to pieces. It did considerable damage in the destruction of forest and fruit trees, and sugar
maples. It was also felt at Branford, and probably ended its disastrous career
on the Sound.

Chapter xli.

THE LONG STORM OF NOVEMBER 1798

The long and severe winter of 1798–99 began on the morning of Saturday, the seventeenth of November, 1798, with one of the severest snow storms that has ever been known in New England.

On Sunday it became quite moderate, and for a time appeared to be clearing off, but when night came on the snow began to fall fast again, and the wind blew from the northeast with the force of a gale. The storm continued all day Monday and Tuesday and until the night of Wednesday, when the weather cleared, the wind ceased to blow and the snow to fall.

The great quantity of snow that fell was unprecedented so early in the winter, and in but few instances had the settlers experienced such a snow storm during any part of the year. The mail carriers, or post-boys, as they were called, were obliged to ride through fields for miles at a time, the roads being impassable in all parts of the country. The snow was so deep that in some places where the highways had been shovelled out the banks of snow on both sides of the road were so high that men on horseback could not look over them. Many houses were so deeply buried in the snow that the families which lived in them found it very difficult to make an egress without tunnelling through the drifts.

The snow fell so densely, and the wind blew so terrifically, that great damage was done to the vessels along the coast. One of them that sailed from one of the northern ports for the West Indies a few days before the storm began was commanded by Captain Hammond. He was in the height of the storm off Cape Cod, and though his was one of the vessels that weathered the gale he was nearly driven on shore, all but one of about forty horses that formed part of the cargo perishing on the deck. As soon as it as possible the vessel returned to the port from which it had sailed.

Many vessels were wrecked on the Cape, and seven of them went to pieces, all the people on board being lost. The bodies of twenty-five of the men who lost their lives here in this storm washed ashore, were found and buried. One of the ill-fated vessels was the schooner *Rachel,* of one hundred tons burden, nearly new, and commanded by Capt. John Simpson of Frenchman's Bay, Sullivan, Maine, who was then about thirty-five years of age. He was the sole owner of the craft. With a cargo of lumber he sailed

Running Before the Storm. Oil on canvas, anonymous. Museum of Fine Arts, Boston.

from Sullivan for Salem, Massachusetts, about the middle of the month, his crew consisting of William Abbot, mate, Zachariah Hodgkins, Stephen Merchant, and James Springer. There was also on board a passenger, Paul Sargent, a young son of Paul D. Sargent of Sullivan, who was on his way to attend a school in Salem during the winter. As far as Herring-gut Harbor, St. George, Maine, they kept company with another schooner, which bore the name of *Diana,* whose commander was a brother of Captain Simpson. The weather had then become quite threatening, and the wind began to blow very strongly from the northeast. The two schooners were so near each other at this time that their captains discussed the situation. They were of diverse opinions, and the result was that the *Diana* made a harbor, while the *Rachel* kept on its way before the wind, its captain believing that the strong breeze would enable him to reach his destined port before the storm should come upon them. His calculations proved to be erroneous, for he had accomplished but a small part of the distance when

The black clouds the face of heaven defined,
The whistling wind soon ripened to a storm,
The waves tremendous roared, and billows rolled.

Snow began to fall, and blasts from the northeast swept the craft on through the blinding storm. Fearing the wind would drive them ashore they steered away from the land as far as possible, and though the general line of the Massachusetts coast was cleared they did not escape the sandy peninsula of Cape Cod, that great arm of the Commonwealth that is thrust out into the sea as if to grasp the vessels as they pass. With many others the schooner was driven upon the beach a short distance below where the Highland light-house at Truro stands, between the second and third sand hills. Every per-son on board was lost, all their bodies being found, some on the wreck and the rest on the beach. That of the captain was easily recognized by his cloth-ing and the articles found in his pockets. The young passenger was identi-fied by his apparel, which was better than that of the crew. Many little things belonging to the captain were found, carefully preserved and forwarded to his family. There were among them a small trunk covered with sealskin, also a pearl-handled pocket-knife and a small handkerchief, the latter having been put into his pocket by his five-year-old daughter the day he sailed from home. The bodies of the drowned were all tenderly interred in the old cemetery at North Truro, where there has been erected to their memory a tablet of fine Italian marble set in a base of granite, quarried near Captain Simpson's home in Sullivan.

The brig *Hope,* commanded by Capt. James Hooper, sailing from Demerara, British Guiana, South America, was off the coast when the storm commenced. A harbor could not be made, and at length the gale came on so terrifically that they were in the utmost danger. They cut away their mainmast and dropped both their anchors, but were still driven before the blast. Fearful that they would run upon some rocky shore and be dashed to pieces, the captain and his crew left the vessel and embarked in an open boat, hoping that it would live among the furious billows. They were then about six miles from the nearest lighthouse in the direction of which they sailed, and finally reached a harbor in safety. After they left the brig it parted both cables, and at last was driven upon the beach at Hampton, New Hampshire. The seamen remained at the place where they were until the storm was over and they had learned the fate of their vessel, when the captain with the owners went to Hampton, where the brig was found high on the beach in an upright position. Its hull has suffered but very little damage, and the cargo, consisting of rum, coffee and sugar, was but slightly injured.

Chapter xlii.

HAIL STORM IN CONNECTICUT IN 1799

There have been several very destructive hail storms in New England, but the most disastrous of them all was that which occurred in Connecticut on the afternoon of Monday, July 15, 1799. The shower passed over Litchfield County, crossed the Connecticut River near its mouth, and then went in a northeasterly direction, being most severe in the southern portion of Lebanon and in the towns of Bozrah and Franklin. The path of the shower grew wider as it advanced, and in Franklin, the last place where hail fell, it was about four miles in width. Beyond the town rain fell in great quantities.

About five o'clock in the afternoon of the day mentioned, a dark and fierce looking cloud was seen rising from the western horizon. As it came up it grew darker and moved with ever-increasing rapidity. Half an hour later, in front of it, a brassy colored cloud rolled up like a volume of smoke, and diffused itself over it, growing brighter and becoming much agitated and very wild in its appearance. Then, a little to the north of the place where the first cloud arose, another one, large and black, and similar to it in its general aspect, was seen to ascend until the two met, when the summits of both shot up and overspread the heavens. It was almost as dark as evening at six o'clock, when forked lightning, sharper than the people then remembered ever to have been seen before, darted from the clouds, followed by continuous peals of heavy thunder, and the rain fell in torrents. After a short time there was a lull in the storm, during which birds and animals, being greatly frightened, fled to various places for safety. Some of the people thought that the worst of the shower was over. The calm continued but a few minutes, however, and then the wind breezed up and soon blew violently. It quickly increased to a gale, and was accompanied by a roar which penetrated to the very hearts of those that heard it, being doubly awful amid the darkness, the rain, the intense lightning and terrific crashing of thunder. Next came sounds like bricks being thrown from the chimneys upon the roofs of the houses, and the windows were smashed in as though with rocks.

Hail stones were falling, at first scatteringly, but in a moment so thickly that there was an unbroken shower of them. It seemed to many as if the day of judgment, with its sheets of flame and stones falling from heaven and tremendous thunder, was at hand. The elements were in an awful and sub-lime uproar. Hail fell for about fifteen minutes in all, but for only a few moments with great rapidity and in large quantities. A heavy shower of rain immediately followed, and the water ran with violence, washing the hail into large ridges and the fragments of plants it had destroyed into heaps and bearing them away together to the streams and lowlands. An hour had passed since it began, when the shower ceased, the clouds rolled away, and the setting sun shone brightly over a wet and ravaged country.

The larger hail stones were carefully measured in several places and found to be from two to three inches in diameter, and from four and a quar-ter to six inches in circumference, even after the rain had washed them and they had probably become somewhat smaller than when they fell. They were not perfect globes, but somewhat flattened, with uneven edges. Banks of hail five or six inches deep remained on Saturday and Sunday following, nearly a week after they fell, and the larger specimens then measured three and a half inches in circumference. They were driven by the wind against everything in the track of the shower with almost as much force as if they had been fired from a gun.

Nearly all the windows on three sides of the houses that were in the storm's path (the wind probably being variable) were broken; and not only the glass, but in some instances the sashes also were destroyed. Shingles on the roofs of buildings were badly split and beaten off, and fences and build-ings were so deeply indented with the hail stones that the marks always remained. Vegetation and fruits were almost entirely destroyed by the hail and wind combined. Flourishing cornfields were wholly cut down and swept away, and in some of them not a single stalk remained standing. Rye, oats, flax and similar crops were nearly ruined. Many fields were immediately plowed up, and in others only about one-sixth of a crop was obtained, and that cost more than it was worth. The stoutest grass was not only beaten down level with the ground, but cut to pieces and blown or washed away or driven into the earth with great force. The hail stripped great numbers of apple trees of their fruit, leaves and twigs, and then the wind blew them down. The smaller fruit trees, as the peach and plum, were so barked and bruised that they died. Even the hard-wood trees had their trunks more or less bruised, and were so much wounded in their tender branches and stripped of their leaves that at a distance of two or three miles they appeared as if a fire or a blight had been through them. The wind also overturned forest and ornamental trees, unroofed or removed several barns and destroyed many fences.

It was providential that so few human beings were injured by the hail. Only two or three men and one or two children were knocked down, one child, who was about fourteen years old, being so bruised and stunned that his senses did not return to him for two days. But few animals were killed, although many were very badly injured, some cows being so much wounded that their backs were bloody. Several horses had their legs greatly bruised, cut and swollen. The smaller animals suffered much more severely than the larger ones. Some pigs four months old and a number of sheep were killed by the hail, and geese, turkeys and other domestic fowls met with the same fate. Quantities of birds were found in the fields and gardens either dead or with broken legs and wings.

Chapter xliii.

THE FRESHET OF 1801

On Wednesday, March 19, 1801, began a rain storm, which continued until the next Saturday, four days in all, causing the greatest flood ever known in some sections of New England.

At Groton, Massachusetts, it was very severe, and in the southeastern portion of Vermont, mills, bridges, and other property were washed away or destroyed to the value of more than two hundred thousand dollars.

Fourteen bridges, seven grist-mills, five saw-mills, two clothiers' shops and works, one dwelling-house, two barns and several small outhouses in Connecticut, situated on the Farmington River and its branches, were carried away and destroyed, besides great quantities of lumber and fencing material. From the banks of the river, near the residence of Capt. Dudley Case at West Simsbury, were seen floating down the stream, one after another, a grist-mill, a saw-mill, a dwelling house, a clothier's shop and a bridge intact. It is impossible to estimate the amount of damage done on this stream. No other freshet had equalled it.

Two incidents of this flood have been found recorded in the journals that were current at that period. One of them relates to two boys, who on Saturday, the last day of the storm, were travelling along the turnpike in

Thompson, Connecticut, half an hour after sunset. One of them was Cushion Brown and the other Otis, son of Gen. Daniel Larned. They reached the Quinebaug River, and attempted to cross it, the water being above the road and running very swiftly. Larned was a little in advance of Brown, and after walking in the water a distance of about three rods, suddenly plunged into a hole that had been made by the raging flood. The current swept him into the middle of the stream, and he was not seen again. Nine days later his body had not been found. Young Brown continued on his way through the water with great care and reached the other side in safety.

The other incident was much sadder than the foregoing. A boy, whose age was fourteen, and his sister, children of Josiah Adkins of West Simsbury, Connecticut, went into a mill belonging to a Mr. Cleveland to take down and remove an old weaver's loom that was owned by the family. They began to work upon it, and became so deeply engrossed in what they were doing that they did not observe that the mill was afloat until it began to move off its foundations. The girl was the first to discover it, and she quickly ran to the door to make her escape. Water had surrounded the building before they had entered it, and a plank had been placed from the bank to the threshold of the mill door. She attempted to reach the shore by way of the plank, and had placed but one foot upon it before the other end of it was drawn off the ground by the moving building, causing her to tumble head foremost into the raging current. She was carried down the stream about thirty yards, to a point where some shrubs hung over the water. She made an effort to reach them, and being successful clung to them till she was able to draw herself to land. Her brother found his way of escape cut off, and he was forced to stay in the mill, which was borne down the stream a considerable distance in its ordinary position. The people along the shore saw the boy standing at the door and heard him beg for assistance, but no one could help him. His parents were among the crowd looking at him while he faced the dangers that would probably sooner or later prove fatal to him, and they followed along the banks of the river, keeping abreast of the floating mill. This continued some distance farther, and then the building struck a large rock, causing it to suddenly turn. The boy was heard to cry for help once more, and then there was silence within the mill. The building trembled for a moment and then crumbled to pieces. Then followed minutes of agony to the parents, as they stood on the shore watching for some sign of their son. Oh, what agonizing thoughts and feelings thrilled them when they saw their child in such terrible danger and were powerless to lift a hand to save him! They did not distinguish his body as it was carried down the stream with the debris from the mill, and which a few hours later was taken from the water about half a mile below. His death was undoubtedly instantaneous, as his head was found to be shockingly bruised, and there were many other wounds which were apparently caused by blows from falling timbers. His remains were carried home to his almost broken-hearted parents, and the next day interred in the family lot.

Chapter xliv.

THE GREAT SNOW STORM OF FEBRUARY 1802

The winter of 1801–02 was very mild, the month of January being so warm that on the twenty-fourth, the ice on the Merrimack river began to move down the stream, and on the twenty-eighth, at Salem, Massachusetts, the thermometer indicated sixty degrees above zero. It was the warmest January that the people remembered. There had been but little snow, and they congratulated themselves upon the pleasant winter and the prospect of an early spring.

On Sunday, the twenty-first of February, the aspect of the weather wholly changed. The first part of the day was remarkably pleasant, but the wind soon changed to the northeast, and a fierce snow storm came on. The storm continued for nearly a week, covering the earth with snow and sleet to the depth of several feet. Intense cold prevailed, which produced much suffering among all classes, and caused the sleet to freeze upon the snow, forming a crust so hard and thick that the people, not distinguishing the location of the roads, drove in their sleighs across lots over fences and walls. Hon. Bailey Bartlett, Ichabod Tucker and several others of Haverhill, Massachusetts, drove from that place to Ipswich a distance of sixteen miles, in a large double sleigh upon the crust of snow across fields and pastures. The mail carriers were also greatly interrupted in the performance of their duties.

This was one of the winters to which the old folks of two generations ago were wont to refer, when no roads were broken out, and the farmers dragged their grists of corn on hand sleds upon the crust of the snow across fields, through woods and over fences and walls to the mills to get it ground.

The storm proved very disastrous to the vessels along the coast of Massachusetts. A schooner came ashore at Plum Island, and a brig and a sloop were cast away at Cape Ann. On Chelsea Beach a ship and a schooner were wrecked. The brig *Eliza,* commanded by Captain Ricker and owned in Berwick, Maine, while on its trip from Demerara to Boston, by way of the Vineyard, was driven on shore near the place of its destination on Monday, the twenty-second. Two schooners were also cast ashore at the same time and place, one of them being from Havana and bound to Salem, and the other belonging in Marblehead. Fortunately, no lives were lost from either vessel. Two pilot boats belonging to Messrs. Cole and Knox were driven ashore in the bay at Braintree, and a schooner, bound from Halifax to Boston, was wrecked on Cohasset rocks, one or more of the crew perishing. At Marshfield, the ship *Florenzo,* commanded by Captain Ham, bound from St. Ubes to Portsmouth, New Hampshire, by the way of New York, was driven on shore, a pilot, whose services they had secured at the Vineyard, and three of the crew being lost. Cape Cod, however, was the scene of the principal shipwrecks, among them being that of a schooner from Martinico, which was driven ashore at Sandwich, her crew and cargo of molasses being saved.

Fifty years ago, the storm was best remembered by the people living on Cape Cod, on account of the wrecks there of three East-Indiamen, from the port of Salem, Massachusetts. They were all full-rigged ships, and were named *Ulysses, Brutus* and *Volusia,* being commanded by Captains James Cook, William Brown and Samuel Cook, respectively. The first two were owned by G. Crowninshield and sons, and the other by Israel Williams and others of Salem. On that lovely Sunday morning, the three vessels proudly passed down the harbor of Salem, the *Brutus* and *Ulysses* being bound to Bordeaux, in France, and the *Volusia* to a port in the Mediterranean. A few hours after their departure, snow began to fall, the temperature descended very quickly, and before the next morning dawned, the wind blew a gale.

The storm came on so suddenly and was so furious that the people in Salem, to many of whose families the officers and crews belonged, were anxious to learn something from the vessels, and their owners also were interested as the ships and their cargoes were valuable. The first information that was received indicated that all the vessels and their crews were lost. Gloom rested upon the faces of the people as they conversed about the probable accuracy of the report.

There is waiting, anxious waiting, for the tidings of the missing—
And tearful eyes are looking in sadness to the shore;
And the mother's heart is aching as the child she's fondly kissing
Whispers softly from its cradle, "Will papa come no more?"

They were kept in suspense several days, and not till the fourth of March did they begin to learn the particulars of the great disaster that had come to the vessels and their crews. The story has been told thousands of times around the hearth-fires of a past generation, always being listened to with great interest. A warm summer-like day in February would bring the tale to the minds of those who remembered how lovely that quiet Sunday was, and what a terrible storm of snow, sleet and wind immediately followed.

At sunset on that beautiful day, the ships were about ten miles south-southeasterly from the Thachers Island lighthouse at Cape Ann, the wind was blowing lightly from the southeast, and all three vessels were sailing together toward the east northeast. Snow began to fall soon after, and a storm seemed to have begun. During the latter part of the evening the captains spoke each other, and discussed the situation. Had they better return to wait until suitable weather came, or push out to sea as fast as possible? They finally concluded to continue on the voyage, and turning their prows toward the east added to their sail. They made but very little progress, however, as the breeze was so light it had but slight effect upon the canvas, and at times seemed to leave them entirely. They continued together until midnight, when the snow fell faster and the wind grew strong, having suddenly changed to the northeast. The weather had now become so threatening that the captain of the *Volusia* regretted that he had consented to continue on the voyage, and at half past two in the morning, concluding to risk the trip no farther, he put about on his return to Salem. The other vessels were so far from him that he could not see them, and he therefore started back without informing them of his change of mind and course.

Before the *Volusia* could reach Cape Ann, the snow fell so thickly, and the wind blew so hard that it was found impossible to enter the harbor. Thwarted in their design they were now under the disheartening necessity of running before the wind, and endeavoring to keep the ship away from the dangerous coast. With reefed topsails, they managed to do this through the early morning hours and most of the forenoon, though the wind was blowing a gale from the east-northeast. At eleven o'clock they saw land to the leeward, which was immediately recognized as Cape Cod, whose perilous shores they knew full well. They saw that it was almost impossible to weather the cape, and that the only thing they could do would be to tack and try to run into the cape harbor. Just then the wind parted the fore-topsail sheet and tore the sail into shreds, at the same time carrying away the slings of the foreyard, which brought the yard down on deck, and rendered the headsails useless. Their hope of reaching the harbor was now utterly gone. They could do nothing but let the vessel drive on shore, and if they succeeded in reaching it all would be well; but how little hope any of the men had that they would survive the terrible breakers and the powerful undertow. They had spent their lives on the ocean and knew how slight their chance of preservation was. They thought of Salem, of their homes, their wives and children, that they would probably never see again, and they seemed to love them all then with an affection that was a thousand-fold stronger than they had ever felt before. Kindred thoughts filled their minds during the ten minutes that elapsed before the ship struck the bar, about a mile from the shore, off Truro near the Peaked Hills. The crew had already cut away the mizzenmast, and now the main lanyards were severed, and the mainmast fell over the side of the ship. After a short time the vessel beat over the bar, and was driven quite near the shore. Hope came to them again. They knew at what time of the day low-tide would occur, and so they patiently waited until the afternoon when the tide was at the lowest point. Many of the inhabitants of the cape had gathered on the beach, and with their assistance the land was successfully reached by the entire crew. The vessel and part of the cargo were also saved, although much damaged.

Let us now return to the *Brutus* and the *Ulysses* that the *Volusia* left in the night, plowing their way oceanward in the storm. The *Volusia* had left them at half-past two in the midnight darkness of the early morning, they not being aware of what had become of her. An hour later the captains of the two vessels spoke each other, and now agreed that the safest plan would be to tack to the north-northwest till daylight came, and then endeavor to run out of the south channel. They accordingly changed their course, and continued in the proposed direction until six o'clock. The *Brutus* then turned to the southeast, but the *Ulysses* headed for Cape Ann as the *Volusia* had done earlier in the morning. Captain Cook of the *Ulysses* kept his course until eight o'clock, then brought the ship round and stood out of the bay, under as much canvas as she could possibly carry. The gale increased, and they were obliged to reduce the amount of sail in the afternoon. At five o'clock they sighted the highlands of Cape Cod, and immediately tacked to the westward. The sky was dark and gloomy, the snow was falling thickly and the wind blew with so great fury that the only canvas the ship could carry were her foresail and mizzen-topsails. They did not dare to expect that they would weather the shoals, and thought they must strike immediately. The waves dashed over the deck carrying away from the bows one of the anchors, and more than an hour was spent in heaving it into place again. At ten o'clock in the evening the ship struck on the bar at the northern pitch of Cape Cod. The bowsprit and foremast were soon carried away by the wind and waves, and the mainmast, the mizzenmast, the boats and everything on the deck followed a few moments later. The hull only remained, and the crew fled to the cabin for protection. The ship lay thumping upon the bar but a few minutes, when some gigantic waves lifted it over, and carried it toward the beach. There they remained all night in almost utter hopelessness. The ship had bilged, and the men watched it fill with water until the floor of the cabin was covered. Their situation was now most serious, as the vessel was filling with water and they were far from shore. Before morning dawned, the tide had reached its extreme ebb, and the ship was happily left on the beach, near the water's edge, only about a mile from the wreck of the *Volusia*. The crew easily reached the shore, and received assistance from some of the people of Provincetown. A part of the cargo was saved, though it was much damaged, but the vessel finally went to pieces.

When the *Brutus* separated from the *Ulysses* at six o'clock on Monday morning, it changed its course to the southeast, carrying all the sail it possibly could. It weathered the gale all through that day, but was constantly driven shoreward. During the day Andrew Herron, who belonged in Salem, while engaged in reefing the foresail was blown from the yard, and fell, being instantly killed. He was a foreigner by birth, and a prudent and industrious young man, who by hard labor had accumulated considerable property. He was engaged to be married to a worthy lady of Salem, who was greatly affected by his death. About eight o'clock in the evening, the ship struck on the bar, two miles from the lighthouse and near the place where the *Volusia* and *Ulysses* came ashore. She remained on the bar some time, and at length was lightened by throwing overboard a large part of the cargo. The waves then carried her over, and she ran upon the beach. The mizzenmast was now cut away, and a few moments later the mainmast also. Hardly had this been done, when the crew were horrified to discover that the ship was parting in the middle. They must get on shore immediately, or perish in the waves. But how could they reach the land? Fortunately, the mainmast had fallen toward the beach, and on that they crawled as far as they could, Captain Brown bravely leading the way. He was the first man to get on shore. The two mates followed, and then came the seamen. All but one man, George Pierce of Marblehead, reached the beach in safety. He was overcome by the terrible waves, and drowned. The men were wet and cold and exhausted, and it seemed to be as fatal to remain on the beach as to have stayed on the vessel. Something must be done for their preservation immediately. They determined to keep in a body, and if possible to cross the neck of land and seek a place of shelter. This was the coldest night of the winter, the temperature being below zero, and the strong northeast wind pierced them through and through. Captain Brown was very thinly clothed, having lost his thickest garment as he left the ship. He soon succumbed to the intense cold and the fatiguing march through the deep snow, which was too exhausting for his weak limbs to continue further. Mr. Ruee, the first mate, and other seamen tenderly assisted him as well as they could, but they could not rally his waning strength and will. When they had reached the western side of the bay, about a mile from Provincetown, between that town and Truro, the captain gave up entirely, and soon after expired. It was now nearly midnight. One by one the men began to give out, Jacob Ayers of Manchester, the second mate, a worthy and promising young man, being one of the first to perish in the snow. Soon after, several others of the crew, becoming exhausted, dropped into the drifts, and froze to death. The survivors travelled about, not knowing whither they went, till about four o'clock in the morning (Tuesday), when they discovered a lighthouse. The party was now reduced to five persons only. They had wandered about, back and forth, in the course of the night, more than twenty miles. With limbs stiffened by cold and fatigue, they were just able to drag themselves to a small house situated in the vicinity of the lighthouse. They made their presence known to the people within, who opened wide their doors, and assisted the wretched mariners to enter. Here the sufferers received the most humane treatment. Search was immediately begun for those who had fallen in the snow during the night, but not one of them was saved. Had the wrecked seamen varied their course either to the right or left, they would have seen either the town of Truro or Provincetown, and probably fewer of them would have been lost. One of the men, Benjamin Ober, who belonged in Manchester, was found buried in the sand and snow, after having been there for thirty-six hours, being all that time in his full senses, and perceiving people continually passing near him, but powerless to move his body or make the party of rescuers hear his feeble voice. At length he held up his hand through the snow, and a boy saw it. Willing and strong arms immediately bore him to a warm room, but it was too late to revive his feeble life, which soon ebbed away.

The following is a list of the names of the crew of the *Brutus*. Those that perished were William Brown of Salem, captain; Jacob Ayers of Manchester, second mate; and Benjamin Ober of Manchester, Andrew Herron of Salem, Samuel Flagg of Andover, George Pierce of Marblehead, and three Negroes belonging in Salem, named Benjamin Birch, John Lancaster and John Tucker, seamen. The five men who survived were Thomas Ruee of Salem, first mate; and Joseph Phippen Jr., Robert Martin and William Rowell, all of Salem, and Daniel Potter of Marblehead, seamen. The bodies of those that perished were found the next day, and properly interred. Captain Brown, being found near Provincetown, was buried there, but the rest of the men having perished near Truro, were there given their last resting place. Captain Brown's death was sincerely mourned by a large number of people, as he had been a most valuable member of society.

During an easterly storm in 1880, the waves washed away a portion of the bank where the wreck of the *Brutus* had lain, and under it was found the skeleton of a man, who was supposed to have been an officer of that ship. With his bones were found some silver coin, and a watch that had stopped at two o'clock, which was shortly after the hour that the wreck occurred. The author of the History of Truro adds, "The wheels of the watch and the wheels of life stood still, and had been wrapped in their sandy winding-sheet for seventy-eight years."

Chapter xlv.

STORM OF OCTOBER 1804

At about nine o'clock in the morning of Tuesday, October 9, 1804, the temperature fell very suddenly, and a storm of rain and snow, accompanied by thunder and lightning, began. In the southern part of New England it rained, and in the northern portion the storm began with snow. The wind blew from the southeast until one o'clock in the afternoon, when it changed to the north-northeast, and before sunset became so powerful that it blew down houses, barns, chimneys and trees. The wind reached its height in the evening, and at midnight began to blow less violently, abating considerably before morning, though the storm of rain and snow continued until

Thursday morning. People sat up all that night, fearing to retire lest their houses would blow down. Wednesday morning revealed the streets in towns encumbered with sections of fence, whole or parts of trees, and many other things that the wind could carry away; and the country roads were everywhere obstructed with fallen trees.

In the southern portion of New England the rain fell in extraordinary quantities until the wind grew less violent, when snow began to fall, continuing all day Wednesday, that night and until the storm ended the next morning. In Vermont, the snow fell till Wednesday morning only, covering the earth to the depth of four or five inches, though along the higher lands the wind blew it into such large drifts that the roads were blocked, thus giving it the effect of a much greater storm. At Concord, New Hampshire, the snow was nearly two feet deep, and in Massachusetts from five to fourteen inches. In the southern portion of New England it melted in a few days, but in the northern states it remained in places until the next spring.

It was the earliest snow storm that the people of eastern Massachusetts had experienced for fifty years; and "the oldest inhabitant" did not remember so violent a storm, occurring there before. It did not reach far either north or south, but was felt inland beyond the limits of New England.

The effect of the storm on apples and potatoes was very disastrous. The fruit was blown from the trees, and in the norther sections large quantities of potatoes that remained undug were frozen into the ground, where they were left until the next spring, being harvested after the frost was out. The storm also caused the death of large numbers of cattle and sheep, and fowls of all kinds, especially around Walpole, and at Newbury and Topsfield, Massachusetts. At Newbury nearly a hundred cattle were killed, thirty being found dead in one section of the town. The snow also greatly damaged the fruit, shade, and ornamental trees, being so damp that it clung to the boughs and broke them down by its weight. The noise of breaking limbs of trees was continually heard in the woods.

The gale was very injurious to the pine and oak timber trees of the forests, destroying the larger portion of the best oaks that were useful in ship-building. It has been said that so many of the great oaks were destroyed that the building of vessels declined in Massachusetts, and that the great gale of 1815 brought about its entire abandonment in several places. At Thomaston, Maine, a sixty-acre timber lot was almost entirely blown down. Such great sections of the woods were levelled that new landscapes and prospects were brought into view to the surprise of many people. Houses and other buildings and hills that could not be seen before from certain places were now plainly visible. The change was so great in some localities that the surroundings seemed to have become entirely different, and people felt as if they were in a strange place.

Buildings and chimneys were blown down or greatly damaged by the wind. At Danvers, Massachusetts, the South Church (now included in that part of the town which was afterward incorporated as Peabody), and also the Baptist church at the port were unroofed, the latter having one of its sides blown in and the pews torn to pieces. At the brick-yard in that town belonging to Jeremiah Page, thirty or forty thousand unburned bricks were ruined by the rain, the wind blowing so violently that no covering could be kept over them. At Beverly, the spire of the lower meeting house, as it was then called, was broken off. At Salem, the dome and belfry on the Tabernacle church were torn to pieces; and a barn belonging to a Mr. French was blown down, killing one of his truck horses. Several sheds were also blown down. Many chimneys could not withstand the blasts, and fell. The three chimneys on the ancient court house that stood in front of the Tabernacle Church in the middle of Washington Street, being observed to be broken near the roof and tottering as if about to fall, were pushed over before they had caused injury to any one. Among the other chimneys blown down were three on William Gray's house in Essex Street, and two on Captain Mason's house in Vine Street, one of the latter falling upon the roof of Asa Pierce's house, which it broke through. No one in Salem suffered personal injury, fortunately. At Charlestown, the roof of the Baptist church was blown off, the spire on Rev. Dr. Morse's church was much bent, and two large dwelling houses were demolished. A brick building in the navy yard that had recently been erected was very much injured and had to be taken down. The brick-yards there were also much damaged, many bricks being destroyed. The wharves in Boston were somewhat injured, particularly May's, and the damage to buildings was considerable. Several new buildings were badly shaken and twisted, being so much injured that they had to be taken down and built anew. At the western part of the city, the wind blew the battlements from a new building upon the roof of an adjoining house, which was occupied by Ebenezer Eaton. Shortly before, a neighbor noticed that the battlements were giving away, and directed the attention of Mr. Eaton to it. He accordingly took his wife and children, and went to a safer place. A few minutes later the battlements fell and demolished the house, burying in its ruins the four persons who remained in it. These were a servant woman, named Bennett, who was killed, and another woman, a man and a boy, who were seriously injured. The roof was torn from the tower of King's Chapel, and conveyed two hundred feet. The beautiful steeple on the North Church fell, and demolished a house, the family that lived in fortunately being away on a visit. While the wind was blowing very violently, a stage was upset at the bridge at the west-end, some of the passengers being considerably hurt. Houses were also damaged at Newport and Providence, Rhode Island.

The shipping was also very much injured by the wind all along the coast from Rye, New Hampshire, to Newport, Rhode Island. Many vessels in the harbors dragged their anchors or broke their cables, and dashed against each other or the wharves, or were driven upon lee-shores and wrecked. The lives of many seamen were lost. In Vineyard Sound a sloop was upset, and all hands perished, and on the back of Cape Cod the schooner *John Harris* of Salem was lost with all on board. Five miles south of Cape Cod light-house, the ship *Protector,* of about five hundred tons burden, while on a trip from Boston to Lima, ran on the outer bar, about two hundred yards from the beach. This was a large vessel for those times, and was quite attractive, having yellow sides and a white figure-head. She went ashore stern first. Her bowsprit remained for some time, but the quarter deck, a part of the stern and the anchor on the larboard bow, with the boat, sails and rigging were soon washed away, some of the wreckage coming ashore. Of her cargo, which was worth a hundred thousand dollars, a considerable part was saved. One man was lost. Several vessels were driven ashore at Plymouth, and the dead body of a mariner was found on the beach and those of two others in a wreck. Vessels were driven out to sea from Marblehead, Manchester and other places and lost.

The brig *Thomas* of Portland was returning from a voyage to the West Indies, when she went ashore on Scituate Beach. The cargo of sugar and molasses was safely landed, and the vessel was gotten off without much damage being done to it.

The sloops *Hannah* of North Yarmouth, Capt. Joshua Gardner, master, and *Mary* of New Bedford, which was commanded by Captain Sanson, drifted together out of the harbor at Cape Ann, and were driven on shore at Cohasset at about the same time. The *Hannah* struck on a ledge some distance from the shore on Wednesday noon at twelve o'clock, and the first sea that swept the deck carried off the master, who was drowned. Two of the men lashed themselves to the boom, and remained on deck about two hours, until the vessel went to pieces, when the boom with the men still lashed to it washed ashore. Several of the citizens of Cohasset saw the men plunging in the surf, and came to their assistance, saving them when they were nearly exhausted. The people on board the *Mary* were all saved, and the vessel was afterward gotten off. Three other vessels came ashore at Cohasset, and were wrecked.

At Boston, many vessels in the harbor were damaged by being forced by the wind violently against the wharves. The *Laura,* belonging in Gloucester and commanded by Captain Griffin, was nearly beaten to pieces at Long Wharf, and her cargo was very much damaged. Many of the small craft were so blown about and strained that they bilged and sank, several of them being staved to pieces. Some of the larger vessels also bilged, and several had bowsprits, sterns and other sections broken. Cargoes were also damaged. Several men were drowned there during the gale, two being cast into the water from a boat that upset at May's Wharf, and drowned before they could be rescued. A lad was endeavoring to keep a sloop free of water near Four Point Channel, but his efforts proved unsuccessful. When the vessel was sinking he clasped a plank, but was soon washed off and drowned.

The vessels in the harbor at Salem also drifted about, their anchors failing to hold them. Very few were injured, however, except two schooners, one of which drifted in from Gloucester, and the other, the *Success,* commanded by Captain Robbins and laden with fish, oil and lumber, put in here while on a trip from Passamaquoddy to Boston. They were both cast ashore, and damaged more than any of the others. The *Success* lost her anchors and her main and jib booms, and finally bilged.

Near Fresh Water Cove in Gloucester, a sloop belonging to Kennebunk, laden with rum, was lost. The master and crew were saved, but a lady passenger perished. A schooner, belonging in Connecticut, with a cargo of corn, also went to pieces there, the people on board being rescued. Several other vessels were wrecked on different parts of the cape; and six large crafts there had to cut away their masts, among them being an English ship from Newfoundland. Four or five vessels were driven out of the harbor, some of them being lost, with their crews. A fleet of fishing vessels were off the northern part of the cape, and for a while the people were much concerned for their safety.

The schooner *Dove,* of Kittery, was wrecked on Ipswich Bar, and all of the seven persons on board perished. An eastern vessel was lost on Rye Beach, in New Hampshire, and a woman, who was a passenger in it, was found dead on the sand, with an infant clasped in her arms. Near Rye was also wrecked the schooner *Amity,* from Philadelphia, commanded by Captain Trefethern. All the people on board were saved, except a passenger named Charles Schroeder, of Philadelphia, who was drowned.

Chapter xlvi.

TOTAL ECLIPSE OF THE SUN, 1806

The only total eclipse of the sun visible in New England during the present century occurred on Monday, the sixteenth of June, 1806. The day was unusually beautiful, scarcely a cloud being discernible in any part of the New England sky. The air was dry and serene, and so still that the very gentle breeze which came from the northwest was hardly distinguishable. Nature gave every opportunity for observation.

The eclipse came on at six minutes past ten and went off at ten minutes before one. During the period of five minutes, at about half past eleven, it was total, the moon during that time being surrounded by an illuminated white ring, from which issued minute and vivid corruscations.

There had been a slight frost on the preceding night, and the morning was quite cool for the season. When the eclipse came on the temperature was sixty-three degrees above zero at Salem, Massachusetts, and the heat decreased until the time when the disk of the sun was entirely covered. The thermometer then stood at fifty-five and one-half degrees above zero, a diminution of seven and one-half degrees. In some places sufficient dew fell on the grass to wet one's shoes. The change in the temperature was so sudden and so great that many people, who were in a state of perspiration from their morning's labor, became chilled, and some died from its effects.

The better educated classes of course expected that a certain degree of darkness would come over the land, but it was found to be much more intense than any one had supposed it would be. When the eclipse came on the sky was of the brightest azure, but as the moon covered the sun's disk the color became darker, and soon grew dusky. One star after another came into view, until Venus shone brightly in the west, Sirius in the southeast, and Aldebaran sparkled in the zenith. Mars, Mercury and Procyon also came, and the larger stars in Orion and Ursa Major were plainly visible to the naked eye. Venus was seen for more than half an hour.

As the sun began to be covered everything around assumed the appearance of twilight for ten or fifteen degrees above the horizon. From that time the scene was sublime. Night seemed to be settling over the land at noon-day. As the darkness increased a feeling of awe came over the people, and though it inspired neither dread nor anxiety among the great majority of the people, as the dark day did, even the most educated persons could not repress the feeling of gloom and solemnity that comes over mankind generally when anything of this nature occurs. The wonder workings of the universe compel our notice and veneration. What display could be more sublime than this exhibition of the grandeur of nature, arranged on such a stupendous scale that the inhabitants of a hemisphere could gaze at it with perfect ease and freedom!

The darkness became so intense that the seconds on the dial of a clock could not be seen without the aid of a candle, except by very sharp eyes, and then with much difficulty. The effect of the darkness upon animals was about the same as if night were coming on, except that they seemed to be somewhat surprised and perplexed. Cattle in the pastures ceased feeding, and started for the bars. Fowls retired to their roosts, and bees returned to their hives. When the darkness began to disappear, and light to come again, the cocks jumped down from their roosting places and crowed as lustily as when they awoke that morning.

Ramsey, in 1715, wrote the following lines on an approaching solar eclipse, which are as applicable to this one of 1806 as to that. He sees

> *Black night usurp the throne of day,*

and prophesies that

> *. . . thoughtless fools will view the water-pail*
> *To see which of the planets will prevail;*
> *For then they think the sun and moon make war:*
> *Thus nurses' tales ofttimes the judgment mar.*

He concludes that

> *When this strange darkness overshades the plains,*
> *'Twill give an odd surprise t'unwarned swains;*
> *Plain honest hinds, who do not know the cause,*
> *Nor know of orbs, the motions or their laws,*
> *Will from the half-plowed furrows homeward bend*
> *In dire confusion, judging that the end*
> *Of time approacheth; thus possessed with fear*
> *They'll think the general conflagration near.*
> *The traveller, benighted on the road,*

Will turn devout, and supplicate his God.
Cocks with their careful mates and younger fry,
As if 'twere evening, to their roosts will fly.
The horned cattle will forget to feed,
And come home lowing from the grassy mead,
Each bird of day will to his nest repair,
And leave to bats and owls the dusky air;
The lark and little robins' softer lay
Will not be heard till the return of day.
Not long shall last this strange uncommon gloom.
When light dispels the plowman's fear of doom,
With merry heart he'll lift his ravished sight
Up to the heavens, and welcome back the light.
How just's the motions of these whirling spheres,
Which ne'er can err while time is met by years!
How vast is little man's capricious soul,
That knows how orbs through wilds of aether roll!
How great's the power of that omnific hand,
Who gave them motion by his wise command,
That they should not, while time had being, stand!

Chapter xlvii.

THE FRESHET OF 1807

The first great flood in New England during this century occurred in February, 1807. It was occasioned by heavy rains, which melted the snow and swelled the rivers until they overflowed, carrying away bridges and mills, entering warehouses and stores, and doing great damage.

It carried away several bridges at the eastward of Portsmouth, New Hampshire, and one over Little River in Haverhill, Massachusetts. The principal bridge at Lawrence,[1] and others farther up the Merrimack River were destroyed. The Watertown bridge and the Milford bridge were also carried away. At Pawtucket, Rhode Island, the bridge was destroyed, and the

---

1. This bridge then connected Andover and Methuen, but by the incorporation of the city of Lawrence and change of town lines, it is now wholly within the bounds of Lawrence.

cotton factory that was then flourishing there, and four or five other buildings floated off.

In Connecticut, the stone bridge over Swallow-tail Brook at East
Chelsea, that had been built in 1795, was destroyed. It was reconstructed,
and is now beneath the street. The Willimantic and Mount Hope rivers
began to break up on the night of Saturday, February 7, and the sound of
the cracking of the vast cakes of ice was like the crashing of thunder. The
Shetucket River rose from eighteen to twenty feet, and at Norwich the
stream could not contain the water that came down. Lord's and Lathrop's
bridges were swept away, and Lovett's was considerably damaged. Lathrop's
Bridge was rebuilt. The abutments of Geometry Bridge had to be replaced,
and Wharf, Courthouse and Quarter bridges were somewhat injured. The
river overflowed its banks here, and the water ran into the cellars and buildings along the shores of the stream. The water rose in the houses until it
reached the first stories, and compelled the inmates to go into their chambers to escape the flood, which had come upon them so suddenly that they
found themselves imprisoned. The water continued to rise higher and
higher until it was within a few inches of the chamber floors, when it was
considered unsafe for people to remain in the houses longer, and they were
taken away in boats, into which they stepped from their chamber windows.
Captain Rockwell's and other families were removed in this way. The flood
extended from East Main to Franklin streets, and from hill to hill, the
topography of the city then being somewhat different from what it is now,
some portions of the streets having been filled in. That the flood should
spread no further, the people erected with great expedition a temporary
embankment out of timber, spars, rails and wood, securing it in place with
heavy stones. It was filled in with hay, straw, canvas, and everything that
would resist leakage. It extended from the site of the Wauregan Hotel to the
opposite side of the valley where the streets cross each other. The effect of
the erection was satisfactory. The water trickled slightly over this breast-
work, but the embankment was effectual in keeping back the great body of
water until the river subsided in the course of a few hours.

Chapter xlviii.

THE METEORITE OF 1807

At about six o'clock on the morning of Monday, December 14, 1807, when it was yet an hour to sunrise, and dark enough to make it startlingly visible, the people of the western portion of New England who were lucky enough to be out of doors saw a ball of fire pass through the air from north to south. It was a rare meteorite, and its course lay over Rutland, Vermont, the western part of Massachusetts, and into Connecticut as far as Weston, where it exploded. The temperature was quite mild that morning, the air was still, the heavens were somewhat clouded, and near the earth considerable fog had gathered. The meteorite was seen by a considerable number of people, especially in Vermont and Connecticut, being noticed particularly by parties interested in such things. This was a specimen of the meteoric stones which suddenly and unexpectedly appear and are seen for such a brief space of time that it is hardly possible to make observations that are sufficiently accurate for scientific calculations. This meteorite was one of the most remarkable that ever fell in this region.

The course of this ball of fire, which was called by some of the people of those times a "terrestrial comet," was a few degrees west of south, and its altitude was variously estimated to be from one to five miles. It was about three feet in diameter, having a conically-shaped train of pale light resembling sparks about two rods in length. It appeared like a ball of fire, being bright red, and in those sections where it passed through clear sky a brisk scintillation was seen about the body of the meteorite, the whole appearing like a brightly-burning fire-brand carried against the wind.

The speed at which the meteorite travelled was duly estimated and found to be about one hundred and sixty miles per minute. It remained in sight at no place for more than thirty seconds. It did not vanish away instantly at last, but apparently made three successive leaps, and disappeared with the last, its light growing dimmer at every effort. These movements were caused by explosions, and about thirty seconds after the last one three loud and distinct reports, like those of a four-pound cannon fired near at hand, were heard. They followed each other rapidly but distinctly, and all occupied less than three seconds of time. A rapid succession of reports less loud then followed, which ran together so as to produce a continued rumbling, being sometimes loud and sometimes faint. At New Milford, which was more than twenty miles from the place over which the meteorite burst, the explosion was severer than in Weston. The cause assigned for its extinction in this manner was the dampness and density of the atmosphere.

Sections of the meteorite fell in different parts of Fairfield County, some of the pieces being six miles apart. One mass was driven against a rock and dashed into small pieces, a peck of which remained on the spot. A piece weighing thirty pounds fell in Weston, and was secured entire, being exhibited the next day at the town meeting that was held there. Some pieces weighed as much as thirty-five pounds, and others that fell on rocks were estimated to weigh one hundred and fifty pounds. A small mass was sent to Yale College, and examined by a number of the faculty, who reported that it contained a large percentage of iron. As far as history shows this was the first instance in the United States where iron was thus found. Scientists said that the stones consisted of silex, magnesia, iron, nickel and sulphur, the light coming from the last three substances, which were probably in a state of combustion. Where the stones came from is not so easily answered, but they are supposed to have been formed of the ingredients of the air.

Chapter xlix.

COLD FRIDAY, 1810

January 19, 1810, is the date of the famous day known in the annals of New England as "Cold Friday." It was said to have been the severest day experienced here from the first settlement of the country to that time.

To this date the winter had been unusually moderate. December had been quite warm, even milder than November. Very little snow had fallen and the ground was bare in southern New England, but in New Hampshire and other northern states there was good sleighing. The preceding day and evening had been mild for the season, with a warm south wind, but at about four o'clock in the afternoon there was a squall of snow, the wind sprang up, and immediately changed to the north-northwest, increasing in force until it blew with great violence. The temperature was then forty-five degrees above zero at Salem, Massachusetts, and it suddenly began to descend. The next morning, only eighteen hours later, it was five degrees below zero, having fallen fifty degrees. At Amherst, New Hampshire, it was fourteen

degrees below zero, and in other places thirteen, having fallen as many
degrees as it had at Salem. At Weare, New Hampshire, the temperature fell
fifty-five degrees in twenty-four hours, from Thursday morning to Friday
morning. The strong piercing wind enhanced the cold to a great degree, and
penetrated the thickest clothing, driving the cold air into all parts of
dwelling-houses, and making the day almost insufferable in common
houses and terrible out of doors. Few people ventured out, and those that
did had their hands, noses, ears or feet almost instantly frost-bitten. Many
people were frozen to death while travelling along the highways. At times
and places the wind was so strong that it was difficult to keep on one's feet.
The gale continued all day, and houses, barns, and vast numbers of timber
trees were blown down, or broken to pieces in such a way as to render them
unfit for timber, being left to decay where they fell.

At Chester, New Hampshire, the wind lifted a house, letting one corner
of it fall to the bottom of the cellar. At Sanbornton, the three children of
Jeremiah Ellsworth perished with the cold on this morning under very sad
circumstances. As Mr. Ellsworth and his wife were uncomfortable in bed,
they rose about an hour before sunrise. Shortly after, a part of the house was
blown in, and it was thought that the whole structure would be demolished.
Leaving the two elder children in bed, because their clothes had been blown
away, Mrs. Ellsworth dressed the youngest child and went into the cellar for
safety, while her husband started for assistance to the house of the nearest
neighbor in a northerly direction, which was a mile distant. He found it to
be too hazardous to face the wind and so changed his course toward the
house of David Brown, which was the nearest in another direction, being
only a quarter of a mile away. He reached it as the sun rose, his feet being
considerably frozen, and his whole person so benumbed by the cold that he
could not return with Mr. Brown to bring his wife and children in a sleigh.
Having arrived at the house, Mr. Brown put a bed in the sleigh and placed
the children upon it, covering them with the bed clothes. Mrs. Ellsworth
also got into the sleigh; but they had gone only six or eight rods when it was
blown over, and all the persons and every thing were lodged in the snow.
Mrs. Ellsworth held the horse while he reloaded the sleigh. She decided to
walk, and started off ahead, but before Mr. Brown's house was reached was
so overcome by the cold that she thought she could not go farther, and sank
into the snow. She thought that she must perish, but at length she made
another effort and crawled along on her hands and knees until she met her
husband, who was searching for them. She was so changed by her experiences that he did not at first recognize her. By his help she reached the

house. Mr. Brown had not yet come. After Mrs. Ellsworth left him, he again started, but had gone but a few rods when the sleigh was torn to pieces by the wind, and the children thrown to some distance. He collected them once more, laid them on the bed and covered them over. He then hallooed for assistance, but no one answered. He knew that the children would soon perish in that situation, and as their cries of distress pierced his heart, he wrapped them all in a coverlet, and attempted to carry them on his shoulders. But the wind blew them all into a heap in the snow. Finding it impossible to carry all three of the children, he left the child that was dressed by the side of a large log, and took the other two upon his shoulders. But again he failed to carry them against the strong wind. He then took a child under each arm, they having on no other clothing than their shirts, and in this way, though blown down every few rods, he finally reached the house, having been about two hours on the way. The two children, though frozen stiff, were alive, but died a few minutes after reaching the house. Mr. Brown's hands and feet were badly frozen, and he was severely chilled and exhausted. The body of the child was found before night. Mr. Brown lived many years after this experience, but never recovered from its effects, becoming blind in consequence.

The cold continued to be extreme until the forenoon of the following Monday, when the wind changed to the southwest, and the temperature began to rise.

At Springfield, Massachusetts, on the cold morning, a heavy fog seemed to be passing down the river. The cold air congealed it into fine snow, which rose as high as forty feet above the water. It continued through the day, but was most conspicuous about two o'clock ill the afternoon. A similar phenomenon was seen at the same time in Salem. It there had a smoky appearance, being so dense that it was opaque, but rose only a few feet above the surface of the water.

Chapter C.

THE FRESHET OF 1814

In May, 1814, a great and disastrous freshet occurred in Maine. The weather had been very inclement for the season nearly all the month. From the second to the ninth, there were but two pleasant days, and on the night

Bridge out. Mill Street, Brunswick, Maine. Pejepscot Historical Society.

of the thirteenth rain commenced to fall in torrents, continuing without intermission until the night of the seventeenth. During those four days and nights more water fell than the people remembered to have fallen in the same length of time. The weather did not clear, nor the rain wholly cease until the nineteenth. It then became very warm, the temperature rising to seventy-eight degrees, and a greater freshet than had been known in that region for a third of a century followed, doing incalculable damage in several places.

The Mousam River was so raised by the great rain that the bridge in the village of Kennebunk was entirely swept away, and for some time afterward foot travellers were carried over in boats. The dams and mills were also much injured.

The Saco River, which is so quickly affected by heavy rainfalls, became a roaring flood of waters. At Conway, New Hampshire, where so much loss was occasioned by the deluge of 1785, a carding- and fulling-mill and a dwelling-house were taken down before the freshet in order to save them. The dam of the iron works there was carried off, and the people greatly feared that the works themselves would also be swept away. A short distance down the stream, at Fryeburg, in Maine, a bridge in the southeastern part of the town, leading across a branch of the Saco River, was destroyed. The flood then rushed down to Brownfield, where all the bridges on the main road were carried away, and thence to Hiram, where the bridge over the Saco and part of that across the Great Ossipee River were lifted and set adrift down the stream. The principal part of the mills, several dwelling-houses, an immense number of logs and boards, and all the bridges between Buxton and the mouth of the Saco River, including the two bridges in Saco, were carried out into the ocean.

The losses sustained on the Androscoggin River by the freshet were equal to those on the Saco. Eight saw-mills, a valuable aqueduct, and part of the bridge between Topsham and Brunswick were carried away, and a hundred thousand dollars' worth of logs and much other valuable property floated out to sea.

In almost all the towns in that section of Maine there was more or less damage done. The bridge, between Long Pond and Brandy Pond at Otisfield, was swept away on the night of Wednesday, the eighteenth, and strange to say it floated up the stream until the next day at noon, when the current turned. Many parts of the bridge floated back to the place where it had stood, and were pulled out of the water. The dam and five grist- and saw-mills in Waterford and vicinity were also carried away. The mill pond above the mills of C. Johnson, Esq., and others in Windham rose so high and pressed so hard that a new outlet was formed through the sandy banks.

Chapter Ci.

THE TORNADO IN NEW HAMPSHIRE IN 1814

At about five o'clock on the afternoon of Saturday, May 21, 1814, in New Hampshire, there was a violent storm of wind and rain, accompanied by hail. It passed over Litchfield, Merrimack, Londonderry, North Chester, and some of the adjoining towns. It crossed the Merrimack River near Read's Ferry, in a northeasterly direction, and continued as far as Chester, a distance of seventeen miles, its width being from fifty to a hundred rods. It was severely felt, a considerable number of houses, barns and other buildings, trees of all kinds, and fences being destroyed. The injury to wood lots was very great. Few trees could withstand the violence of the wind, strong oaks, ancient maples, and lofty pines alike yielded and fell prostrate. Some were broken or twisted off from five to thirty feet above the ground, but most of them were turned up by the roots. Many fences were wholly destroyed, being torn to pieces and the fragments scattered everywhere. One or two persons were killed and several injured by falling buildings. It also proved fatal to cattle in several places. Much window glass in houses was broken by the hail-stones which were said to have been extremely large. A journal of that time says that some of the pieces were of an enormous size, weighing more than half a pound, and measuring eleven inches in circumference.

In Litchfield, two houses and two barns were demolished, and Jonathan Coombs was badly injured by a part of one of the buildings.

The tornado first appeared in Merrimack about half a mile west of the house then owned by Lt. Samuel Foster. One of Mr. Foster's barns was demolished, the pieces being scattered in every direction. In it were a horse and two calves, none of which were injured. He had two other barns unroofed, and otherwise considerably damaged. Benjamin Hartshorn also had a barn unroofed. About half a mile from the house of Nathan Parker, Esq., in his field, three of his sons and two other persons were at work with him. They saw the storm approaching, and speedily made their way to the barn, which they entered for shelter. But in a few moments, realizing that they would not be safe there, they all ran out, and had hardly crossed the threshold when the wind struck the barn, demolishing it. One of Mr. Parker's sons, a lad of about eleven years of age, was struck on the neck by a stick of timber, and instantly killed. Another of the boys was severely wounded.

In Londonderry, seven barns and sheds were demolished. An incident connected with the tornado in this town is related of Dr. Bartley, as follows. He was returning home in his carriage, and perceiving the storm approaching with great rapidity, with singular forethought he alighted and unharnessed his horse. A moment later the wind carried the carriage over a fence about twenty rods away, and dashed it to pieces.

At North Chester, a house and barn were damaged to the extent of a thousand dollars. A pair of oxen were taken up by the wind, and carried some distance, being finally thrown into a pond and killed.

Chapter Cii.

THE GALE OF SEPTEMBER 23, 1815

The summer of 1815 was remarkable for exceptionally violent and dis-astrous storms all along the Atlantic coast, and the columns of the newspa-pers were filled with accounts of the great destruction of life and property on both land and sea. The equinoctial gale of September, however, exceeded them all in violence, and caused greater and more general disaster than any that had preceded it, not that year only but since the settlement of the country.

The storm began at three o'clock on the morning of Friday, the twenty-second, when the wind was at the northeast, and rain fell copiously until sunrise. Shortly after, the clouds partly broke away, and fair weather seemed about to return. During the forenoon, however, the clouds became thicker, the sky darkened, and in some sections of New England rain fell to a considerable amount. In the afternoon the wind blew with increased force, and rain continued to fall in small quantities. Through the night the wind was moderate, and there was a slight fall of rain, but before sunrise next morning the wind again became violent having changed to the east in the night, and about nine o'clock was very strong, having veered to the east-northeast. At ten o'clock it shifted to the southeast, and continued to increase in force until it blew so fiercely that buildings, fences, trees, vessels along the exposed sections of the coast, and all kinds of movable things, were swept away before it. But little rain fell during the tornado where it was the fiercest. The wind did not blow steadily, but came in gusts, and contin-ued its work of destruction until noon, when it changed to the southwest, after which it quickly subsided. Then a little more rain fell, but before night pleasant weather had come.

During the heaviest part of the gale fires could not exist in the houses, being blown out as fast as they were lighted. This might have been the result of the peculiar condition of the air, which at about the time that the wind changed to the southeast was very oppressive and almost suffocating. Respiration was laborious and difficult. This was particularly noticeable at Worcester, Massachusetts, where a hot wind seemed to envelope the town and render the air non-elastic.

The gale swept away buildings of all sizes and varieties from churches to sheds, unroofed an exceedingly great number of others, and damaged many thousand more to a greater or less extent. On the roofs of some of the structures shingles were stripped off in rows from the eaves to the ridge-poles. In some places the air seemed to be full of shingles and fragments of timbers and boards, forced hither and thither by the blasts. Great quantities of forest, shade, ornamental and fruit trees were uprooted or broken down, many of them being twisted like withes. Fruit of all kinds was blown from the trees and destroyed. The gale of October, 1804, had blown down many timber trees, and this wind came from the opposite direction and prostrated the great oaks and pines that had escaped at that time. The loss in timber trees was exceedingly great; and in order to save as much as they possibly could from the ruins of their forests the owners had the logs sawed into lumber, with which they constructed houses, barns and other buildings. Probably New England never knew another season of such building activity as prevailed in 1817 and 1818, the logs having been sawed in the winter of 1813-1816, and the lumber seasoned during the following summer. This occurred in hundreds of towns and villages, and in one case, at least, a church was erected on this account. This was the old South Church at Reading, Massachusetts, the timber on the "ministerial" lands being almost wholly blown down. Had the storm occurred a little earlier, when there was so much more corn and grain in the fields, it would have produced a great deal more suffering. As it was, besides the great quantity of hay that had been gathered into barns, and was now scattered to the winds, much of the apple crop was ruined, and also corn and grain. Many persons were killed by falling houses and trees, and others were drowned from the wrecks of vessels along the coast. The lives of a large number of animals were also destroyed by falling trees. The next day was Sunday, and the religious services held that day were scantily attended, as the men were busy in caring for their property, and in building or repairing fences to protect from cattle the crops which had escaped the fury of the wind.

The surface of the sea, bays, harbors and inland waters was made smooth by the force and velocity of the wind, no waves or other unevenness being seen upon them when the gale blew the strongest. Along the coast the wind so drove in the water that the tide rose to a great height, deluging wharves, streets and cellars.

The wind carried the salt water of the ocean more than forty miles into the country destroying the foliage of the trees, crisping and curling the leaves of plants, and giving to all vegetation with which it came in contact the appearance of having suffered from a severe frost. Along the Massachusetts coast, a thin layer of salt was formed on the sides of houses and other things that were exposed to the wind, especially on windows, owing undoubtedly to the comminuted particles of salt carried that great distance by the terrific wind. The brooks and small rivers became quite brackish, and the rain-water that fell as far inland as Worcester and Sterling, in Massachusetts, more than forty miles from the sea, had a strong briny taste. In some localities fresh water was long a rarity, and it has been said that some of the springs did not fully recover from the effects of this deposit of salt for years. Some people have thought that so much of this saline substance could not have been carried to such a great distance by the wind, and that it must have been generated in the air in the localities where it was noticed.

Many birds, whose home is on the ocean, were driven with the spray twenty miles inland. Flocks of sea-gulls were seen in the meadows at Grafton and Worcester, in Massachusetts, in the forenoon, but during the afternoon, after the storm had subsided, they speedily returned to their lonely abode on the deep. Several sea-swallows, properly petrels, or what the sailors call "Mother Cary's chickens," were also seen quite a distance inland. Their usual abode is on the deepest water of the ocean, and they are rarely seen within many miles of land. They alight on vessels at sea, and are so tame that mariners call them chickens. The people did not remember to have ever seen them on land before, and to the knowledge of the writer such an instance has occurred but twice since, the last time being a few years ago, during a severe easterly storm, when they were driven inland a distance of at least fifteen miles. They were so tame that they would allow themselves to be handled by the people. They had never received other than kind treatment from sailors, and therefore had no reason to suspect harm from landsmen.

As blast after blast of the wind blew down buildings, the people closed windows and doors, but what more to do they did not know. A writer has said that if the windows and doors on the leeward side of the buildings had been left open a far less number of roofs would have been blown off. The gale came against the sides of the houses bearing them in and compressing the air inside, and when the force was withdrawn the inside air expanded and raised the roof; or, according to the more reasonable view, the pressure on the side caused the air to press the roof upward, that being the portion of the building that would most readily yield to a force from within.

The countenances of the people during the gale bore an expression of awe and fear. Men spoke in low tones in the lulls of the wind, but were silent and held their breath when it raged again. Each one thought that his house might be the next to be shattered to atoms, and that the lives of his family might be taken. The first intimation that the wind had begun permanently to abate cheered the hearts of the people, hope and joy taking the place of doubt and fear, and they felt as if a burden of insufferable weight had been rolled from their shoulders.

The gale was felt as far south as Delaware, and inland to a considerable distance beyond the New England states in a westerly direction. Just how many lives were lost, many of them being those of husbands and fathers, and how much property was destroyed cannot be ascertained. Neither can any one know how many fond hopes were forever blasted, how many changes in life and its plans were caused, nor the pain of body and heart that followed.

The force of the gale was principally and most severely felt in Narragansett Bay in Rhode Island. The wind swept the bay, and Providence suffered from its effects more than any other place. From ten to half-past eleven o'clock it blew a hurricane. About the wharves and lower part of the town generally confusion reigned. High water was about half-past eleven o'clock in the forenoon, and the wind brought in the tide ten or twelve feet above the height of the usual spring tides, and seven and a half feet higher than ever known before, overflowing and inundating streets and wharves. The vessels there were driven from their moorings in the stream and fastenings at the wharves, with terrible impetuosity, toward the great bridge that connected the two parts of the town. The gigantic structure was swept away without giving a moment's check to the vessels' progress, and they passed on to the head of the basin, not halting until they were high up on the bank. All the vessels were driven ashore, or totally destroyed. There were wrecked in the cove four ships, nine brigs, seven schooners and fifteen sloops. After the storm they lay high and dry, five or six feet above high-water mark, in the streets and gardens of the town. One sloop stood upright in Pleasant Street before the door of a Mr. Webb, and a ship was in the garden of General Lippet. Nine of the vessels that were driven ashore were successfully launched again, but more than thirty were totally lost.

The owners of the stores, wharves, and other property in the inundated district exerted themselves to the utmost to save all they possibly could from destruction, but with little success on account of the terrible violence of the gale. The water was rising rapidly, trees were falling, chimneys were crashing through roofs of houses or into the street, tiles and railings from the tops of buildings, and other dangerous missiles were flying through the air, making it hazardous to be out of doors.

The storm raged with increasing violence, and the water was rapidly rising and deluging the lower parts of the town. Wharves were being washed away, stores and other buildings on them were about to leave their foundations, and the water surged around the houses of the people who resided in the lower sections. All considerations of property soon gave way to a more important concern. Every one in the more exposed parts of the town became solicitous for his own personal safety and that of his family and friends. Stores and dwelling houses were seen to reel and totter for a few moments, and then plunge into the deluge. A moment later their fragments were blended with the wrecks of vessels, some of which were on their sides, that were passing with great rapidity and irresistible impetuosity on the current to the head of the cove, to join the wrecks already on the land.

On the west side of the river the water rose nearly to the tops of the lower windows of the houses, and people were removing, in boats and scows, from their dangerous situation. Most of the stores and other buildings were destroyed and the fragments carried into the cove above the bridge. On the east side the water rushed impetuously through Weybosset Street, which was the principal thoroughfare, nearly a yard in depth, turbulently carrying along with it boats, masts, bales of cotton, etc., with almost resistless force. It seemed as if that portion of the town was doomed. The store on Bowen's wharf just below where the bridge had stood still maintained its place, though much injured, but all the stores below, on the east side, were either carried away or so much damaged that they were in a great measure useless. Several dwelling-houses on Eddy's Point were carried off, leaving not a vestige behind. In Westminster Street, the water was from six to eight feet above the pavements. The Second Baptist Church, which was located near the water, was entirely demolished and that of Rev. Mr. Williams, which also stood in a very exposed place, was considerably injured, and if the tide had continued to rise but a few moments longer that, too, must have been destroyed. All the space which but an hour or two before had been occupied by valuable wharves and stores filled with goods, and the river that had been crowded with vessels, were now one wide waste of water raging and furious. Along the higher portion of land were heaped together lumber, wrecks of buildings and vessels of every description, carriages, and bales of cotton, mingled with household furniture, coffee, soap, candles, grain, flour and other kinds of merchandise. Those who witnessed it said that it was a prospect of such widespread desolation and havoc as was beyond description.

A brig, that was laden with living stock and ready for sea, was driven by the gale against the end of a wharf, her head resting on it. There the vessel hung, and from time to time it seemed as if she must upset and plunge into the raging flood. Her crew, consisting of nine persons, clung to her, and awaited their fate. It was not safe for the people on shore to venture to their relief, as the space between them and the vessel was filled with roofs and other parts of stores tumbling about with the violence of the wind. Becoming desperate the sailors made an effort to reach the shore. They quitted the vessel and crawled along on the rolling, bounding debris, the wind threatening them with instant destruction. They endeavored to gain a foothold on something, and as they struggled the people looked on. At length the seamen came near some houses that were still standing, and some of the men were pulled in at the second-story windows by the people in the houses. The rest of them could not come within reach, and at length plunged into the clearer water between two houses and safely swam ashore. Similar incidents were constantly occurring.

The third story of the handsome Washington insurance office building, which was occupied by Mount Vernon Lodge, was much injured by being perforated by the bowsprit of the ship *Ganges* when she was impetuously forced up the stream with the other vessels. India Bridge at India Point and Mill Bridge at the foot of Constitution Hill were also swept from their foundations. Five hundred buildings in all, large and small, were destroyed in this gale and flood, which, with other property that was lost, were valued at fifteen hundred thousand dollars.

Beside those persons who were wounded and maimed, many valuable citizens were carried with their houses into the water, and others were crushed to death between the planks and the vessels as the latter dashed through the great bridge. No one knows how many human lives were lost in Providence, nor how many cattle were drowned. After the inundation had subsided, a military force of about three hundred was stationed there for several days to prevent pillage of the remaining property that was exposed. No business but that in connection with the storm could be done for some time, the streets having first to be cleared, and then buildings, bridges and wharves rebuilt.

Providence profited, however, by the great calamity in the general improvement of the town. In the place of dilapidated warehouses, spacious brick buildings arose, new bridges far surpassing the old ones in strength and beautiful design were built, and an elegant and much larger church occupied the site of that which had been destroyed. Four years after the storm the greatly improved appearance of the place indicated an era of prosperity rather than one of loss and disaster, in spite of the general inactivity of business that had then prevailed for a year or two.

At Bristol, a short distance from Providence down Narragansett Bay, all the vessels were driven a great distance in on the land, and considerably injured. There the tide rose seven feet higher than it was ever known to rise before, and the wharves were completely swept away. The building then occupied by the post office, and several houses and stores were also carried off. A long row of brick stores on one of the wharves, with their contents, which were very valuable, were carried away. A great many trees were also blown down, and much other damage done. The grist-mill at Glenrock Village in the Narragansett country and at Point Judith the lighthouse were destroyed, the large fishing rocks at the latter place being removed from their beds.

The section of country that suffered next to Providence in amount of damage was that around Buzzard's Bay in Massachusetts, which had the full sweep of the wind. No rain fell there, but the tide was eight feet higher than usual, and salt water was driven in on the land so far and in such quantities that it killed the vegetation—grass, Indian corn, potatoes, etc. Wells and springs, the principal sources of the people's supply of fresh water, were also ruined. Some of the fields near the shore were so washed by the overflowing tide, or covered with sand, that they resembled beaches, and in some places where the English grass was killed, wild grasses or clover appeared the next year, and still again where only mosses had grown, grass sprang up. Generally, the land was made better. The salt water killed the trees in the cedar swamps along the shore of the bay. Trees and buildings were blown down and vessels driven on shore by the terrific wind.

At New Bedford, all the vessels in the port, except two, were driven ashore, and several of them beaten to pieces. One ship was left on a wharf, and another on one of the islands. All the warehouses on the lower wharves were swept off, many houses being injured, and four men and one woman perished. A merchant, by the name of Russell, was in his store trying to save some of his property. While he was in the building it floated off its foundation, and he leaped on board a vessel that was lying near. He soon discovered that he was in as dangerous a place as the floating building, for in a few moments the vessel was dashed upon the shore, but he fortunately escaped unhurt.

The salt-works were swept away by the tide, and those on Mashena Island were torn to pieces, the fragments being carried into the woods of Wareham, where they were afterward found. In one instance, a large portion of one of the works floated a distance of several miles entire, and then striking a ledge was torn to pieces. One salt-house after sailing along several miles foundered in a road nine feet above common high-water mark, and was found there standing in its ordinary position on corner-stones properly adapted to it. The owner conveyed it back to its original site. The coasting vessels were not only driven ashore, but several of them were found in the adjacent forest, where they had been blown on the tide. One was discovered in its usual position being supported on either side by trees, and was gotten off with but little damage. Another was driven over a bluff and deposited so near a house that the front door could not be used. Everything movable on the surface of the water in the bay was swept from it.

Some slight damage was done at Falmouth, but in Vineyard Sound the water was not so much affected by the wind as in Buzzard's Bay. At Hyannis, a brig was driven upon the shore by the wind. At Sandwich, a vessel bound for Newport was dashed furiously against a wharf while the captain was endeavoring to enter the harbor of New Bedford, and a young lady passenger, Miss Temperance Perry, was drowned in spite of the strenuous efforts that were made to save her. Farther out on Cape Cod the wind blew much more moderately, and at Provincetown nothing suffered from it.

Hundreds of vessels other than those mentioned were lost, the newspapers of that time saying that they had not space enough to record the marine disasters. At the eastern end of the Connecticut coast the storm was almost as severe as in Narragansett or Buzzard's bays. At Stonington, the tide rose seventeen feet higher than usual, and swept almost entirely across the town, which is built on a tongue of land running into the water. Everything was washed from the wharves, and then the wharves themselves were demolished. General disaster prevailed among the twenty vessels in the harbor, every one of which was either driven ashore or sunk. The schooner *Expert*, Capt. William Pousland, master, on a trip from Norfolk, Virginia, to Salem, Massachusetts, with a cargo of flour, ran into this port for safety, and was driven ashore, becoming bilged. A new ship belonging to New York was carried up among the houses, and the schooner *Washington*, Capt. Lewis Folsom, master, bound from Cape Francois to Newburyport, which had also put in there for safety, was entirely beaten to pieces in the gale, not a single article of the cargo or personal effects being saved. The persons on board, among whom were a lady and her child, who were passengers, were all saved. A small sloop, which was out from Providence with a pleasure party, among whom were His Excellency Governor Jones and Messrs. Brown and Ives, had also run into Stonington, where it became involved in the general destruction of the shipping, though none of the party on board were lost. A number of dwelling-houses and many other building were destroyed. One man's house, rope-walk and blacksmith's shop, with all their contents, were swept away, and his wife, his daughter, his wife's mother and a young lady visitor perished in the deluge. The fury of the powerful elements so changed the appearance of the place that it was hardly recognizable. Where there had been gardens and fertile fields there were now sandy beaches, and an island with an area of several acres, situated a short distance from the town, was so changed that only a small rock that was on it could be seen.

At New London, the storm was severe, and the tide rose so high that it carried away outhouses and fences, and filled cellars, it never having been known to rise there so high before. Entering many brooks and wells in the town it made them brackish even as late as October 4. In Main Street the water rose at least three feet, and many trees drifted up the street, barricading it. The wharves were almost demolished, that of N. Ledyard being entirely carried away with all the goods that were upon it. The store of Mr. Kimball, the stone-cutter, together with a considerable number of other buildings near the wharves, was also carried off. Almost every vessel in the harbor was driven on shore and stove to pieces. A new brig, belonging to S. Peck, was upset and sunk, and a gun-boat, drifting on the rocks, was beaten to pieces.

Across the Thames opposite New London lies Groton. There the waves ruined three wharves and some tan works, and by the combined forces of wind and water two dwelling-houses, three barns and other buildings were destroyed.

The wind forced the tide up the beautiful and romantic river so far that at Norwich (then known as Chelsea) the water was so high that it swept off several stores that were situated on the wharves, and carried them out into the river, and several warehouses were damaged more or less. The water rose five or six feet above Wharf Bridge, as it was called, and beat over it so furiously that it carried away the markethouse and an adjoining store. The market drifted up the stream and grounded on the east side of the cove, some thirty or forty yards above the bridge. The brig *Mary* and several schooners and sloops were driven ashore, in some instances knocking in the sides of the stores and lodging almost in the streets of the town.

No portion of the New England coast north of Cape Cod suffered from the gale except that which lies between Boston and Cape Ann in Massachusetts Bay. In Boston Harbor, some sixty vessels received more or less damage, among them being the schooner *Nancy* of Salem, whose bowsprit was carried away. The schooner *Three Brothers* of Beverly was run into by the ship *Ariadne*, which was driven from the end of Long Wharf, and had the whole of her stern above water and part of each quarter stove in. Many wrecked vessels were lying at the wharves after the gale had subsided. James Colman was drowned from the new brig *Washington;* a son of F. C. Lowell, Esq., was badly injured by a boat on board the *Borneo;* and at the same time a seaman had an arm broken. The wind was very severe, being described by one writer as "an awful, tremendous blast." Many of the church steeples were blown down, and a number of private residences were much damaged, losing chimneys, turrets, battlements, slates and shingles. Many of the wharves were swept away, and from two hundred thousand to three hundred thousand feet of lumber were lost.

At Cambridgeport, a schooner was carried up into Main Street, two houses were blown down, and forty other buildings were unroofed or otherwise injured by the wind.

At Marblehead, fourteen vessels went ashore and became bilged. Seven chimneys on the almshouse were blown down, James Merritt being killed by their fall.

In Salem, the vessels in the harbor escaped damage, but several of the buildings in the town were destroyed, the most important being the beautiful summer house of E. Hersey Derby on Castle Hill, which had been a landmark for several years. Chase's oil-mill and several small buildings and fences were also destroyed, and more than a dozen chimneys were blown down, one of which belonged to the court house. A chimney on the house next to the Pickman mansion fell directly over a school room, and crashed its way into the cellar. The school, fortunately, had been dismissed a few minutes before, else several of the children must have been killed or maimed. A number of ornamental trees were also torn up by the roots.

At Gloucester, the United States gun-boat numbered seventy-seven, the schooner *New Packet,* Captain Tilden, master, of Damariscotta, Maine, the schooner *Washington,* of Warren, Maine, commanded by Captain Vose, and a sloop commanded by Captain Blasdell, were all driven ashore and became bilged. The sloop was ladened with bread for the navy department at Portsmouth, and nearly all the cargo was damaged. A block of unfinished buildings and several stores were blown down, and other structures were injured.

The wind was also severely felt in many other places beside those mentioned. In Connecticut, at Plainfield, two churches were blown down, and at New Haven the West Bridge on the Milford turnpike was rendered impassable by the destruction of the causeway on either side. The greatest material injury sustained in the town was that done to Long Wharf, which was entirely inundated, everything on it that was movable being swept away. The water in some of the stores was two feet deep, but no extraordinary loss of property occurred.

Several places in Rhode Island, other than those already mentioned, suffered great loss. In the village of Pawtucket, situated on the river of that name, several houses were carried away, and in one of them was a man named Smith, who was drowned. At Newport, all the stores on Long Wharf were washed off, and a family of five persons perished.

The gale swept across Massachusetts, displaying its greatest energy a little east of the centre of the state. On Cape Cod and in the extreme western part of the state it was felt but slightly. In Plymouth County, several barns were blown over, a number of houses were much damaged, and a man was killed at Hingham. A greater loss seems to have been suffered at Abington. The town historian says that the morning there was fair and pleasant, and a stillness, such as precedes hurricanes, was noticed. A sailor who had become accustomed to the violent winds of the West Indies frequently started as if he were conscious of the approach of one of those unwelcome visitors, and when asked why he did so he replied that there would be a terrific wind before the day had passed, for there was a crackling in the air and it loomed up as he had noticed it in the tropics before an unusual wind. He was not deceived: the sky soon became hazy, the wind freshened, and grew stronger and fiercer until it became a hurricane indeed, sweeping almost every movable thing before it. Barns were blown down and houses unroofed, some of the buildings being carried some distance from their foundations, and boards and shingles lodged miles away. Hay from the barns was distributed over the whole region, many chimneys on the houses that resisted the gale were blown down, and whole orchards and many fences were laid flat. The author of the History of Abington says: "Within two miles of where I was several barns were blown completely down, over twenty barns and houses were unroofed, roofs being taken off entirely whole, carried to a distance of twenty or thirty rods, and broken to pieces." Many of the leading highways there were blocked up for several days by prostrate trees and fences, and roads through heavy forests were obstructed for several weeks. The driver of the New Bedford stage, on account of trees falling across the road, was obliged to unharness his horses and take them to a place of safety. While he was absent his coach was turned over, though he had ballasted it with stones. The narrow escape of a Mrs. Dyer from instant death, by the thoughtfulness of a young man, is worthy of notice. Having become much frightened, she left her house, and stood behind a large apple tree. The young man saw her there, and warned her of the danger of standing beneath the tree, which was much more liable to be blown over than the house. She left the tree and had gone but a few rods when it fell prostrate, and she would doubtless have been killed instantly had she remained there.

In Norfolk County, the wind was as severe as in any other part of Massachusetts, the church at Needham being blown over and several persons killed.

In the neighborhood of Boston, considerable damage was done. At Dorchester, seventeen houses and forty barns were unroofed, some of the barns being demolished, sixty chimneys were blown down, and more than five thousand fruit and other trees were torn up by the roots. The South Church was also partly unroofed, and the North Church was injured so badly that it had to be taken down. In Charlestown, the upper story of a large brick building was blown in, the Universalist church was partly unroofed, and a portion of the base of the steeple on Dr. Morse's church was blown away. In Chelsea, a great elm situated near the ferry, measuring seventeen feet in girth, and having upon its limbs a portico capable of holding thirty persons, was blown down.

At Newton, many windows were blown in, and a baker, who was making his daily calls, had his cart overturned by the wind, and all his gingerbread and other goodies scattered over the ground to the delight of the boys, who profited by the disaster.

At Reading, the steeple on Rev. Mr. Emerson's church, and many barns and sheds were blown down. Some houses were also damaged, and two men were severely injured. A suit at law was being tried on that day before John Weston, Esq., in which Deacon Caleb Wakefield was a witness. The deacon was captain of the military company, and it became necessary for him to produce his commission. He went home in the gale to get it, and the wind was so strong that on the way his horse was thrown down. Getting him up, he started on, and had gone but a short distance when the animal became frightened at the fall of a chimney on Silas Smith's house. Deacon Wakefield said that he saw sea-gulls, which the wind had driven from the ocean, trying to descend into the Quannopowitt, but they failed in the attempt, and were carried by the wind out of sight. Eighty thousand feet of boards were sawn from his timber that was blown down by the wind.

In Essex County, the gale was perhaps the fiercest ever known there. Beside the places on the coast that have already been named, others suffered. At Newburyport, many buildings were much injured, and the beautiful rows of shade trees were nearly all destroyed. In Boxford, a house and several other buildings were blown down.

The wind was so powerful that persons were lifted bodily from the ground and carried some distance. An instance of this kind occurred at Boxford. Capt. John Peabody, who is still living and in his eighty-sixth year, was nine years of age at the time of the gale, and was residing in the house now known as the Spiller place, within a few feet of which was a mill-pond. He was standing on the ridge by the edge of the water, when the wind took him off his feet and dropped him into the pond two or three rods from shore, to his great danger as the water was very deep. He was rescued by other members of the family.

At Wenham, the steeple of the church was blown down, part of it falling on a dwelling-house, which it damaged considerably.

In Danvers, barns, sheds, chimneys, fences and trees were prostrated. Orchards and forests suffered severely, majestic oaks that had withstood the tempests of a hundred years being torn up by the roots and dashed headlong to the ground. The venerable pear tree that had been brought from England by Governor Endecott in 1630 lost about half of its branches.

At Saugus, many houses and barns were damaged, but the greatest loss fell upon John Bullard, whose two large barns, one seventy and the other fifty feet in length, were blown to pieces and the hay that was in them, they being full, was blown away and lost. Two sheds, each seventy feet in length, all the back buildings adjoining the farm house, and a small house connected with one of the teams were also levelled.

At Worcester, it rained hard from nine to eleven o'clock in the forenoon, and the gale was severely felt.

We do not find that the wind blew very severely in Vermont. Rain fell heavily during Friday night and Saturday forenoon, raising the streams in the vicinity of Brattleborough to an unusual height, and destroying bridges, dams, and other property. Considerable damage was done to the grist-mill in that town. At Newfane, the oil-mill and clothing works of Captain Williams, and a grist- and saw-mill owned by Deacon Hill were much injured, and a grist-mill owned by D. Norcross was swept almost entirely away.

In New Hampshire, it was a rainy day, and the wind blew less severely than farther south, although for two hours it seemed to threaten destruction to every movable thing. Sturdy oaks and stately elms yielded to it, many buildings were blown down or unroofed and orchards destroyed, growing crops were considerably damaged, and apples were blown from the trees. At Amherst, several barns were demolished, and a number of buildings were unroofed. At Concord, the destruction of the forest trees was very extensive, and many cattle were killed by the trees falling upon them. At Sanbornton, the loss was estimated at fifteen thousand dollars. At Portsmouth, the shipping was not injured, but the buildings felt the shock severely.

In Maine, trees were blown down as far east as Wells, where a man was killed by a falling tree while travelling in the highway.

The old people still tell of the wonderful power of this September gale, almost every person living in central New England having had some interesting personal experiences that they could relate. The venerable and ever light-hearted Doctor Holmes was then six years old, and in his inimitable style he relates, in his poem entitled "The September Gale," how he was affected by the storm, as follows:

> I'm not a chicken; I have seen
> Full many a chill September,
> And though I was a youngster then,
> That gale I well remember;
> The day before my kitestring snapped,
> And I, my kite pursuing,
> The wind whisked off my palm-leaf hat:—
> For me two storms were brewing!
>
> It came as quarrels sometimes do,
> When married folks get clashing;
> There was a heavy sigh or two,
> Before the fire was flashing;
> A little stir among the clouds,
> Before they rent asunder,—
> A little rocking of the trees,
> And then came on the thunder.
>
> Lord! how the ponds and rivers boiled,
> And how the shingles rattled!
> And oaks were scattered on the ground
> As if the Titans battled;
> And all above was in a howl,
> And all below a clatter,—

The earth was like a frying-pan,
Or some such hissing matter.

It chanced to be our washing-day,
And all our things were drying;
The storm came roaring through the lines,
And set them all a flying;
I saw the shirts and petticoats
Go riding off like witches;
I lost, ah! bitterly I wept,—
I lost my Sunday breeches!

I saw them straddling through the air,
Alas! too late to win them;
I saw them chase the clouds as if
The devil had been in them;
They were my darlings and my pride,
My boyhood's only riches,—
"Farewell, farewell," I faintly cried,—
"My breeches! O my breeches!"

"That night I saw them in my dreams,
How changed from what I knew them!
The dews had steeped their faded threads,
The winds had whistled through them;
I saw the wide and ghastly rents
Where demon claws had torn them;
A hole was in their amplest part,
As if an imp had worn them.

I have had many happy years,
And tailors kind and clever,
But those young pantaloons have gone
Forever and forever!
And not till fate has cut the last
Of all my earthly stitches,
This aching heart shall cease to mourn
My loved; my long-lost breeches!

Chapter liii.

THE COLD SUMMER OF 1816

The coldest summer known to have been experienced in New England was that of 1816. Since that time the year has been generally called "poverty year," a name given because so many of the crops proved a failure and it seemed at the time as if nothing would be produced, many of the farmers being brought to want. Some have spoken of it as the year of "eighteen hundred and froze to death." In New Hampshire but little pork was fattened on account of the scarcity and consequent great cost of corn, and the people used mackerel as a substitute for it. For this reason the name given to the year there was "mackerel year." There were frost and snow in all the summer months, and in the northwest section of New England a severe drought prevailed, which added to the disastrous effects of the season.

Many persons have endeavored to ascertain some cause for the extraordinary nature of this summer, though no opinion has gained much ground. A large number of the people of that time believed that the large spots which appeared on the sun's disk that spring lessened the number of rays of light and consequently the earth was to that extent cooler than usual. The spots were so large that, for the first time in their history, they could be seen without the aid of a telescope. They attracted a great deal of attention from the common people, and their appearance added to the gloom of the season.[1] They were seen by the naked eye for several days, beginning on the

---

1. At the time of the appearance of the spots upon the sun, some writer published the following humorous lines in the *Connecticut Herald,*–

> *All ye wha tell why stars do wink,*
> *Come ease my fears;*
> *Wha' means this spat? that folks maun think*
> *Sae strange appears:*

> *As if wi'in this ball o'fire*
> *Some haule were dug;*
> *Or something black had settled there,*
> *Like ony bug.*

third of May, and, reappearing on June 11, they were again seen for a few days only.

For the most part, April was a dry month, but on the twelfth snow fell at Warren, Maine, to the depth of several inches, and remained on the ground nearly a week, causing good sleighing. In the vicinity of Danby, Vermont, rains continued through the month, and during the last few days of it in other sections of New England the weather was dry, fine and warm.

The rains that the people of Vermont had enjoyed through April terminated with the month, being followed by an excessively dry May. No other part of northern New England is known to have suffered from lack of rain, but in the southern portion of Bristol County, Massachusetts, and in Rhode Island and Connecticut refreshing showers had not come to enliven vegetation, and the surface of the ground became so dry that forest fires of great

---

Some canna' tell, an' some nae care
Wha' means this creature;
Whether auld Nick hae put it there,
Or laws o'nature.

An' some will swear it o'er and o'er,
Wi' looks fou' furious,
A comet there hae run ashore,
Or auld Mercurius;

Wha' since this spring, sae coldly blows,
Hae ventur'd nigher,
An' there will stick, as lath to lose
Sae warm a fire.

An' ithers think some one supplies
The sun with food;
An' sae this spat they wad surmise
A laud o'wood.

An' some will say, wi' dismal fear,
Auld Nick's broke loose;
An' there they've stapt his sly career,
An' hau'ld him clause.

An' some, nae doubt, will tell how
There is a drought there;
An' sae this haule they've dug just now
To come at water!

extent raged in many places. At Dartmouth, Massachusetts, a pile of brush was injudiciously set on fire, and in a few hours the fire had spread over several square miles of field and forest, destroying fences, trees, etc., to the amount of twenty thousand dollars in value. Near Providence, Rhode Island, more than a thousand acres of wood and timber land were set on fire in a similar manner, and everything growing thereon was destroyed in a few hours' time. Similar instances occurred in Oxford, North Haven, Bristol, Derby, and New Milford, in Connecticut, resulting in serious loss to owners of woodland and farmers. In northeastern Massachusetts, however, vegetation was as forward as usual. Apricots opened their buds May 3, peaches began to blossom, and asparagus to be cut on the fifth, cherries were in full bloom on the sixth, currants and gooseberries were in blossom on the ninth, plums on the twelfth, and pears began to open their blossoms on the thirteenth, the prospect of plentiful crops at that time and section being indeed flattering.

The month was not only dry but unseasonably cold and uncomfortable. At Chester, New Hampshire, on the fifteenth, land that had recently been plowed froze hard enough to bear a man, and snow fell in some of the northern parts of New England. In the vicinity of Weare, New Hampshire, there were no blossoms on the fruit trees until about the twentieth, and on the twenty fourth some rain fell, congealing on the branches, buds and blossoms. But in spite of the cold, drought, and general backwardness of the season, farmers bravely continued their planting, believing that winter always "lingers in the lap of May." Throughout the entire summer the weather was the subject of remark. People asked themselves and each other, if a change had not come over the climate, especially when they heard that in Ohio it had snowed on May 22, and on the thirtieth of May there had been frost as far south as Virginia.

June at length came, and although there were some excessively hot days in the month, it was as disagreeable as May had been, perhaps even more so. At Salem, Massachusetts, there were three very hot days, the twenty-third of the month, when the thermometer stood at one hundred and one degrees above zero, being the hottest day there had been for ten years. On the fifth of June, the heat was extreme in every part of New England, but the next day was uncomfortably cold, and travellers suffered from the severity of the weather. At Bangor, Maine, the night of the fifth was so warm that a blanket over one was sufficient for warmth, and at Hallowell it was the warmest day of the season. At Salem, Massachusetts, soon after noon on the fifth, the temperature was ninety-two degrees above zero, and the next day at

sunset it had fallen to forty-three. At Chester, New Hampshire, on the fifth
the heat increased to eighty-eight degrees above zero, and on the next day
fell to forty. On the morning of the sixth, at the latter place as well as in
other sections, ice formed to the thickness of an eighth of an inch on bodies of standing water. The weather was cold and squally, and snow fell in
Maine, New Hampshire and Vermont, and in Cheshire, Peru, Windsor and
other mountain towns in Massachusetts. In Maine the change came suddenly, with squalls from the northwest, and snow and hail fell for one and
a half hours, the flakes being so large that when they struck the ground they
spread out two inches and a half in diameter. The frost and cold chilled and
killed the martins and other birds, and froze the ground, cutting down corn
and potatoes, and compelling workmen to put on great coats and mittens in
order to keep warm. In Vermont, the snow melted as fast as it fell, but in
Massachusetts it was blown about as in winter. The whole month, in fact,
was so cold that apple trees, which began to bloom at its commencement
were not out of blossom at its close, and the yellow cucumber bug was so
effectually destroyed that it was not seen again in its old resorts for ten
years.

Snow fell again on the seventh of June sufficient to cover the ground at
Newton, Massachusetts, and at Hopkinton, New Hampshire, it was four
inches deep on a level. Snow also fell in Hallowell, Maine.

At Salem, Massachusetts, on Saturday, the eighth, there was a slight fall
of snow, but it was not deep enough to make good sleighing. Along the
northern portion of Massachusetts, large icicles were pendent, and the
foliage of the forest trees was blasted by the frosts. Snow fell that morning
at Hallowell, Maine, for three hours, the wind being about west-southwest.
At Waterbury, Vermont, snow began to fall on Friday night, and continued
on Saturday forenoon until it was of a considerable depth in many places.
In Williamstown, it was twelve inches deep, and in Cabot eighteen inches.
Joseph Walker, an old gentleman of eighty-eight years, lost himself in the
woods at Peacham in the snowstorm on the night of the seventh, and
remained there through the night, his feet becoming so severely frost-bitten that it was necessary to amputate one of his great toes. The oldest
inhabitants did not recollect such an extraordinary cold June as this. On
the morning of the eighth, there were drifts of snow on many of the hills in
and around Montpelier, and on the mountains it was more than a foot deep.
No one in that region remembered to have seen snow on the earth in June
before. A person writing from that place at the time said, "This part of the
country, I assure you, presents a most dreary aspect, great coats and mittens

are almost as generally worn as in January, and fire is indispensable." Many sheep perished with the cold, birds flew into houses for shelter, and great numbers of them were found dead in the fields. Throughout Maine, vegetation seemed to have been suspended, and nature presented a most dreary appearance. Even in Berkshire County, Massachusetts, the foliage was killed by frost over a considerable portion of the higher lands so that for several days the woods appeared to have suffered from fire.

> *The trees were all leafless, the mountains were brown,*
> *The face of the country was scathed with a frown,*
> *And bleak were the hills, and the foliage sere,*
> *As had never been seen that time of the year.*

On the morning of Sunday, the ninth, at Chester, New Hampshire, the thermometer stood at thirty-seven degrees above zero, and at Salem, Massachusetts, ice was drawn from a well at the toll-house on the turnpike after sunrise. The next morning there was frost again at Salem, and it was so severe at Montpelier, Vermont, that it killed the foliage of the trees. At Hallowell, Maine, the earth was frozen half an inch deep, and ice was observed to be a quarter of an inch thick, being strong enough on some of the mud puddles to bear a man. A great variety of birds, among them being the humming-bird, the yellow bird, the martin, and the beautiful scarlet sparrow, were so benumbed that they allowed themselves to be taken in the hand, and great numbers of them actually perished with the cold. The continued frosts rendered the prospect gloomy to the husbandman. "Still," says the author of the History of Henniker, New Hampshire, "the strong-hearted, industrious men and women of the town toiled on bravely, trusting and hoping that brighter days were in store for them, and in God's own time would be theirs; and they waited not in vain."

On the morning of Tuesday, the eleventh, there was a heavy white frost in the northern part of New England, and it was so severe in Berkshire County, Massachusetts, that vegetables in gardens were destroyed, and Indian corn was cut down to the ground, though it started up again after a few days. During the day the wind changed to the south, and the weather became warm and pleasant. In several sections of New England the drought that began in May still continued. At Weare, New Hampshire, on the eighteenth, there was a refreshing summer rain, which was again followed by cold, windy and dry weather. On the twenty-second, there was ice in James Wason's tanyard at Chester, New Hampshire. It was so cold that at

Gilmanton, New Hampshire, the men who were engaged in hoeing corn often repaired to the house to warm themselves, and some wore overcoats and mittens at their work. On that date, however, at Salem, Massachusetts, the weather had greatly moderated, and the thermometer indicated ninety-three degrees above zero. The next day it was one hundred and one, and on the twenty-fourth, one hundred. The heat started vegetation into a strong and rapid growth in spite of the dryness of the earth.

Strange as it may seem, there were frosts in northern New England in July, which did considerable injury to crops, and in Amherst, New Hampshire, snow fell. On July 8, the frost was so severe at Franconia, New Hampshire, that it cut off all the beans. At Warren, Maine, on that day and also on the next, when corn was being hoed for the first time, the frost cut it down again; and in the latter part of the month it had not spindled out. July 10, there was frost in the low land at Chester, New Hampshire. On the seventeenth, there was an abundant fall of rain in the northwestern part of Massachusetts, and in New Hampshire and Vermont, and all the small grains in those parts, especially rye and barley, then seemed to promise a heavy yield. In eastern Massachusetts, large quantities of grass were cut that week, the crop being greater than it had averaged for the preceding ten years. During the week the appearance of Indian corn greatly improved, the crop of potatoes promised to be heavy, and a newspaper of that vicinity said that vegetables were free from blemish. The fruits were also in great abundance, and possessed of fine flavors. The cold weather had indeed annihilated the caterpillars and canker-worms, but the king-bird and others, which usually feed on such insects, now resorted for sustenance to cherry trees and pea vines.

In Massachusetts, however, July was a warm month. At Salem, on the evening of the twentieth, was a plentiful rain, which was followed the next day by bright sunshine, giving a new freshness to the fields. On the twenty-eighth, rain fell incessantly for six hours, the greater part of the time pouring down in such quantities that the water ran along the streets in torrents. Much thunder and lightning accompanied it. The earth never looked fresher, nor the grass greener, and the warm sunlight produced a new spring. In Vermont, however, the drought still continued.

In August, there was frost, and at Amherst, New Hampshire, snow fell. In Maine, haying was begun in the first week of the month, and the crop was so light everywhere in that region that farmers sought substitutes for hay, some using potato tops, mowed and dried while they were succulent.

To the twentieth of the month the weather had been warm and pleasant, but on that day squalls occurred in New Hampshire, rain falling at
Chester, and snow on the mountains at Goffstown. At Keene, the change
in temperature on that day was greater than had ever been observed in this
variable climate. On the night of the twenty first, there was a frost, which
at Keene and at Chester, New Hampshire, killed a large part of the corn,
potatoes, beans and vines, and also injured many crops in Maine. It was
felt as far south as Boston and Middlesex County in eastern
Massachusetts, and in the western portion of the state as far as
Stockbridge, where it injured vegetation. The mountains in Vermont were
now covered with snow, and the atmosphere on the plains was unusually
cold. In Keene, New Hampshire, the oldest persons then living said that
they never saw such a severe frost in August. It put an end to the hopes of
many farmers of ripening their corn, especially in the low lands, and they
immediately cut the whole stalks up for fodder, but being in the milk it
heated in the shocks and spoiled. By the twenty-ninth of the month the
frost had reached as far south as Berkshire County, Massachusetts, where
it killed the Indian corn in many of the fields in the low lands. The farmers there saved much of it by cutting it up at the roots and placing it in an
upright position, where it ripened upon the juices of the stalks. If frost had
kept off two weeks longer there would have been a very good crop of corn
in Massachusetts.

On September 11, two or three inches of snow fell at Springfield,
Massachusetts, and the Vermont mountains had then been covered with
snow for several days. At Hartford, Connecticut, the next day, there was a
rain storm continuing for twelve hours, and it was as cold as it usually is in
November, with the wind blowing from the northeast. In the neighborhood
of Hallowell, Maine, on the twentieth, frost killed the corn and injured
potatoes in low grounds. In New Hampshire, toward the last of the month
occurred four of the greatest frosts ever known. At sunrise, on the
twenty-sixth, the thermometer indicated twenty-three degrees above zero,
the twenty-seventh and twenty-eighth, twenty degrees, and on the
twenty-ninth, twenty-five degrees. The small crop of corn and potatoes that
the drought had spared was destroyed. These frosts were also very heavy in
central Massachusetts, and Indian corn, which was then mostly in the milk,
was much injured. Before the month closed snow fell at Boston,
Massachusetts, and in Wiscasset, Maine, for several hours.

The drought was still severely felt in Vermont, there having been no
rain of any consequence there for one hundred and twenty days. The fail-

ure of the crops seemed certain. It was one of the most discouraging features of the summer. Devastating fires swept through the woods of Vermont, New Hampshire and Maine. In New Hampshire, Gilmanton, Guilford, Alton, Barnstead, Grafton, Rochester, and other towns, suffered severely from them, and in Maine, along the Kennebec River, and as far east as Frenchman's Bay, they were burning as late as October 11. In Paris, Maine, a dwelling-house and two barns were destroyed by the fires. In some places, the atmosphere was so filled with smoke that the sun could not be seen for a considerable time.

In New Hampshire, the drought continued, except for a few showers, until October 22, when there was a heavy rain. In the vicinity of Haverhill, however, on the night of the seventeenth, snow fell to the depth of twelve inches, and the next day there was sleighing.

The crops of rye and other small grains were excellent, though but little wheat had been sown in New Hampshire and Maine, on account of the previous unfavorable fall and spring. Few potatoes had been planted for the same reason. In Massachusetts the potato crop was large and the tubers were of good quality, but in the northern states the crop was very light. A very small corn crop was produced in the northern states, though in some parts of Massachusetts it was nearly an average crop, and in other portions of the state not more than an eighth of the usual quantity. But a small proportion of that which was raised was fit to shell, being as the farmers of New Hampshire called it all "pig corn." In some sections the hay crop was good while in others only about half the usual amount was produced. In Massachusetts, apples were plentiful and of good quality. The weather had not been extreme in Rhode Island and Connecticut, the season was somewhat backward, but the crops were not so materially affected as they were farther north.

There was great destitution among the people the next winter and spring. The farmers in some instances were reduced to the last extremity, and many cattle died. The poorer men could not buy corn at the exorbitant prices for which it was sold.

In the autumn, stock was sold at extremely low prices on account of lack of hay and corn, a pair of four-year-old cattle being bought for thirty-nine dollars in Chester, New Hampshire.

Some favored spots in the northern New England states produced a little corn for seed, which commanded a great price the following spring. Abraham Sargent Jr. had removed from Randolph, Vermont, to his father's farm in Chester, New Hampshire, and brought with him a very early kind of corn. He raised a crop of tolerably sound corn which he sold for seed the following spring at four dollars per bushel, and the farmers esteemed it a great favor to obtain it at that price even.

The next spring hay was sold in New Hampshire in a few instances as high as one hundred and eighty dollars per ton, its general price, however, being thirty dollars. The market price of corn was two dollars per bushel; wheat, two dollars and a half; rye, two dollars; oats, ninety-two cents; beans, three dollars; butter, twenty-five cents per pound; and cheese, fifteen cents. In Maine, potatoes were seventy-five cents per bushel, the price in the spring of 1816 having been forty cents, which was the usual price. Pumpkin seeds were sold in Massachusetts for one dollar per hundred, and other seeds proportionately. Fine crops of Indian corn were raised for many successive years following this cold summer of 1816.

Ever since that cold year, old people have continued to tell about its unfruitfulness, and some of their stories were exaggerated as stories will become by repetition. For example, Jacob Carr of Weare, New Hampshire, used to boast of the large crop of potatoes that he raised that year, and said that he did not get less than five hundred bushels to the acre, and that he never allowed one to be picked up that was smaller than a tea-kettle.

Chapter Civ.

THE TORNADOES OF SEPTEMBER 9, 1821

On the afternoon of Sunday, September 9, 1821, occurred two famous tornadoes, one in New Hampshire and the other in Massachusetts. It is claimed that they were two branches of a tornado that originated at Lake Champlain, and became divided, one branch proceeding easterly and the other southeasterly. The easterly section crossed the Connecticut River at Cornish, New Hampshire, and the southeasterly one rushed into Massachusetts where the states of Vermont, New Hampshire and Massachusetts meet, neither of them, however, coming near enough to the earth to do much damage until the Connecticut River was reached. It is not known that these tornadoes were noticed west of the Connecticut River, unless the whirlwind which passed through the town of Berlin, Vermont, in an easterly direction, on the same afternoon, was the beginning of them. There, its course was marked for two miles by potato tops, bushes and brakes, which it twisted off near the ground. It crossed Onion River, raising the water in a body, like an ocean water-spout, about the diameter of a barrel.

Whether or not the Connecticut River had anything to do with causing the wind to descend to the earth, is an interesting question. Both branches of the tornado were, perhaps, the most terrible that were ever known in New England. Pen cannot describe the desolation they made, destroying crops and trees, demolishing buildings of all kinds, and killing persons and animals.

The Sunday on which the tornado occurred was warm, the air was balmy, and the sun shone brightly. During the afternoon there was a breeze from the southwest, and the air was hot and sultry. At about five o'clock dark thunder clouds gathered in the northwest and soon overspread the sky. The stillness that usually precedes a storm was soon interrupted by mutterings of distant thunder, and the clouds grew darker. Livid lightning lit up the black, angry masses, and in some localities rain fell. This continued for a brief period, however, and at about half-past five, the wind having suddenly changed to the north, as the sky cleared, a peculiar looking cloud was seen in the northwest about ten degrees above the horizon. It was brassy in color, dense and portentous, and small clouds from all directions rushed to it. As it approached, there was seen suspended from it a cylinder of very dense vapor, in the form of an inverted cone, or, as some called it, a trumpet with the small end downward, or like the trunk of an immense elephant, hanging down from the heavens. It moved along steadily and majestically, and from it came incessantly flames or sheets of lightning like liquid fire, and frightful peals of thunder. It was a sight sufficient to strike terror to the hearts of the beholders, and those that witnessed it never forgot it. The nearer it came the grander and more awful it seemed. It whirled with great rapidity, bending round and round in a serpentine form, and the wind within it roared with increasing vigor and vehemence. It was distinctly heard several miles away on either side of its course. Some thought it would do no damage, but it generally excited most fearful apprehensions, although no one had any adequate conception of what it was able to accomplish. People listened and held their breath in silence as the awful cloud came nearer and nearer, fearful that their houses might lie within its track. The relief of those that escaped was great, though they were sorry for their neighbors whom they believed must have suffered from its terrible ravages. At last, the great arm was let down to the earth, which shook under the wind's terrible force for two or three miles. An instant later it burst upon the terror-stricken inhabitants, and in another was gone. There was no time to meditate on means of safety, or to escape, as the wind travelled more than a mile a minute. The horror of those moments to the people living in the track of the tornado cannot be imagined. They were caught up, their houses dashed to pieces, and almost everything movable was whirled into the air and torn apart. The people were indeed taught of the irresistible power that Omnipotence holds in his hands, and the utter impotence of man and all his works. The track of the wind appeared as if a mighty stream had been pouring down for many days, buildings, fences, trees and all things were swept away, the earth was torn up in places, grass withered, and nothing fresh or living was to be seen. Desolation was certainly in its path. The wind was felt, and hail fell in adjoining towns on either side of the track of the tornado. Though the sun was yet an hour high, there was almost total darkness in the space covered by the cloud while it was passing over, and the air was filled with gravel, leaves and fragments of trees. At some places a little water fell, probably not rain, as some writers have said, but water that had been taken from ponds and streams which the tornado had passed over. It was said that the water in a small pond in Warner, New Hampshire, was lowered about three feet, and the water in Sunapee Lake appeared to be rushing up toward the heavens.

The width of the tornado's track was from six rods to half a mile, varying with the height of the cloud, which rose and fell. It was much wider on high grounds than on low, and the deeper the valley the narrower it became. Its force, however, increased when it became more compact.

Entering the state at Cornish, the New Hampshire branch of the tornado passed easterly of Grantham Mountain in Croydon, then over Sunapee, Sunapee Lake, a part of New London, and Sutton, then over the west branch or spur of Kearsarge Mountain, which caused it to take a course more southerly, and over Kearsarge Gore (which was a part of the town of Warner), then over another spur of the mountain into the easterly part of Warner, touching a corner of Salisbury, and into the woods of Boscawen, where it was lifted from the earth, its havoc ceasing.

In Cornish, the wind caused much devastation in the woods. At Croydon, beside other damage, it injured the house of Deacon Cooper, and blew down his barn, scattering its contents. The course of the tornado was then turned to the east-southeast, and its path was very narrow as it went over the lowlands.

The next town that the tornado entered was Sunapee (which was then called Wendell). There it did a large amount of damage, destroying trees and buildings. The residence of Harvey Huntoon, situated about eighty rods from Lake Sunapee, was in the track of the wind. The family saw the cloud as it approached, and were alarmed at its appearance. As it came nearer they saw that the air was filled with birds and broken boughs of trees, and they became frightened. Mr. and Mrs. Huntoon were standing in the kitchen as the terrible cloud swooped down upon them. In an instant, the house, two barns and some outbuildings were demolished, and their contents swept away. One side of the house fell upon Mr. and Mrs. Huntoon, but the next moment it was snatched away and dashed to atoms. They both escaped without injury, although Mrs. Huntoon was carried across a field by the raging wind. Their baby, eleven months old, was asleep upon a feather bed in the western part of the house, and the wind took the child and the bed, dropped the child in Sunapee Lake, carried the bed to the town of Andover, and the bedstead into the woods, eighty rods away in a northerly direction from the house. The mangled body of the child was found the next Wednesday on the opposite (western) side of the lake, where it had floated, and the dress that it had worn when it was snatched so ruthlessly from its peaceful bed, was picked up on the shore of the lake one hundred and fifty rods away. The other seven members of Mr. Huntoon's family were injured, some of them severely. A Mrs. Wheeler was living in another part of the house, and when the cloud approached she took a child that was with her, and fled to the cellar for protection, but was somewhat injured by falling bricks and timbers. Bricks were blown more than a hundred rods, and pieces of the frame of the house, seven and eight inches square and twelve feet long, were carried eighty rods. A bureau was blown across the lake, a distance of two miles, and with the exception of the drawers, was found half a mile beyond the water. Other pieces of furniture, casks and dead fowls were carried to a much greater distance, and a large iron pot was found seven rods away. A pair of wheels was separated from the body of a cart, carried sixty rods, and dashed to pieces, one of them having only two spokes left in it. The only furniture found near the house was a kitchen chair. Beside these, other wonderful feats were accomplished by the wind. From the buildings the land rises about one hundred feet in a distance of fifty rods, and then descends on the other side of the hill to the lake. A horse was blown up this rise a distance of forty rods, and was so much injured that he had to be killed. A door-post of Mr. Huntoon's barn, measuring eight by twelve inches, and thirteen feet in length, was carried up the hill a distance of forty-four rods. A hemlock log, sixty feet long, three feet in diameter at the butt, and nearly two feet at the top, was removed from its bed in the earth, where it had lain since the gale of

September 23, 1815, and carried by the wind six rods up the hill, passing on the way over two rocks, which were only six feet from the place where the log was taken, each being seventeen inches high. It then struck a rock, and was broken into two parts. The rise of the land in the six rods was ten and a half feet. Not only were orchards destroyed, but some of the larger trees were torn up and carried from seventy to a hundred rods. After leaving the farm of Mr. Huntoon, the tornado proceeded a hundred rods further and blew down every tree in a tract of timber land of forty acres in area. No human lives were lost in Sunapee, except that of Mr. Huntoon's child.

The tornado then passed over the northwestern end of Lake Sunapee, its pillar of cloud foaming and writhing as it plowed its way to the very bottom of the lake, drawing up the water as it went. The cloud's appearance was most grand and terrifying. It was about twenty rods in diameter at the surface of the water, and expanded as it rose toward the heavens. It was quite black, but was occasionally illuminated by the most vivid flashes of lightning. Parallel to the shore of the lake was a stone wall, which the tornado struck, scattering the stones at various distances. Some that weighed seventy pounds were carried more than two rods up a rise of at least four feet in that distance. The shore of the lake was literally covered with timbers, boards, shingles, broken articles of furniture, and the fragments of demolished buildings, that had fallen from the cloud into the water and been washed ashore.

On leaving the lake the tornado entered the town of New London, where it did considerable damage, though no lives were lost, as few houses were in its track. It passed over the southerly part of the town, destroying first the two-story house, barn and the wood-house of John Davis. Not a timber or a board was left upon the ground where the house had stood, and not a brick in the chimney remained in the place where it was when the wind struck the house. All the furniture, beds, bedding and clothing that were in the house were swept away, and lost. A huge hearthstone weighing seven or eight hundred pounds was removed from its bed and turned up on its edge. Three barns belonging to Josiah Davis, with their contents, were blown entirely away, and his house was also much damaged. Lt. Jonathan Herrick's house was unroofed, the windows broken out, and a part of the furniture and clothing in the house blown away, but none of the family were injured. The frame of a new two-story house, which was nearly covered, belonging to Nathan Herrick, together with his two barns, was blown down. A house and a barn of Asa Gage were unroofed, and two sheds carried away.

Anthony Sargent had one barn demolished, another unroofed, and two sheds blown to pieces. Deacon Peter Sargent had one barn blown down, another unroofed, and a shed destroyed. A house belonging to the widow Harvey was unroofed, and a barn of J. P. Sabin was shattered. Levi Harvey's barn was blown into fragments, his saw-mill demolished, and his grist-mill moved some distance, being left on dry land. His hog-house, in which was a hog weighing three or four hundred pounds, was carried several rods entire, and dropped on the top of a stone wall, where it fell to pieces, releasing the hog, which, with a grunt of satisfaction at his freedom, walked away uninjured. Some twelve thousand feet of boards were blown away from the mill-yard of Mr. Harvey, and a few of them were found in the Shaker Village in Canterbury, thirty miles away. A pair of cart wheels, strongly bound with iron and nearly new, together with the tongue and axle to which they were attached, were carried ten rods, the tongue being broken off in the middle, and all the spokes but two taken from one wheel, and more than half knocked out of the other. One writer says that two more houses were destroyed and two others injured, that a cider-mill was demolished and three sheds other than those already mentioned, were damaged. One cow was killed, and several others injured. Eight orchards were utterly swept away, most of the trees being wrenched out of the ground by the roots. The trunk of one of these trees, divested of its principal roots and branches, was found half a mile away, at the top of a long hill. A piece of timber, apparently part of a beam of a barn, ten inches square, and ten or twelve feet long, was carried up the same hill for a distance of a quarter of a mile. Near the top of the hill was found an excavation some forty feet long, and in places from two to three feet deep, partly filled with broken boards and timbers, having been made apparently by the fall of a side of a barn that must have been blown whole at least a quarter of a mile. A birch tree, whose trunk was ten inches in diameter, was blown across the lake (which was at that place nearly two miles wide) to a point ten or twelve rods beyond. But the most wonderful feat of the wind there was the rending of a large rock one hundred feet long, fifty feet wide, and twenty feet high, into two pieces, which were thrown twenty feet apart. The space covered by the wind in New London was about one-fourth of a mile wide and four miles long. In that area the timber on three hundred and thirty acres of woodland was blown down, and this loss, together with the destruction of buildings and crops, amounted to ten thousand dollars.

The wind then passed through Sutton, where considerable injury was done, though the country was sparsely settled, and few houses were in its path. It then passed over Kearsarge Mountain at a point about two miles south of the highest peak, and swept down the steep descent into the valley on the other side, known as Kearsarge Gore, which is in the town of Warner. In the valley were seven dwelling houses. The people could not see the cloud until it was driving down upon them with the velocity of lightning. The first building that was struck was the barn of William Harwood, which was instantly carried away. Then the wind injured the houses of F. Goodwin, J. Ferrin and Abner Watkins, completely destroyed Mr. Ferrin's barn, and unroofed that of Mr. Watkins. Five barns were utterly demolished.

The first house that was struck by the terrible tornado was that of Daniel Savory, and after the wind had passed only part of the floor and some bricks remained to mark the site. Seven persons were in the house: Mr. Savory's parents, himself and wife, and their three children. His father Samuel Savory, who was an old man of seventy-two, saw the cloud as it came over the mountain, and, supposing it to contain wind, went into one of the chambers to close a window, his son's wife starting to assist him. While he was shutting the window, the tornado struck the house, whirled it around and lifted it into the air, demolishing it in a moment. The old gentleman was carried six rods, and dashed head foremost upon a rock, being killed instantly. The other six persons were covered by the ruins. Mrs. Elizabeth Savory, wife of Samuel, though badly bruised by timbers that had fallen across her person, extricated herself and assisted the rest of the family from under the debris. She was hardly able to move, yet she had the most surprising strength in removing the timbers and bricks beneath which could be heard the cries of the sufferers. Mrs. Mary Savory, wife of the son Daniel, was bruised on head, arms and breast, and she still held her infant child, which had been killed by a falling timber while it lay in her arms. The other children, Laura Little, Leonard N. and Jesse, were also much injured. All of Mr. Savory's buildings, furniture, implements, wagons, fruit trees and crops were swept away.

A few rods from the house of Daniel Savory stood that of his brother Robert Savory, which was also entirely destroyed. In it were eight persons, one an infant, and all of them were buried beneath the ruins. They were all much bruised and wounded, but none dangerously. Mrs. Abigail Savory, Robert's wife, saw the cloud, and went into a bedroom to take up a child, and knew nothing more until pain brought her to her senses. She found herself confined under some timbers, greatly bruised, but the child was unharmed. Their other children, Levi, Isaac and George, were much hurt. Mr. Savory was entirely buried in the bricks, with the exception of his head, being much injured, and two of the children were completely covered with splinters and other debris. Two girls, Charlotte and Ruth Goodwin, were in the house at the time, and were also hurt. Mr. Savory, as well as his brother, lost the whole of his property.

Passing on, the wind tore up everything in its course. Buildings were not only levelled, but shattered into small fragments which with the contents were spread abroad for a mile in every direction. The farming utensils, carts, wagons, sleighs, ox-sleds and plows, many of which were new and strong, were carried from twenty to sixty rods and dashed into pieces small enough for fire-wood. Ten hives of bees were destroyed, and legs, wings and heads of domestic fowls were torn from their bodies. Several acres of corn and potatoes adjacent to the buildings were swept down, hardly an ear of corn being left. Stone walls were levelled, and rocks weighing from two to five hundred pounds and half buried in the earth were turned out of their beds, being carried several feet. A bridge, made of large oak logs, split in halves, instead of planks, was torn up, and some of the timbers carried for ten rods in the direction from which the wind came, others sixty rods in the direction it went, others still were dropped near the margin of the stream to the right and left. A hemlock log, sixty feet long, lying half buried in the ground, was taken from its bed and carried six rods forward, while a knot from the same log was carried fifteen paces backward and driven with great force two feet under the sward. In one instance, at least, one large hemlock log, sixty-five feet long, was lying across another one that measured forty feet in such a position that it was thought that ten yoke of oxen could not have moved the lower one from its bed; but both were removed by the wind to the distance of about twelve feet and left in the same position. Near the rock where old Mr. Savory was killed, an elm tree, whose trunk was seventeen inches in diameter, the roots being too deeply embedded to yield, was twisted like a withe to the ground, and was thrown across the path like a wilted weed. A few ash trees were stripped of their bark and limbs, and were literally made into basket stuff. Not an apple or forest tree was left standing. The power of the wind was so great that one barn was taken up whole, with its contents of hay, grain, etc., and after being carried several rods, came to pieces, its fragments flying like feathers in every direction.

Half a mile from the Savory houses up a rise of the hill lived John Palmer. He was out at his door when the tunnel-shaped cloud came over the mountain, filling the air in its path with trees, branches, etc. He immediately attempted to enter the house, but the wind forced the door to, catching his arm, and at the same instant the house was caught in the vor-

tex of the tornado. The chimney gave way, and a part of the frame buried
Mrs. Phebe Palmer, wife of the owner of the house, under the bricks and
timbers, as she was trying to force open the door that held her husband. She
was considerably injured, but the rest of the family escaped with slight
wounds.

The tornado then passed over a spur of the mountain, a distance of two
miles from Palmer's house, and swooping down on the other side about a
hundred feet, violently swept away the house and other buildings of Peter
Flanders. The house was so located under the mountain that the family had
no intimation of the horrible event that was to befall them before the ruin
was wrought and the death-dealing arm had carried two of the nine persons
that were in the house into eternity. All the inmates were more or less
injured. Mr. Flanders was dangerously wounded, and his wife was almost as
seriously hurt. For several days his life was despaired of, but he finally
recovered. Their daughter Mary's arm was broken, and she was otherwise
somewhat bruised. The widow Colby, who was there, was also injured. Mr.
Flanders' daughter Phebe, only three years old, was carried from the house
on her bed, asleep, but was badly hurt, and another child named True, was
slightly injured. Lorn Hamah, a girl that lived in the family, was severely
hurt. One of the number killed was Mr. Flanders' infant child, and the
other Miss Anna Richardson. Nearly everything that Mr. Flanders possessed, buildings, furniture, crops, etc., was destroyed.

A few rods from the Flanders house, over the town line in a corner of
Salisbury, lived Joseph True.[1] Seven persons were in the house when the
wind struck it, and all of them, except two children, were wonderfully preserved. Mrs. True's parents, bearing the name of Jones, who lived about half
a mile away, were there on a visit, and the family had just left the tea table.
Mr. True and Mr. Jones were at the door, and seeing the ominous cloud,
thought at first that, as they were sheltered by the hill, it would pass over
without harming them, but they were soon convinced that its track was
marked with desolation. Mr. True gave an alarm to his family, then ran
under one end of his shop, which stood a few paces from the door of the
house just one side of the path of the tornado, and therefore was preserved.
Mr. Jones stood still till the wind struck the barn a few rods to the northwest of him, and he saw the fragments of it flying thick in the air above him,
then threw himself upon the ground by a pile of heavy wood. A moment
later a rafter fell endwise close to him, entering the ground to the depth of

---

1. One account gives Mr. True's name as John.

one or two feet, the other end falling on the pile of wood and protecting him from a beam that grazed down upon the rafter immediately after, and lay at his feet, but he was unharmed. Of the new, strong house, not a timber remained upon the foundation. It was blown into fragments, which were scattered over a wide extent of territory. The cellar stairs, even, were carried away, and the hearth, which was made of the brick tiles of the period, eight inches square, was removed. The bricks of the chimney were scattered along the ground for some distance, partly covering Mrs. True a foot in depth. The oven in the chimney had been heated, and some brown bread was being baked when the tornado struck the house. The bricks were hot, and Mrs. True was badly burned by them. Mrs. Jones was also burned. Of the children, Caleb and Joseph were wounded, and Mary Sally was greatly bruised and burned. Piercing shrieks and cries from two others, who were ten or twelve years old, called their father to a pile of hot bricks, which he removed as quickly as possible, burning his fingers to the bone in doing so, and they were taken out alive, but suffering intensely from burns and bruises. One of them was so disfigured as hardly to be known, and after suffering extremely for several weeks died. All the persons of the household were now accounted for except the baby, who was only seven weeks old. Where was the little one? We can imagine the anguish of the father's heart when we learn that although his hands were already burned to the bone he began to remove other piles of bricks supposing that the child was under them. But his efforts were fruitless. A few moments later, from the direction of the wind came a faint, baby cry, which was responded to most alertly by all who could run. The lost one was soon found lying safe upon the ground underneath a sleigh bottom about ten rods from the site of the house. When the wind struck the buildings the sleigh was in the barn, which stood six or eight rods north or northwesterly from the house; and it is an interesting coincidence that the child and the sleigh should meet at exactly the same place. The top of the sleigh could not be found. The materials of the buildings were not simply separated, but broken, splintered and reduced to kindling, and scattered like chaff over the region. It was the same with beds and bedding, bureaus, chairs, tables, etc. A loom was to all appearances carried whole about forty rods, and then dashed in pieces. Nearly all Mr. True's property was destroyed. He saw one of his trees whirling in the air perpendicularly at an immense height. One or two other unoccupied buildings in the neighborhood were somewhat injured.

The tornado then passed into Warner again, tearing down a barn. It went over a pond, the waters of which seemed to be drawn up into the centre of the cloud. When the tornado reached the woods of Boscawen, the terrible arm that had reached down to the earth was lifted up and did no further damage, passing out of sight behind a black cloud.

Many people visited the Gore to see the ruins. Among them was the
editor of the *New Hampshire Patriot,* who in the next issue of his journal
said, in reference to the authenticity of the accounts of the havoc wrought
in that state, and after giving his authority from the other towns, "What
relates to Warner and the destruction near Kearsarge Mountain we know to
be true, having ourself visited the spot. We saw the stone against which Mr.
Savory was crushed, the place whence were dug the children of True and
Savory, the children themselves, mangled and torn, the mothers mourning
the death of an aged husband and an infant child. We witnessed the awe of
the survivors of these distressed families. We stood at the foot of the mountain and saw the track of the whirlwind. It appeared as if a mighty torrent
had many days poured down the mountain; the earth torn up, the grass
withered, and nothing living to be seen in the path of desolation. May God
in mercy avert another such catastrophe."

The wind was also felt in New Hampshire in several other towns than
those that lay in the track of the cyclone. At East Weare, the wind mowed a
swath through the woods in the valley, twisting great trees off as if they were
straws, leaving the hill-tops untouched. Thousands of dollars' worth of timber was destroyed. The wind was felt slightly at Concord, where trees and
fences were blown down. Considerable hail fell there, and also in
Canterbury, some of the hail stones in the latter place measuring five inches
in circumference. In Pittsfield, which is twenty miles from the track of the
tornado, pieces of boards, shingles, strips of clapboards, and half the panel
of a door were picked up the next morning. Shingles were seen at a great
height in the air at Loudon and Canterbury on the evening of the eventful
day.

The southeasterly branch of the tornado moved almost southeast, and,
as was said at the beginning of this chapter, proceeded into Massachusetts,
crossing the Connecticut River where the states of Vermont, New
Hampshire and Massachusetts meet. This place is forty miles from the spot
where the New Hampshire branch passed over the river. As soon as it had
crossed the stream its havoc began, as in New Hampshire. The first town it
entered was Northfield, and the time was about six o'clock, the same hour
as the New Hampshire tornado occurred. In all respects the two were identical. The cloud appeared black and terrible, and nearly in the form of an

inverted pyramid and moved very rapidly, being accompanied by a horrible roaring noise. It was an awful yet sublime spectacle.

Its track, which varied in width from twenty to one hundred and twenty rods, was a little south of the centre of Northfield, and over the south part of Warwick and Orange, to the southwesterly part of Royalston, where its force was broken by Tully Mountain. It prostrated all buildings, fences, stone walls, and trees that came in its way. Along its path, and for the distance of twenty-five miles beyond, through Winchendon, Ashburnham and Fitchburg, were strewn fragments of buildings, sheaves of grain, bundles of corn stalks, clothing, etc. Trees stripped of their small branches were found at a considerable distance from the place where they had formerly stood. Several persons were killed and wounded, numerous houses, barns, and other buildings were demolished, and many domestic animals killed. Large trees were carried two hundred feet into the air, and great logs were swept out of the bed of Tully River, where they had lain for more than fifty years. The ground was torn up from the river to the mountain, a distance of about forty rods, from one to six feet deep, appearing as though it had been struck by successive discharges of cannon balls. Stones of many hundred pounds' weight were rolled from their beds, one that weighed half a ton being forced several feet and overturned.

An agitation among the clouds was first noticed, and a few minutes later they were raging furiously. The wind cloud then assumed the shape and appearance of a column of dense smoke ascending from a burning building, becoming more compact, retaining a regular cylindrical form, and moving along in grand majesty. The bottom of it swept everything before, or rather into it, for it revolved with great velocity, drawing into the vortex whatever movable things came within its influence and carrying them high up into its top, whence it threw out in all directions the broken articles, timbers, boards, shingles, limbs of trees, leaves, grass, etc., filling and darkening the air. Birds, especially hawks and crows, sailed round and round high in the sky, and screamed dismally. But above all other noise was the tremendous crashing, stunning, deafening roar of the wind in the cloud, which sounded like heavy thunder, and the earth trembled under the mighty power that thus stalked abroad on its desolating tour, giving the people most appalling sensations.

It began its destructive work in Massachusetts near the top of the high ridge of land called the Northfield Mountains. The first buildings it destroyed were the house and barn of Mr. Garland, who was thrown a considerable distance from the house, but not materially hurt. Then Chapin

Holden's house and barn were destroyed. Mr. Holden was very much injured, being knocked down several times in his retreat to the cellar of the house. Reuben Wright's barn was also entirely destroyed.

Then the tornado passed into Warwick, and shivered to atoms the house, barn and outbuildings of Jonathan Wilson, the pieces being scattered like chaff. Several members of his family were badly injured, six persons being in the house at the time of the disaster. Mr. and Mrs. Wilson and their son Joseph and his wife were taken from the ruins, all of them being much bruised and wounded, with the exception of Mrs. Wilson Sr. who was but slightly hurt. A cow that was standing in the barnyard was thrown by the current a number of rods and killed. A tavern day-book was carried from this house to the southerly part of Groton, forty-five miles away, and a piece of a bureau to Leominster. From this place the whirlwind was traced to a large pond, where a great quantity of water was taken up in the form of a waterspout. Thence it passed to the house of Elisha Brown, which was almost wholly destroyed. In it were himself, his wife, and nine children. One of his daughters, about thirteen years old, was buried in the ruins and killed, and another daughter was permanently injured. The next buildings that stood in the track of the tornado were four barns, which were entirely destroyed.

Still retaining its violence the wind passed through the northwesterly part of Orange, Capt. Moses Smith's large tavern with barns, blacksmith shop, and sheds being all swept from their foundations in a moment of time. So strong was the whirlwind that the chimneys and part of the foundation stones were swept away, and much of the cellar wall thrown down. Eleven persons were in the tavern, and they were carried in all directions, one of them, a young woman named Stearns, being found dead under the rubbish, after one and a half hours' diligent search, forty feet from where she was last seen, having been instantly killed. Only these two persons were killed, but several were severely injured. One young man had his shoulder fractured, and Mrs. Smith was taken out from among the timbers with a young child in her arms, neither of them being much injured. Several cattle were killed, and others were considerably hurt. Captain Smith's loss was very great, scarcely an article of furniture being saved. Two barns belonging to neighbors were also destroyed.

The tornado then passed to Tully mountain in the easterly part of Orange, doing but little other damage, its fury having abated.

The next day the people of Warwick assembled and chose a committee to ascertain the extent of the damage in that town, and they also voted to raise four hundred dollars to be distributed among the sufferers in proportion to each one's loss according to the estimate of the committee.

The accounts of the damage done by the tornado were so astounding that people in other sections doubted their truthfulness. Among others the editor of a New York journal was incredulous, and a reply was made to him by the editor of the *New Hampshire Patriot,* who had visited the spot. He closed his article as follows: "Some uncommon cause, incomprehensible by human ken, on that day operated upon the surrounding atmosphere—there was a power in the wind which seemed to exceed all combined animal strength—to those who felt that power, or were witnesses of the ravages made, it was most fearful and appalling—it defied all human art or strength—it exceeded all human belief—it can be resolved only into that Divine Power, which 'rides in the whirlwind, and directs the storm.' "

Chapter IX.

THE SPRING FRESHET OF 1823

In the southern portion of New England, during the last part of February, 1823, the snow lay very deep upon the ground, and on the fifth of March began a rain that for twenty-four hours poured down in great quantities, causing a disastrous freshet in Rhode Island and Connecticut on the next day. About one o'clock that night, the bridge on the Providence and Pawtucket turnpike, which spanned the Pawtucket River at Natick, in Rhode Island, was carried away whole. The bridge on the old road, which was then commonly called Natick Bridge, and a bridge on Olneyville were also destroyed. The bridge at the Arkwright factory, and another at the Hope factory were considerably damaged, but remained passable. At Pawtucket, the river had risen as high as the bridge the next day, and its abutments tottered, but still held. A bleach-house that had been recently built there was also somewhat injured.

In Connecticut, the Yantic River was so full and the force of the water so great that the channel was considerably deepened in some places by the removal of large stones. One that weighed more than a ton, and which had been placed in the bed of the stream many years before to support a foot bridge, was raised and carried up into a meadow where it was thrown against a large tree. The six bridges that then spanned the river were all carried away. Three of them were at Norwich, two in Bozrah (one at Colonel Fitch's iron-works, and the other at Bozrahville), and one in Franklin. The oil-mill at Bean Hill was swept away, and the oil-mill and the machine-shop near the falls at Norwich were much injured. A considerable amount of flax-seed was carried away from an oil-mill, and by the middle of May several meadows adjoining the river below the mill were covered with growing flax. At Norwich, a bridge that had been built in 1817 at an expense of ten thousand dollars, and which was supported by heavy stone piers, was lifted entire and carried down the stream in its usual position till it came to the rapids near the mouth of the river, when it separated into three parts, gliding with a graceful motion into the Thames. On the Wharf Bridge, as it was called, several buildings were moved, some being partly turned round. The most interesting feature of the freshet was the carrying away of the Methodist chapel which stood on the bridge. It had been decorated with evergreens for some festive occasion, and they had not been removed when the building was swept from its foundations. It moved along like a majestic ship, bowing to the waves, then righting itself again. For a mile it retained its upright position, and the frame held together until it had passed into the Sound. The incident gave rise to many exaggerated stories, the newspapers alleging that the church bore off both pastor and flock who were singing as they passed New London. Another report came that the church had successfully landed on one of the islands, and that notice had been given that services would be held there in the future. The schooner *Fame,* bound from Charleston, South Carolina, to Bridgeport, was in the harbor, and nearly collided with the building. The crew reported that it gallantly sailed by them in the night, being brilliantly lighted. The poet Brainard heard of the incident, and wrote some lines about it, which he entitled "The Captain." The following are a part of them:—

> *Solemn he paced upon that schooner's deck,*
> *And muttered of his hardships:—"I have been*
> *Where the wild will of Mississippi's tide*
> *Has dashed me on the sawyer; I have sailed*
> *In the thick night, along the wave-washed edge*
> *Of ice, in acres, by the pitiless coast*
> *Of Labrador; and I have scraped my keel*
> *O'er coral rocks in Madagascar seas;*
> *And often, in my cold and midnight watch,*
> *Have heard the warning voice of the lee shore*

Speaking in breakers! Ay, and I have seen
The whale and sword-fish fight beneath my bows;
And, when they made the deep boil like a pot,
Have swung into its vortex; and I know
To cord my vessel with a sailor's skill,
And brave such dangers with a sailor's heart;—
But never yet, upon the stormy wave,
Or where the river mixes with the main,
Or in the chafing anchorage of the bay,
In all my rough experience of harm,
Met I—a Methodist meeting-house!

"Cat-head, or beam, or davit has it none,
Starboard nor larboard, gunwale, stem nor stern!
It comes in such a 'questionable shape,'
I cannot even speak it! Up jib, Josey,
And make for Bridgeport! There, where Stratford point,
Long beach, Fairweather island, and the buoy
Are safe from such encounters, we'll protest!
And Yankee legends long shall tell the tale,
That once a Charleston schooner was beset,
Riding at anchor, by a meeting-house!"

Chapter Cvi.

THE SPRING FRESHET OF 1826

In the spring of 1826, occurred a freshet that had been unparalleled in New England for more than thirty-five years. It extended not only through the northern New England states, but into Canada and New York. In the evening of Friday, March 24, the wind began blowing a gale from the southeast, and rain fell in such torrents that it seemed as if the very flood-gates of heaven were open. It continued all night, and ceased the next morning.

In Vermont, much damage was done to the roads and small bridges in the vicinity of Brattleboro', the greatest loss being the destruction of the bridges over West River between Brattleboro' and Newfane. In Weathersfield, Black River rose so high that it flooded a certain barn yard and drowned eighty merino sheep. At Bellows Falls, buildings and other property of much value were destroyed. A large paper-mill that had been built a short time before by B. Blake at Rockingham, on Saxton's River, was entirely carried away, the loss being five thousand dollars. A saw-mill, two bridges and a dye-house connected with the woolen factory of N. Whitcomb & Co., on the same stream, were also lost. On Williams' River, two bridges were carried away, and much damage was done by the swollen streams in the neighborhood of Woodstock. A sad incident that occurred in that town was the death of Nathan Furbush, who, while attempting to leap a stream formed by the overflowing water, fell into the swift current and was carried beyond all human assistance. The village of Montpelier was almost entirely inundated, and the turnpike between that place and Royalton was washed away in so many places that it was impassable. The freshet happened in the night, and in consequence the farmers that lived near the river suffered much in the loss of sheep and young stock.

The Kennebec River in Maine was more affected than any other large stream. When the rain began, the river was covered with ice that was twenty inches thick. The next day after the showers the water rose slowly and in the afternoon it was supposed that the great weight and strength of the ice would prevent its breaking up. The river continued to fill, however, until three o'clock on the next morning, when the ice could no longer resist the powerful pressure beneath, and it burst half a mile above Gardiner. The water raged down on the wharves at Gardiner, covering them four or five feet deep, and the great body of ice that followed pressed down upon them. At the first shock, a warehouse that stood nearly at the end of the upper or Long wharf was swept into the dock below. At five o'clock the water had risen two or three feet higher, and a small quantity of wood, lumber, etc., had gone down the stream, being lost. The ice above Gardiner still remained intact, and by twelve o'clock the water had lowered two or three feet. It immediately began to rise again, and continued rising until four o'clock, when it had attained its former height. A great body of ice had been accumulating for a mile above the town, and at this hour it suddenly started, rushing down the river with tremendous force. The people saw it coming and realized its almost superhuman power. The only hope they had of saving their property lay in the resistance of Long Wharf, from the end of which the warehouse had already been carried away. Adjoining the place where it had stood was a large building which was used as an ice-house, containing at the time about four thousand tons of ice, and piled against it on

the wharf were five or six hundred cords of wood. The wharf extended far
into the river, and it was hoped that the heavy weight upon it would enable
it to withstand the flood. It would thus form a partial barrier to the ice and
water, compelling them to pass down gradually through the town. People
anxiously watched it, fearing lest the wharf should give way and the water
sweep down the stream, destroying the property on the wharves below, and
the fifteen vessels that were lying in the docks. Hundreds of the inhabitants
eagerly gazed at every assault made upon it. The ice leaped twenty feet from
the surface of the water and fell against the building, which withstood the
shock. Masses of ice then pressed against it, but it held firm. A small
schooner that had lain a few rods up the stream was dashed against it, and
in a moment was shattered to pieces, as easily as one would crush an egg
shell. At last, as if to make one last struggle to overcome the obstacle in its
path, the water caused logs twenty feet long and three feet in diameter to
rear their whole length and be thrown against the building,—but it still
stood. For two minutes the conflict seemed doubtful, but in two more it was
decided. The wharf remained, and the property below was chiefly saved. The
terrible breathless anxiety of the spectators gave place, when the danger was
passed, to a general and heartfelt shout of joy. The force of the raging
stream had lessened, but the water had not lowered, neither had the ice and
timber all gone down. A compact mass of ice, logs, trees, lumber, etc., was
floating rapidly by, and in the midst of it were embedded five schooners,
hurrying to what seemed to be certain destruction. The ice continued moving down for a mile or two below the town, where it was finally stopped by
an unbroken field of ice, and jammed so severely that it caused the water to
rise to a height never before known in Gardiner. At six o'clock the water was
thirteen feet above the common high-water mark, an hour later it began to
subside, and in twenty-four hours had fallen about four feet. The loss in
Gardiner alone was about five thousand dollars. The chief sufferers were R.
H. Gardiner, Esq., and J. P. Hunter & Co. The firm's loss was in logs. Mr.
Gardiner was the owner of the warehouse, which was carried away, and in
which were a few goods belonging to parties in Augusta. His causeway across
the basin of the stream was pressed by the ice several rods from its original
location. A boat-builder's shop belonging to Mr. Patten, which stood by the
side of the ice-house, was crushed by the ice and by the logs that were driven
upon it, and the fishing schooner of Enoch Dill was utterly destroyed.
Small quantities of salt, in some of the lower stores, wood, lumber, etc., were
destroyed, and some damage was done to one or two vessels, which were
lodged upon the wharves. In Pittston, on the opposite side of the river from

Gardiner, a large brig on the stocks, in the process of construction, belonging to J. H. and A. Cooper, was lifted from the blocks, and somewhat damaged. The firm also lost one or two small buildings. To show the force of the water at this place it is related that an elm tree five feet in diameter, situated in the ship yard of Capt. J. Tarbox, standing many feet from high-water mark, and protected by a point of high land above it, was uprooted by the action of the water.

At Hallowell, the ice jammed below the village, forming a dam, and the water inundated the town, swept off buildings and filled the lower rooms of the stores on the river side of the main street, destroying large quantities of the articles contained in them. All the vessels on the stocks at that place were swept away, and four or five schooners were driven from their moorings nearly to Gardiner, where they were wedged in the immovable mass of broken ice. In the town thirty or forty families were obliged to abandon the living rooms in their houses, and flee to the upper stories on account of the flood. The loss in Hallowell amounted to more than twenty thousand dollars. The principal part of the bridge at Waterville was destroyed, and two or three small bridges between that town and Augusta were so much damaged that they were impassable. Indeed, every settlement on the river suffered more or less from the inundation.

Chapter Cvii.

THE AVALANCHE IN THE WHITE MOUNTAINS, AND DESTRUCTION OF THE WILLEY FAMILY

All visitors to the White Mountains know of the Notch, a famous pass, thirty miles in length, in which are Crawford's, Bemis and the Glen. East of Crawford's for two miles it is only a very narrow defile, running between two huge cliffs, that were apparently rent asunder by some almost inconceivable convulsion of nature. The high walls of Mount Willey on one side and of Mount Webster on the other, are almost perpendicular, and rise in the highest place three thousand feet. The eastern entrance to this cut is between two rocks, one about twenty feet high, and the other twelve, being only twenty-two feet apart.

The Saco River rises in the mountains, and flows down through this remarkable gap in a southeasterly direction. In the upper part of the Notch, the channel of the stream is only twenty feet wide, about the entire width of the pass, which widens as it approaches North Conway, where it becomes a fertile valley four or five miles in width. There are several streams in the mountains which empty into the river as it flows through the Notch, and on one of them is the Silver Cascade, which is one of the most beautiful falls of water in the world. Here is also the famous flume. All through the pass the scenery is exceedingly grand, and few places in the world exceed it in beauty. The luxuriant foliage of the large trees on either side of it for much of the distance meet, forming an arched covering of green.

This natural pass was taken advantage of by the early settlers of the section of New Hampshire which lies northwest of the mountains, it affording the only direct means of reaching the seaport that was nearest to them. This was Portland, where they exchanged their produce for foreign commodities, and other supplies that they could not procure in their region. Through the Notch, as it was called in very early times, a turnpike had been built, and in 1826, it had become a great thoroughfare for the farmers of the upper counties of Vermont and northwestern New Hampshire for transporting their produce to market at Augusta as well as Portland. Mr. Crawford conducted a public house in the Notch in those days, and he frequently supplied feed and keeping for eighty horses in a single night during the period of good sleighing. A short distance east of Mr. Crawford's was another tavern kept by Capt. Samuel Willey. The history of these old-time hostelries would furnish one of the most interesting chapters of New England history if it could be fully written.

In some places the river runs so near the side of the pass that the mountains overhang it, and again there is scarcely room for the road between the streams and rocks. Thus side by side, the road sometimes crossing the river, they run through the pass.

The sides of the mountain are so steep at many places along the Notch that, after the road was constructed, heavy rains frequently caused the earth and rocks to dislodge and slide down, carrying all the trees, shrubbery and everything else from the rocky foundation of the mountains. These slides usually began near the highest limits of vegetation, and widened and deepened as they descended, sometimes covering a space of several hundred acres and cutting into the side of the mountain to the depth of thirty feet. During the first week in July, 1826, a great rain had dislodged a large mass of stone and gravel from one of the mountains, and came down, filling up the road for a long distance.

The month of August that summer was as wet a month in Massachusetts, Rhode Island and Connecticut as was ever experienced there. At Salem, Massachusetts, fourteen inches of rain fell during the month, and from the tenth to the fifteenth, eight and seven-tenths inches; the greatest quantity falling in one day, being two and one-half inches, fell on the fourteenth. Lowlands were inundated and mill-dams injured. The air was remarkably humid nearly the whole of the month, and profuse showers constantly wet the earth.

In the White Mountains, however, no rain fell until nearly the close of the month. The roads were like beds of ashes, two or three inches deep, and the country around showed the usual effects of a long drought. On the morning of Monday, the twenty-eighth, the mountains were enveloped in clouds, and a cold heavy rain began to fall moderately all through New Hampshire, increasing in the afternoon, and falling in torrents most of the night. The next morning was clear and serene.

In different parts of the state, great quantities of hay and grain were injured, roads washed so badly that travel over them was suspended, and many bridges were carried away. All five of the bridges over the Ammonoosuc River were swept away. The Contoocook River rose higher at Henniker than it was ever known to rise before or since that time. The Souhegan and Merrimack rivers were as high as they usually are in spring freshets, and several bridges and mills located on them were carried away. In the mountain region it caused the most remarkable flood ever known there. At daybreak on the next morning the water of the Saco River in the Notch was sixteen feet above its usual height, and had spread to three times its width. The next day it flowed rapidly between steep banks covered with hemlocks and pines, and over beds of rocks, which broke its surface into raging billows. Down through the Notch were carried sand and driftwood, to an extent never known before, and they were deposited with the water on the fields below. Fences and bridges were carried away, and logs thrown into the roads, blockading them. In some places the turnpike was excavated to the depth of fifteen or twenty feet, and in others was covered with earth, rocks and trees to a greater depth. For a mile and a half along the Notch, from Crawford's to Willey's, the road was not visible, except in one place for a distance of two or three rods. Large patches of the surface of the mountains, first on one side of the road, then on the other, and in some places on both sides had slipped down into this narrow pass, along its whole length. Thirty slides were counted on the mountains, many bare spots appearing that were never seen before. A large area on one side of Mount Pleasant slid down and covered a considerable portion of Ethan Crawford's pasture, which contained between thirty and forty acres. The water rose two feet in his house, and many of his cattle and sheep were lost, eight hundred bushels of oats being also destroyed. On the Saco River below Conway, the damage was considerable. At Bartlett and Conway the loss was severe in the destruction of crops, mills and bridges, and at Fryeburg great quantities of corn, potatoes, meadow hay and fences were destroyed and some cattle drowned.

By Wednesday, the water had subsided, and the weather was clear and pleasant. Nothing had been heard from the Notch House, which was conducted by Captain Willey, at the eastern terminus of the pass, several miles from any human habitation. The house stood on the westerly side of the road, only a few rods distant from the high bluff which rose with fearful abruptness to the height of two thousand feet. The buildings consisted of a house and barn, which were connected by a woodshed. Mr. Willey and his family had recently moved there from Fryeburg and were amiable and obliging people, being much respected by their neighbors, and commended for their neatness by travellers who were their guests.

Mr. Crawford became alarmed for the safety of the Willey family, and with a guest started up the pass on foot, so much earth, and so many stones and trees having fallen that a horse could not travel on the road which in fact was not to be seen in many places, being covered in spots thirty feet deep. After a tiresome journey they arrived at the Willeys. The road appeared to have been overflowed with water for a mile south of the place, and the beautiful little meadow opposite the house, which had been covered with crops, was a pond. The house was found to be uninjured, but the barn was crushed, and under its ruins were found two dead horses. The house was entirely deserted; the beds were tumbled, their sheets and blankets were turned down, and near them upon chairs and on the floor lay the wearing apparel of the several members of the family. On the bar were lying Mr. Willey's money and papers. The visitors were convinced that the entire family was destroyed, and a brother of Mr. Crawford, who then appeared from his father's place, which was six miles further east, confirmed the supposition.

After a slide in June, the family were more ready to take the alarm than they had been, though they did not consider their situation dangerous as no fall had ever been known there. On the night of the great rain, however, probably at about eleven o'clock, the family was alarmed by the noise of rushing wind, flowing torrents, and the tumbling, crushing earth, rocks and forest trees from the extreme point of the westerly mountain above them. They all sprang from their beds, and in their night clothes ran, in the utter darkness, for their lives. But the immense mass descended with terrible velocity, toward the sleeping family. When within about five rods of the house, its course was checked by a large block of granite, and the mass separated into two streams, one of which rushed down by the north end of the house, crushing the barn and spreading itself over the meadow. The other part passed on the south side, overtaking and destroying the unfortunate family. They probably attempted to reach a stone embankment a few rods distant, which, it is said, had been erected for a place of refuge in a similar emergency. This shelter, whatever it may have been, was deeply buried under the earth, rocks weighing from ten to fifty tons being scattered about the place, and indeed in any direction escape was utterly impossible. The house alone remained undisturbed, though large stones and trunks of trees came within six feet of its walls, and the moving mass which separated behind the building again united in its front. The house therefore was the only place of refuge from the terrible avalanche, and in their beds the family would have been preserved from their horrible fate.

> *An everlasting hill was torn*
> *From its primeval base, and borne,*
> *In gold and crimson vapors dressed,*
> *To where a people are at rest.*
> *Slowly it came in its mountain wrath,*
> *And the forests vanished before its path,*
> *And the rude cliffs bowed, and the waters fled,*
> *And the living were buried, while over their head*
> *They heard the full march of their foe as he sped,*
> *And the valley of life was the tomb of the dead.*

The bodies of Mr. and Mrs. Willey, their daughters Eliza and Sally, Mr. Willey's hired man and boy named Allen and Nickerson, were found about fifty rods from the house horribly mangled, but the remains of the three other children were never discovered, probably having been deeply buried under the rocks and earth. Those that were found were all buried in a quiet nook in the field then belonging to Mr. Willey's father, the parents and children being interred in one grave. It was the family burying-ground, Mr. Willey's parents and other members of the family being buried there. It is in

North Conway, and as one passes the Bigelow farm he cannot fail to notice a stone stile built into the wall. A path leads from it for about ten rods to the iron gate of the little country graveyard, which will swing open grumblingly on its rusty hinges, as though resenting the intrusion. Within the enclosure there are about twenty graves, and one is attracted to a slate headstone by the down-trodden grass in front of it. At the top of the slab is engraved a figure of a weeping willow, which was such a popular ornament on gravestones three-quarters of a century ago, and beneath it is this inscription:—

To the memory of the family which was once
destroyed by a slide from the White Mountains
on the night of 28 August, 1826.

> *Samuel Willey, ae 38.*
> *Polly S. Willey, 35.*
> *Eliza A. Willey, 12.*
> *Jeremiah S. Willey, 11.*
> *Martha G. Willey, 10.*
> *Elbridge G. Willey, 7.*
> *Sally Willey, 3.*

The first two named are the parents and the rest are their children.

It seemed as if the Notch road could never again be made passable, but the citizens of Portland, who were interested because of the trade they carried on with the farmers beyond the mountains, called a meeting of the people of the town and vicinity to see what could be done about it. A committee was chosen to examine the road and estimate the cost of repairs. The movement resulted in the road being made passable, though at great expense, and by the last of November wagons passed over it.

Chapter Cviii.

THE WRECK OF THE *ALMIRA*, 1827

The month of January, 1827, was the coldest January there had been in New England for twelve years. On streams and lakes the ice was extremely thick. During the month there was a warm spell for several days, which was succeeded within a few hours' time by a temperature that was below zero. The cold was most intense; several persons were frozen to death, while many lost their hands or feet. Along the coast, vessels were placed in hazardous situations, the cables of many of them being cut by the ice and forced out to sea, or on the rocks and beaches. Several went ashore at Ipswich and at other places along the Massachusetts coast. The perils of sailors are always many, but those of the coasters are multiplied, and disaster often overtakes them. The incident that renders this season of severe cold most interesting is the wreck of a coasting vessel on the Massachusetts shore.

On the afternoon of the sixteenth of the month, a small schooner named *Almira*, laden with wood, was slowly moving out of the little harbor of Sandwich at Cape Cod. After rounding the point sail was hoisted, and she stood toward the north. Until that date the month had been severely cold, gloomy and boisterous. Some of the vessels had been dismantled and laid up for the winter. Others were ladened, and had been waiting for better weather several weeks. Severe cold is generally followed on the Cape by a south wind and rain which pours down in a flood of water. It was so in this instance, and at about noon on the day mentioned the rain ceased, the air grew warmer, and the weather pleasant. The commander of the *Almira*, concluding that there would be a few days of pleasant weather, started down the harbor with a soft, but gusty, spring-like wind. The air was still very damp, and high in the heavens clouds were pursuing each other irregularly.

Upon a hill overlooking the harbor, an old and experienced coaster captain, stood watching the schooner as she glided out toward the sea. Walking up to his side, an acquaintance accosted him, but his gaze was so intent and his thought so concentrated that he took no notice of the intrusion. After the vessel reached the open water and stood away to the north, the old seaman lifted his hands and exclaimed as if to himself, "Gone out! he will never come in again!" His acquaintance, who still stood by his side, remarked that the wind was southerly, but he had again relapsed into his reverie, and walked away with a countenance that indicated plainly the faith that he had in the disastrous results of the vessel's trip.

As the schooner sailed along on its course the breeze became more and more variable. The master of the craft, Josiah Ellis, was a large, noble appearing man, who seemed able to cope with the elements, having many times by his physical energy successfully encountered fierce and pitiless storms during the years he had spent upon the sea. The wind and the tide had seemed to him so favorable that he had started on the trip with a small crew, consisting of his son Josiah and John Smith, a seaman.

The *Almira* soon made but slow progress on account of the fitfulness of the wind, and the early evening came on as they were off Monument Point, Plymouth, when they were working their way across the outer part of the bay. Shortly after, the crew were surprised to suddenly hear Captain Ellis' voice calling them together. He pointed to the northwest sky, which was clear and bright. About midway to the zenith the clouds were hastening toward the southeast. New stars were appearing every moment in the clear section. The sight was indeed beautiful, but to the mariners it was a dreaded indication of an immediate change to severe cold. They knew that the severity of the past few weeks would return, and out on the shelterless ocean they could not hope to withstand it. They must reach shore and shelter! Plymouth was the nearest harbor, but that lay in the face of the wind. However, they must try to reach it by tacking. This was tried several times, but the wind became more violent, the cold more severe, and their efforts were unavailing. At length the main boom was wrenched from the mast by a sudden movement of the vessel, the halyards were let go, and the mainsail came down crashing and crackling, it being already coated with ice. It was impossible to furl or gather it up. The vessel was laid to the wind, the foresail, which was also frozen, being braced fore and aft, and the jib loosened, it not being in their power to haul the latter down. The wind soon cracked the ice and rent the canvas, finally tearing it into shreds. Obeying the helm, the schooner came up to the wind, and so remained.

The whole sky was now swept clear, the moon and stars grew very bright, and the atmosphere was charged with frost and cold. The wind was not simply cutting, but the frozen moisture seemed to be needles of ice. The crew had now become quite wet with the moist air, and drenched with spray, their garments being congealed upon them. Icicles hung from their clothing and hair, and they began to feel the near approach of that stern power which chills and freezes the heart. A considerable distance from shore, their spars,

The Flying Dutchman. Oil on canvas by Elbridge Kingsley. Smithsonian American Art Museum.

rigging and sails ice-covered and useless, and their wet clothing stiff with ice, they knew not what to do. They descended to the cabin, and succeeded in lighting a fire, around which they stood for a few minutes. But the thought of other dangers drew them to the deck, which was also covered with ice, for it had become so cold that the spray froze as soon as it struck. The smallest ropes had assumed the appearance of cables, and the folds of the sails were filled with a weight that caused the craft to careen and threatened to sink it. No remedy seemed to be within their control. The vessel had become so heavy and the helm so encumbered with ice that she could not be guided. They at last concluded to let it drift into Barnstable Bay again, and try to reach their own shore. After a struggle they succeeded in moving the rudder far enough to turn the vessel about sufficiently to head it toward Sandwich, and with the assistance of the wind and tide, Monument Point was cleared and they drifted into Barnstable Bay to a point within eight miles of their homes. It was now some hours along in the night, and the moon shone brightly over land and sea. They could see the shore, and they longed for daylight, in the hope that the people who dwelt along the coast might discover and release them. The long hours passed wearily. The cold steadily increased through the night, and the sun rose upon the coldest morning of the whole winter.

The crew were unable to perform any duty, and the ice still accumulated. They swept pass their homes, hearing nothing and seeing nothing but the smoke curling up from the chimneys. The hope of receiving assistance from their friends were gone. They must now let the vessel float where it would. Their last sail had yielded to the violence of the wind and the burden of ice, and hung in tatters from the mast. Turning broadside to the wind, the vessel floated rapidly along, passing the harbors of Sandwich, Barnstable and Yarmouth, on, on toward the shore. Ahead of them was a reef of rocks, running out into the sea northerly from the town of Dennis. On the west side of the reef is a sandy beach, and on the east is a cove with a similar shore, forming a safe harbor from the northwest wind. But the reef lay between the vessel and the cove.

On this morning, from a hill, one of the citizens of Dennis saw this ill-fated schooner as it drifted toward the rocks, and gave an alarm. With a number of men, most of whom were seamen, he hastened to the shore. The vessel had now come so near the reef that the people looked on the deck, but only saw masses of ice. At length, they thought that there might be human beings on board, and as with one voice gave a shout. The three men emerged from the cabin, shaking with the cold. An old sea-captain shouted to them, "Put up your helm, make sail, and round the rocks," unaware of their utter inability to obey any part of the command. They stood like statues; they could do nothing. The crew felt the rising of the vessel for the last fatal plunge, and clung to whatever they could touch, with more instinct, however, than reason. A great wave lifted the hulk as if had been the body of a man, and dropped it at full length upon the ledges. The waves washed over the deck, filled the cabin, and left no place of retreat but the small portion of the quarter abaft the binnacle, and a little space forward of the windlass. The crew went shivering to the former place, being drenched, and ready to die and expecting each moment that the vessel would go to pieces. The people on shore resolved to make an effort to save their lives. A boat was procured and manned by a hardy, noble crew, who risked their own lives for these unknown men. The surf was very heavy, and largely composed of sludge. It required great effort to shove the boat off, and the men waded into the semi-fluid mass for that purpose. Scarcely had they reached the outer part of the surf when a refluent wave filled the boat. A long and slender warp cast from the shore reached one of the men, and was attached to the boat, all being drawn back again by those on shore. With an all-absorbing interest the crew on the schooner watched these proceedings. They saw the failure, and hope again left them. One went forward and sat down on the windlass; and the cry rang out to him from the shore, "Rise up! rise up, and stir yourself!" The sailor was John Smith. He paid no attention to the warning cry, either because he did not know how fatal it would be to sit down when the cold was so intense, or did not care. However it was, he was soon indistinguishable, the ice having entirely encrusted him. The father and son now stood alone, but the torpor of death was slowly creeping over them. They endeavored to keep in motion, but nature at length conquered the father's resolution and he went forward and seated himself as Smith had done. The cry was again raised in vain. The boat was now manned anew, launched, and this time safely passed beyond the surf. But the vessel could not be boarded. The men in the boat called to young Ellis, and he answered them. The waves and wind swept so violently over the ledges and the wreck that they could not approach nearer; but they encouraged the young man to keep awake, assuring him that the rising of the tide would lift the schooner from the rocks and that they would watch and embrace the first practicable opportunity to save him. The rising tide brought the vessel to a stand, and the people with great effort got on board at four o'clock in the afternoon. Young Ellis was on the quarter deck grasping the tiller ropes to which his hands were frozen. His feet and ankles were incrusted with ice, and he seemed scarcely conscious of the presence of his deliverers. They carried him on shore in their arms, and as they passed his father's body, he faintly uttered, "There lies my poor father." He then relapsed into a stupor, from which he did not wake until the customary remedies had been used for his restoration. Smith's body had been washed away. Young Ellis was given the kindest and best treatment, but he suffered the loss of his fingers and toes.

Chapter Six.

GALE AND FRESHET OF APRIL 1827

At about two o'clock on the afternoon of Tuesday, April 24, 1827, a severe southeast storm of wind and rain came suddenly upon the coast of Maine and New Hampshire. It was accompanied by lightning in some

places, and continued through the night with great violence. Vessels were
driven on shore at Portsmouth and Portland, and other places on that part
of the coast, being wrecked or greatly damaged. Much injury was done to
the shipping in other ways, especially in Portland Harbor, the vessels parting their hawsers at the wharves and being driven about, colliding with other
crafts, sinking some, and greatly damaging others. The bowsprits and jib-
booms of a number were carried away, and several vessels were so strained
that they became bilged.

The greater damage, however, was caused by the rain, a severe freshet
resulting, which carried away many bridges and mills. At Cape Neddick, in
York, Moses Nason's woolen factory and a grist-mill were carried down
stream, sweeping the bridge entirely away, and a bridge at Pettigrew's Hill
was also damaged. About five miles up the Cape Neddick River Cotton
Chase's clothing mills were swept away, carrying with them four bridges and
everything else on the river, with the exception of Norton's grist-mill near
its mouth, which was strongly supported by stone.

On the Kennebunk River, a fulling- and a grist-mill were carried down
against the bridge at Kennebunk, and stove to pieces. A large quantity of
lumber, logs and general debris collected at the bridge, and for a long time
it was thought that the bridge would be forced off its foundations, but it
withstood the onslaughts of the mad waters. Most of the lumber was saved,
and the bridge was injured but slightly, though two small bridges below were
carried away. How much lumber was washed into the stream cannot be
stated, but many piles of boards, which contained from ten to thirty-five
thousand feet each, were taken from the wharves, many of them being saved
by pulling them on shore by means of oxen and long ropes. On the Mousam
River, a house was nearly undermined by the water.

Saco River, of course, was raised by the rain. In the town of Saco all the
roads in the woods were much gullied, and in the river the water was very
high. Fifteen families were taken off the island above Spring's Bridge, the
water being above the first-story windows, and at Poor-house Island three
families were carried off on men's backs. At Biddeford, a bridge was carried
away. The Presumpscot River was also greatly flooded, and mills and
bridges on it were destroyed. Nonesuch Bridge, just outside of Portland, was
covered by the water to the depth of three feet, and Black Point causeway
was five feet under water. The eastern mail-stage driver had to go through
the water at that depth for half a mile. At Scarborough, a grist-mill was so
flooded that it fell ten feet on one side, and the bridge at the end of Storer's
Lane was undermined. The mail carrier's horse narrowly escaped drowning

there while fording the stream. There was no passing at Milliken's causeway, and the water on the turnpike was nearly three feet deep. Pride's Bridge at Portland was entirely covered by the flood, and somewhat injured, but remained upon its piers. Winslow's Bridge at Falmouth and Congin Bridge at Westbrook were carried away. The bridge and Cutler's grist-mill at Saccarappa were swept away, and two saw-mills were much injured, one having its machinery broken.

On the Androscoggin River a great amount of property was destroyed, about two-thirds of the bridge between Brunswick and Topsham being carried away, and also two saw-mills belonging to Dr. Page. The great boom that was located a few rods above the bridge broke away, and two hundred thousand dollars' worth of logs went down the stream, none of them being recovered. Damages were occasioned by the flood all through that section of the country. The rain continued to fall and the rivers to remain very full for several weeks after the water began to lower and the worst of the freshet was over.

Chapter Ex.

THE STORM OF MARCH 1830

A cold northeast storm of wind, rain and snow raged along the coast of New England during the latter part of March, 1830, producing a great tide, which in some parts exceeded the highest tide remembered there. The storm began on the morning of Friday, the twenty-sixth, and continued till one o'clock in the afternoon, the tide being at its height at noon of that day.

At Portland, Maine, several wharves were carried away, and many vessels lost their fastenings, some being driven on shore and others greatly damaged by being beaten against the wharves. One sank while anchored in the stream, and several others were injured. A great quantity of lumber owned by several individuals, and fifteen hundred cords of wood belonging to the Stream Navigation Company, were washed away. A long store-house on Union Wharf was swept away, and several stores on the wharves were displaced. The bridges on the roads leading out of the town suffered much damage.

At Portsmouth, New Hampshire, wharves were injured and several vessels driven ashore.

At Newburyport, Massachusetts, wharves were overflowed and wood and lumber set adrift, but the stores in which was most of the salt in the market were water-tight, and the contents were thus saved. The shipping escaped with little damage, with the exception of the schooner *Lady Howard,* from Boston, having a small cargo, which was driven ashore at Salisbury. The crew and a part of the goods, together with the cables and anchors, were saved, but the vessel was lost, having split open.

At Gloucester, the water was two or three feet deep on the wharves, and much movable property was washed away, the waves being covered with articles and debris of all kinds. The sloop *William Swain,* bound from Nantucket to Boston, with a cargo of oil and candles, was driven ashore at Sandy Bay, and was totally lost. The passengers and crew were saved. One of the passengers was a Mrs. Hayden, who was taken from her stateroom some time after the vessel struck. She was nearly lifeless, and strenuous efforts were necessary for her recovery.

In Beverly, considerable damage was also done. About eighty cords of wood and much timber and lumber were washed off the wharves, which were more or less injured, and Ellingwood's wharf near the bridge was nearly destroyed. Some damage was done by the colliding of the schooner *Agawam* which had parted her cables, with the schooner *Abigail,* carrying away her mainmast.

At Salem, the waves rolled several feet above the wharves, sweeping away great quantities of wood and timber and every other movable thing that was on them. A store on Derby Wharf was undermined in such a manner that it fell partially over, and for a time maintained that position. Strong ropes were attached to it, and it was held there until the Monday evening following, when it went over with a tremendous crash. A store at the head of Crowninshield's wharf was also overthrown by the water. Two of the custom-house boatmen, Messrs. Brown and Peel, were in the building at the time, and very narrowly escaped drowning. A man at the end of the wharf was saved with great difficulty by means of a boat which was sent to his relief. The brig *Washington* was driven from Allen's wharf, carrying away the capsill, and drifted upon the beach at the foot of Hardy Street, but was gotten off without material damage. Other vessels were driven ashore, but were not much injured. The roads over both North and South rivers and several others were rendered impassable by the flood. At high tide, the water was four feet deep on the isthmus connecting the Neck with the town at the head of Fort Avenue. The force of the wind and waves was felt as far inland as Danversport, where the works of the Salem and Danvers iron-factory received considerable damage, and one of the buildings there in which aqueduct logs were bored was destroyed.

In Marblehead, the storm was very severe, several vessels were driven on shore, and others lost their masts, booms, bowsprits and rudders. The wharves were swept of their wood, and several of them were greatly damaged.

At Lynn, the tide broke over the long beach into the harbor, and carried away timber, wood and shingles from the wharves. The old residents of the town said they did not remember a tide that was so disastrous on the beach. About midway of the little beach at Nahant, the schooner *Adventurer* of Hingham, commanded by Captain Churchill, bound from New York to Boston, and laden with flour and grain, went ashore at about nine o'clock in the forenoon and became bilged. The crew and a considerable part of the cargo were saved.

The tide rose at Boston one and one-half inches higher than the great tide of December, 1786, which was ten inches higher than the highest that any person then living remembered. The water broke through the dam along the Roxbury canal, parallel with the neck on the east side, in several places, and flooded the lowlands, sweeping away fences and outhouses, and prostrating buildings. Northampton Street was flooded, and its surface to the depth of about a foot was carried away. The water dashed into the plain between that street and what was then called the town of Roxbury near Lewis' cordage factory, and greatly injured the rope-walks and houses. There were several dwellings of only one story in height, tenanted by the families of persons who were employed in the factory. The water flowed in so suddenly that not one of the families had time to remove a particle of their furniture. On Saturday morning the water was nearly six feet above the floors, and about eighty women and children were taken in boats to the houses that stood on higher ground. The inmates of several two-story houses were driven to the second stories. On the next day workmen were employed in cutting a channel through Northampton Street to drain off the water. Large quantities of rice, flour and coal were either washed away or ruined.

Much property was set afloat at Charlestown and Cambridgeport. The navy-yard was overflowed, and the tide broke through the coffer-dam, about three feet of water coming into the dry dock.

On Scituate Beach, two vessels went ashore. One of these was the sloop *Globe*, Captain Wakeman, master, bound from New York to Salem, with a cargo of flour and corn. She was bilged, one side being completely broken to pieces. A part of the cargo was landed on the beach but the grain washed out through the crevices that had been made in the bottom of the sloop. The other vessel was the schooner *Edward* of Boston, which had sailed from Savannah for its home port with a cargo of logwood. It was cast ashore in the night about four miles south of the Scituate lighthouse. The crew was saved. The vessel was not much injured, the masts having been cut away as soon as she struck.

Chapter Cxi.

THE GREAT FRESHET OF JULY 1830

Till the middle of July, the summer of 1830 had been very cold and wet in Vermont. The weather then suddenly and greatly changed, and the hottest July temperature prevailed, with a clear, calm sky. The thermometer stood at from ninety to ninety-four degrees during the succeeding week. Three days later there was a remarkable freshet. The rivers were swollen to a height never known there before, their banks being overflowed, and much property, including many bridges and mills, was destroyed. The flood desolated and ruined the fields, badly washed highways, and destroyed bridges, greatly delaying travel. Some of the streams formed new channels. A person wrote from Burlington at that time that he doubted if any manufacturing establishment of large size remained within fifty miles of that place.

The freshet was also felt to a considerable extent in New Hampshire, and the Merrimack River was much swollen by the rains, some damage resulting from inundations.

On Saturday, July 24, the day the storm began, the air was sultry, the wind being south. Rain commenced to fall between eight and nine o'clock in the evening, and continued all night. A great deal also fell on Sunday, by which time the mountain streams had become very much swollen. That night and all day Monday there were frequent and very heavy showers, which continued without much intermission until the following Thursday noon. During these five days at Burlington over seven inches of water fell, and more than one-half descended on the twenty-sixth. Much of the time the rain poured down in torrents, and the heaviest sheet of rain seemingly that any one ever witnessed fell on Sunday night at about a quarter before twelve. Thunder and lightning accompanied it. The lowlands on the borders of all the streams were inundated, causing desolation and ruin, destroying property and human lives. The flood was as disastrous on the New York side of Lake Champlain as in Vermont.

The banks of the Missisqui and La Moille rivers were considerably inundated. At the great falls in Milton on the latter stream, where the river descends one hundred and fifty feet in fifty rods, the bridge, a trip-hammer shop, a fulling-mill and one other building were carried away, and the valuable grist-mill there was much damaged.

Winooski, or Onion River, was greatly raised by the rain, being most affected of the Vermont streams. The river passes through a wild and romantic country, and as it leaves the mountains on its way to the lake flows down with great rapidity. At Northfield, the mills and Pine's factory were much damaged. In Berlin, on Mad River, not a mill was left standing, and on Dog River all the bridges were carried away, the intervales being overflowed and crops destroyed. A man by the name of Grant was drowned in the deluge of waters. In Montpelier, which was then a small village, the water rose higher than it had ever been known to rise before, and caused considerable damage. Two of the bridges across the branch of the river in this town were swept away; and that at the upper mills and the arched bridge across Onion River suffered to some extent. A barber's shop that stood near the lower-branch bridge was carried away, and another building was swept down the stream and finally lodged in the top of a tree about half a mile below the village. Many people had narrow escapes from death, but the only life lost in the village was that of a man named Bancroft, who belonged in Calais, he being drowned near Shepherd's tavern. A great amount of damage was done at Middlesex, the mills, carding and cloth-dressing works and the bridge over Onion River being all destroyed. From this place to Lake Champlain not a bridge was left standing on the river. At Moreton, a number of houses and barns were carried away, and the wife of Capt. Harvey W. Carpenter, in attempting to leave the house for a neighbor's, was drowned. In Dolton, where the river passes through the Green Mountains, the house and barns of a Mr. Pineo were carried away. His family escaped by fleeing to the mountains just in season to save their lives. At Hubbel's Falls in Essex, the toll bridge belonging to the Essex Bridge Company, the clothing works and carding machine of a Mr. Haynes, and Capt. R. Butler's hemp machine and saw-mill were destroyed. The stone grist-mill there, which had been erected by John Johnson, Esq., in 1819, successfully resisted the whole current of Onion River, which for several hours rushed against it to a depth of twenty-five feet with incredible velocity. In Colchester, the bridge at F. Brewster and Company's works, which was nearly new, having cost eighteen hundred dollars, was carried away. The works there consisted of a saw-mill, oil-mill and woolen factory, and were valued at ten thousand dollars. They were all destroyed by the flood, but the principal part of the machinery, and the cloth and wool were saved. At Burlington, part of the then new bridge at the lower falls, and the whole of Mr. Catlin's plaster-mill, blacksmith shop, coal-house and the dam above their upper fall were destroyed. It also broke away Messrs. Eddy, Munroe and Hooker's boom, letting about four thousand mill logs down the current. The saw-mill of Messrs. Sinclair and Chittenden, with a large quantity of boards and other lumber, was also destroyed. The turnpike from Royalton to Burlington which follows the course of the Onion River, forming a romantic drive, was made absolutely impassable a great part of the way, and for a considerable distance was washed away entirely. The intervale lands on both sides of the river were so flooded that they were made desolate. Crops of every description were almost entirely destroyed, with most of the fences and many buildings. A small part of the grass had been cut, but the stacks and barns containing much of the hay were swept off. The intervale farm lands along the river in Burlington for a long time appeared like a lake. The wrecks of bridges, fences, barns, houses, mills, furniture, etc., constantly passed down the river, being thrown upon its banks, or collected in the eddies below the lower falls at Burlington.

On the White River, and also on its upper branch, all the bridges from Roxbury to Royalton were carried away. At Braintree, three sawmills were taken into the stream and swept down its current. In West Randolph, Ford's woolen factory and grist-mill, with all their machinery, and two houses were destroyed. At the village of Bethel on the upper branch of the river, Mr. Harvey's store was demolished and the fragments swept away, most of the goods being saved.

On the Middlebury River, Freeman Parkell of Cornwall lost a flock of about a hundred sheep, which were drowned. Both Otter Creek and Lemon-fair River cross this town, and at their junction they were considerably raised by the rain, two bridges being carried away. At Weybridge, Chase's saw-mill with the bridge near it on the turnpike was swept off, and a farmer named Hurd had more than a hundred sheep drowned on the flats. The dams at Lincoln and Bristol gave way before the immense body of water. The greatest amount of damage, however, was done at New Haven. After leaving the mountains the river flows with a rapid current through an open country, forming fertile intervales until it reaches New Haven where the stream becomes narrow, with rugged precipitous banks, and thus continues about a mile until it enters Otter Creek.

At about the time the sun was setting on Monday, a very dark and dense cloud settled over and around the lofty mountains at Bristol, and rain fell in torrents on valley and mountain accompanied by incessant and vivid lightning which enlivened the scene for two hours. A flood of water rushed down the stream from the heights, causing the river to rise ten or twelve feet higher than it was ever known to be before. At twelve o'clock it was at its height. Dams burst before it, and like a great tidal wave it rushed over the banks of the stream, flooding the country on either side.

Just above the mills at New Haven, where the river makes a short turn to the north, a small rocky island divides the stream into two parts, known as the east and west, which however unite again before they reach the Wilson mills, as they were called in those days. The branches are four miles apart, and upon each had been erected mills, around which had grown up small villages, known as East Mills and West Mills.

The small hamlet at West Mills was terribly affected by the flood. Just above the village the river had been dammed by an erection formed principally of timber. On Monday night, when the rain fell in such great quantities, the water rushed down the stream, tearing away every barrier, and overflowing its banks. It filled the intervale on the east side of the river, where the cluster of residences was situated, and carried off about twenty buildings. In the southeast part of the town two houses with a saw-mill were swept away, one family narrowly escaping with their lives.

A few rods below the Wilson mills the river makes a short turn to the west and dashes through a narrow passage between rocks which is known as the narrows. Between ten and eleven o'clock that night the water there rose rapidly. John Wilson, who resided on a flat only a few rods from the stream, became alarmed for the safety of his property, and some of the neighbors came to assist in its preservation. Just above the Wilson mills there was a narrow bridge, and on it Miles Farr and his son crossed the river for the purpose of assisting Mr. Wilson and his son Erskine. While they were busily at work in and about the mill, saving what they could from destruction, the water was rising rapidly in all directions around them. A few minutes later the bridge over which Mr. Farr had come, together with the grist-mill and clothier works was swept away. The floating mass paused a moment at the lower bridge, which gave way, and all was thrown down on the lower mills and dam. The men soon decided that they could do nothing more to save the mill and its contents, and that it was dangerous to remain in the building any longer. They started to go to Mr. Wilson's house, and were greatly astonished to find that a powerful stream of water was rushing along between the house and the high ground beyond. The Farrs went to the Stewart house near by to assist the family to escape from their imprisonment, and Mr. Wilson and his son went to their house, within which were Mrs. Wilson, her daughter Anne, two young children, and Mrs. Wilson's sister. After Mr. Wilson had looked around and observed how fast the water was rising around them, he became alarmed for their safety. They tried again and again to make their escape, but failed each time. Becoming utterly discouraged, Mr. Wilson told his son that they would go into the chamber where the rest of the family were, and if they must perish they would all go together. They accordingly retreated to the upper story, and had been there but a little while when the cellar wall was heard to give way, the chimney falling almost instantly afterward. Erskine was thrown into the water below through the aperture where the chimney had stood, and arose near the place where he fell in, being helped out by his father. He was severely bruised. They watched the water as it speedily undermined the house, and the father and son went to the door that looked toward the road, knowing that they must immediately make an effort to save themselves and the family or they would all be lost. They had stood at the door but a moment when they felt the house move from its foundation. Being frightened and with the instinct of self-preservation, both leaped into the water and struggled to reach the shore, which they finally succeeded in doing. As soon as they were on land they looked after the house. Erskine discovered his sister Anna holding the youngest child in her arms on what seemed to him to be the chamber floor. He distinctly heard her call him by name several times, imploring him to save her and little Sarah. He told her to throw the child into the water toward them, as far as she could, and then jump in herself. Either she did not understand him, or had not the courage to perform such an act, or else she failed to discern a chance of escape by doing so. The house was rapidly approaching the narrows. The father and son ran along on the land as fast as they could, hoping that the current would bring the house nearer the shore that they might be enabled to save the inmates. Anna grew frantic with fright, as she saw that they could not save her. They saw the house enter the rapids as she was still beckoning to them, but they never saw her again, all of the five persons in the house finding a watery grave.

Near Mr. Wilson's house stood the home of Nathan Stewart, a blind man, who had a family of seven. When the Farrs and Wilsons came from

Wilson's mills, the latter went to their own house, and the Farrs to that of Mr. Stewart, knowing that as he was without sight he would probably need assistance as the water was rapidly rising. Lemuel B. Eldridge, Esq., another neighbor, was already there, having ridden on horseback through the current, but with such difficulty and so much danger that he considered it very hazardous to attempt to return that way. With him had come his son, of about twenty years of age, and his hired man by the name of Somers. The family had already left the house, and were seeking refuge in the barn, which stood on ground that was a little more elevated. Mr. Eldridge conceived the idea of a raft on which to take off the family, and the men immediately commenced to build one at the corner of the woodhouse, using the barn doors and other materials at hand for that purpose. They were soon joined by one of the Stewart boys from the barn, who assisted them. The raft was completed, and they were about ready to take the family upon it, when the woodhouse was raised from its foundation, and swept down with the current. At that time they were all on the raft, except one man who was holding it just as the building started. He could no longer restrain the craft from being carried down the stream, and accordingly leaped upon it with his companions. The six men were hurried along toward the narrows, and all maintained their position upon the raft until they had reached that frightful place where in a moment it was dashed into fragments, which were scattered here and there, and all the men were thrown into the seething waters. With his right hand, Mr. Farr grasped a plank that had formed a part of the raft, and soon found some other fragments which he seized with his left. Holding to these as his only hope of escape the current carried him down to the flat about half a mile below the mills, where he lodged against a large pine stump that had come down the stream and grounded. He had found something now, he thought, that would be safer than his planks, and he let them float away from him; but in a moment a quantity of flood-wood came against the stump, and all were driven down the current. He was exhausted and felt that there was no chance of escape, yet he would not give up without one more struggle. He had succeeded in clearing the flood-wood away, when the stump again grounded. There he clung to it until morning came, and he was taken off by friendly hands. Mr. Eldridge was carried nearly through the narrows before he could grasp anything to help support him above the water. Then he fortunately found a board, which enabled him to rest himself. He was driven out of the channel of the stream in the direction that Mr. Farr had been carried, and over a field of corn. There he could touch bottom, and feel the stalks of corn, which he grasped, their roots being strongly enough embedded to enable him to successfully resist the current. Mr. Farr's son and young Stewart had been carried by the force of the stream to a point a little below where Mr. Eldridge was, and there they secured their safety. They caught a clapboard and some pieces of flood-wood, and cut up their suspenders, lashing them together, by means of which they extricated Mr. Eldridge from his position. When morning broke they saw Mr. Farr near them, and assisted him on shore. Of Mr. Somers nothing was ever known, and he must have been drowned soon after the raft broke up. Young Eldridge was helped by his father, who caught him in his arms several times, being repeatedly torn away by the violence of the current and the wrecks of buildings, and at last they separated to meet no more.

When the raft started down the stream the Stewart family were still in the barn. There were Mr. and Mrs. Stewart, and four of their children, the oldest son having been carried away on the raft. They were helpless where they were. They had hoped that the raft which their kind neighbors had made would be the means of their preservation, but that had been driven away from them down the turbulent stream and destroyed, with their son on board, who, as they thought, must have perished in the rapids. The water had now risen so high that they sought refuge on a scaffold, which soon after fell, probably killing some of the family, and intact it was forced out into the current. In passing through the narrows it was crushed to pieces, and all the family perished except the fourteen-year-old son, who was wonderfully saved by being driven against the top of a small tree, to the branches of which he clung until he was rescued the next morning. He said that his mother was confined by some of the timbers of the barn, and that when they were in the narrows, just as the scaffold was dashed to pieces, she had hold of his hand and spoke to him. It was midnight darkness, and he saw her no more.

Two families by the name of Farr had been taken from their houses on rafts in the midst of the storm and the darkness, one of them from the windows of the second story. In Col. William P. Nash's residence, where his wife was confined to her bed by sickness, the water filled the lower part of the house, and the family remained all night in the upper rooms. Outside they heard, but could not see on account of the intense darkness, the water surging and beating around them, and they passed the night in doubt and dreadful suspense. In the midst of the raging and increasing flood, which threatened at any moment to sweep them all into it, certain death seemed to be awaiting them, and there was apparently no means or possibility of escape. But the house held together, and they were saved.

Another family had an interesting experience. They went to bed unconscious that such great danger lurked around them, and in the night the
father, Mr. C. Claflin, was aroused by the noise of the water about the house.
He went to the door, and discovered that it had risen so high they could not
escape. He could not see over the raging flood, but heard it as it came rushing down, apparently growing higher and stronger as he stood there.
Something must be done and that quickly. He thought of an elm tree that
stood near, and conceived the plan of conveying his family into it for safety,
feeling sure that if the house were carried away the tree would hold. He
accordingly, at that midnight hour, placed his children in it and fastened
them there by means of a rope that he took out of a bedstead. He also successfully aided his wife and their youngest child who was only a few weeks
old into the tree, and then climbed up into it himself. There they waited in
this uncomfortable situation, perched among the wet branches of the elm
in the darkness of night, knowing that each moment the water was rising
higher and higher around them. After several long weary hours had dragged
away, the morning light broke, and rescuers came to their relief.

Many people were on the shores of the inundated territory that night,
and they heard cries of distress, and shrieks and supplications for assistance
from their perishing neighbors and friends without being able to afford any
relief. The night was intensely dark, and the waters lashed furiously against
everything with which they came in contact.

Fourteen persons lost their lives in the water at this little village on that
night, and twenty-one buildings were carried away with all their contents.
Among the buildings destroyed were the mills of John Foot and
Champlain's storehouse, and the latter and his wife narrowly escaped
drowning.

On Tuesday noon the river had fallen more than twelve feet, but a vast
body of turbid water was still rushing over the very spot where the houses
and gardens of the unfortunate families had stood the night before, and
nothing remained but naked rock.

At the East mills, the bridge and dam, and a valuable woolen factory, a
grist-mill, a saw-mill, and other mills there were all swept away. The damage done in the county to individuals alone was upwards of sixty thousand
dollars.

Crops on the smallest streams even were greatly injured. A week before,
farmers rejoiced in an abundant harvest and in the prospect of the plen-
teousness of later crops. Now, many a tiller of the soil was in despair at the
desolation that had assailed him in barn and field.

Chapter Lxii.

METEORIC DISPLAY OF 1833

One of the grandest and most remarkable exhibitions of natural phenomena ever witnessed in this part of the world was observed on the early morning of November 13, 1833. In all parts of the heavens, which were clear and serene, meteors fell like snowflakes or shot like sparks flying from a piece of fireworks. They were of various sizes, some being as small as fixed stars and others very much larger. They began to fall and shoot at midnight, and continued until the stars faded away in the early morning, being most numerous at about four o'clock. The shooting meteors left luminous trails or traces of white light behind them of from half a yard to three yards in length, apparently, which slightly curved downward, and remained visible from three to five seconds. The meteors fell at times in such large numbers that they seemed like a shower of fire, by which name similar exhibitions are known in other portions of the world. Now and then, one much brighter and larger than the rest would shoot across the sky like vivid lightning. They fell about one half as thickly as snowflakes fall in a common snow storm, with intervals when but few could be seen. They produced a sound like "whish, whish," gently spoken many times in different degrees of loudness. Great numbers were seen to explode like a rocket, sending forth trains of dazzling sparks, accompanied by an explosive noise. From time to time a sound, as of a body rushing through the air, was heard. The meteors seemed to have distinct nucleuses about half the size of Jupiter, some being larger and some smaller.

The temperature had changed during the night and the morning was somewhat colder, the thermometer at Boston standing at thirty-nine degrees above zero. The slight wind there was came from the west.

From two o'clock to daylight it was calculated that 207,840 of these bodies fell. At about half past five, when they were flashing in the light of approaching sunrise, the heavens presented one of the most extraordinary, beautiful and sublime sights ever beheld by man.

At Boston were noticed two very bright meteors, which reddened the steeple of a church by their light. They generally lighted up the country everywhere so that people were awakened by them, and sprang from their beds thinking that their houses were on fire.

Such exhibitions are not very uncommon in the Arctic regions, and they have been witnessed in other parts of the world several times in the history of civilized nations, but this is the only instance that such a brilliant and magnificent spectacle has been seen by the inhabitants of New England. It may seem surprising that anything of this kind should alarm the people of the nineteenth century. Many persons, however, feared that the meteors would set the earth on fire, and a conflagration ensue, of which no one dared estimate the limits. The people of Amesbury, Massachusetts, and some other sections of the country were considerably agitated on account of it. Such exhibitions have been seen in the older parts of the world before some great convulsion of nature, and the people here may have known of and remembered it.

Chapter Cxiii.

WINTER OF 1835–36

The summer of 1835 was dry and remarkably pleasant, but the winter following was one of the severest seasons ever known in New England. It had many exceedingly cold days, and all the harbors from New York to Nova Scotia were thickly frozen over. Massachusetts Bay was covered by the ice for a long distance from the shore. The first snow fell November 23, and from that time to the end of March snow storms came frequently, covering the earth to a great depth, and making excellent sleighing, which continued for twenty weeks.

December 6, Sunday, was a bitter, cold day, with a high wind from the northwest. The harbor of Salem, Massachusetts, was then frozen over as far as Naugus Head. An incident of that day was the loss of the crew of a small craft bearing the name *Bianca,* in sight of their own homes at Pond Hollow in Truro, on Cape Cod. There were five of them, and they had been to Provincetown to ship their fish to Boston, for they were fishermen, and had started home this Sunday morning against the advice of older and wiser men. The sea was heavy, and the boat was capsized on the bar, all the men being drowned.

Wednesday, December 16, was the coldest day that had been experienced for many years, and taking the whole of the day it was the severest on record, being colder than either of the "Cold Fridays." The sun shone brightly, and a boisterous piercing wind prevailed throughout the day, rendering exposure to the open air scarcely endurable. At Salem, Massachusetts, the temperature at six o'clock in the morning was eight degrees below zero. By nine o'clock it had risen three degrees, but immediately began to descend. At noon it was eight below, and two hours later twelve. During the next hour it rose about two degrees, but again descended, being at eight o'clock in the evening eighteen below. At Greenfield, Massachusetts, at noon on that day it was fifteen below. The next morning it was seven below, and by noon at Salem it had risen to seven degrees above zero. Many fingers, noses and ears were frozen. An instance is recorded of a judge, who, upon entering the court-room immediately after returning from his morning ride on horseback, found that his ears were frozen. The drivers of the stages on the eastern route suffered much from frozen extremities. During the night many buildings were burned, probably on account of the great fires that were made to enable the people to keep warm, and there was such a demand for fuel that the price advanced to an extreme limit.

Through November and December there was that rare affliction, a winter drought. The streams were so low that a considerable number of the manufacturing establishments were obliged to suspend operations, and many poor people were thus thrown out of employment in the middle of a hard winter. All wells were very low, and many dry. Water for domestic purposes was brought from a distance by teams. On Christmas night a slight thaw began, and fog and rain set in, which cleared the ice out of many harbors. The rain fell quite copiously in central Massachusetts, carrying off most of the snow which was on the ground. The springs were not much affected by it, however, the ground being too much frozen to permit the water to go through it.

The month of January was as severe as the preceding month had been. Many disasters to vessels on our coast occurred, and a number of lives were lost. Among the wrecks was that of the brig *Regulator,* bound from Smyrna to Boston, which ran on an island in Boston Harbor. The foremast went by the deck, and the main-topmast followed, taking with it the head of the mainmast close to the rigging and the tops. It was low tide, and the sea broke over the decks, filling her with water. As the tide rose she beat over the island. Some of the crew were lost, but Captain Phelps and several others climbed into the rigging, and there remained until rescued by the crew of the brig *Cervantes,* after they had struggled five hours in the waves trying to reach the wreck. The survivors were all more or less frozen. The rescue was very opportune as the vessel was already submerged, only the bowsprit and a few other projections being above water.

On February 21, the three months' run of cold weather in eastern Massachusetts was broken and another thaw set in. The snow was deep everywhere, in the woods and fields and highways. In most of the streets of Boston the snow and ice had accumulated to from three to four feet in depth, and in many of the narrow streets was even deeper. The roofs of buildings were heavily burdened with it, and they leaked like sieves. As the thaw came on, people were afraid their roofs would break with the weight of snow, and they hurried to relieve them. Cellars were inundated, sidewalks and streets were generally over-flowed and impassable. The scene there was interesting. Axes, hatchets, spades, shovels and brooms were called into use to counteract the effects and avoid the inconvenience of a freshet. Young and old, large and small, black and white, rich and poor, people of all conditions and both sexes, with their various implements, from the ponderous pickaxe to the broom, were industriously delving and digging to open passages for the water in directions away from their own premises.

April 1, snow was four feet deep in the New Hampshire woods, and not a speck of bare ground was to be seen there on hill or in dale. The weather was still very cold.

Chapter Lxix.

THE STORMS OF DECEMBER 1839

During the first two weeks of December, 1839, the weather was uncommonly pleasant, and without the least intimation of the terrible storms that were about to ravage the New England coast. Saturday, the fourteenth, was very mild, with a perfectly clear sky, and many vessels on our northeastern coast left their havens bound for Boston, New York and other southern ports. Soon after midnight snow began to fall and the wind to blow from the northeast, and they were driven down the coast, with the mist that ever exists in the Bay of Fundy, which shielded the breakers and bars from sight. The warning rays of the lights along the shore struggled to penetrate the heavy fog that shrouded the turbulent billows.

The wind suddenly changed to the southeast, and during the night and the next forenoon many of the vessels that had left the ports of Maine and

New Hampshire the day before were run into the nearest port for refuge. At noon the wind had greatly increased in violence, and in the afternoon it blew a gale in many places. The ocean has rarely been seen in such violent agitation, and possessed of such terrible power. Accompanied with mingled rain and snow, the storm continued all day; and all along the coast the harbor scenes consisted of the vessels tossing on the darkened stormy waters, and blown by the wind and thrown about by the waves, being watched with intense interest and anxiety by the dwellers along the coast, who saw the fate of the hapless mariners in the awful breakers on the lee shore. Many people with willing hands and noble, stout hearts hastened to afford assistance if chance should offer, or it could avail. One after another the vessels were seen to drift, and apparently hurry on to destruction, while many silent, earnest prayers ascended from the throngs on the beaches in behalf of the impotent mariners. Some of the crafts turned over and went down at their anchors bottom up, with the crews, who were seen no more. The fearful end of many vessels, however, was checked by cutting away the masts. Others were steered for sandy beaches, upon which the wind drove them, and with assistance from the people on shore, the lives of most of the sailors were saved. Several of them were dashed upon rocks and shivered to atoms in a moment, in some instances the crews being saved in various ways by the strong arms of mariners who had battled with the waves and storms for years. As night came on the storm seemed rather to increase than diminish and the wind blew more violently than it had before during the storm, darkness with all its gloom settling down over the scene that was never to be effaced from the memory of those that witnessed it. The wind blew with mighty power and the sea raged all through the long night. Many persons remained on the beach during those dreadful hours to render aid, but they were rarely able to do so for the fury of the storm. About two o'clock in the morning the wind veered to the northeast, and the gale somewhat abated. It continued to storm and the sea to rage, however, until late Monday night, but most disaster was caused Sunday night. The exact loss of life was never known, but it must have been great. The whole shore of Massachusetts was strewn with wrecks and dead bodies, and the harbors of Newburyport, Salem, Marblehead, Boston, Cohasset, Plymouth and Cape Cod were almost literally filled with disabled vessels. But on the shores of Maine and Connecticut the storm was less severe. On the land the force of the wind was terrific, many buildings being blown down and hundreds of chimneys overturned. The tide rose higher than many of the highest water-marks then known. Inland as far as northwestern Massachusetts the snow fell in great quantities, and its depth rendered travelling almost impossible, the deep embankments in many places extending to the second story of houses. This was the first snow storm of the season.

At Boston, the tide rose higher than the old water-marks, and swept completely across the Neck, the force of the wind being so great that at the south part of the city on Sunday there was no apparent fall of the water for three hours. Many chimneys, signs and blinds were blown down. A corner of the roof of the Maverick House and a part of the roof of the car-house at East Boston were blown away. Several vessels in the harbor had their masts carried away, and many were badly chafed. A ship and a brig were sunk at their wharves. Many vessels dragged their anchors, causing collisions, which sank small crafts and greatly damaged large ones. The schooner *Hesperus*, which belonged in Gardiner, Maine, broke her anchor chain, and was driven by the wind against a dock, carrying away her bowsprit and staving the end of her jib-boom through the upper window of a four-story building.

On the rocky shores of Nahant, at about four o'clock Sunday afternoon, the schooner *Catherine Nichols*, commanded by Captain Woodward, and bound from Philadelphia to Charlestown with a cargo of coal, was literally dashed to pieces. They had run in under the lee-shore, but the wind veered and drove them out. Thirty minutes later they had parted their cables and were driven on the peninsula. With great difficulty and the assistance of the people of the town, the captain and three of the crew reached the shore in safety. One of these, John Whiton of New Bedford, as they brought him from the water exclaimed "Oh! dear," and upon reaching the shore he motioned to them to put him down, which was done, and he immediately died. Levi Hatch, another of the crew, was drowned, or died from the effects of bruises before he came to land. He belonged in North Yarmouth, where he left a wife and two children. The mate staid by the vessel to the last, and died amidst the roaring surf, his body being found jammed in among the rocks almost entirely naked. John Lindsay of Philadelphia, another of the crew, was last seen clinging to the rigging, which with the foremast, the last one to fall, drifted out to sea, and he was never heard of again. The bodies of Whiton and Hatch were taken to Lynn, and buried on Tuesday from the First Methodist Church, the pastor Rev. Mr. Cook, preaching a sermon, after which the citizens followed the remains to the cemetery.

In the harbor of Marblehead several vessels were injured, the masts of some were cut away, and quite a number of schooners were driven on shore.

The schooner *Paul Jones* was forced high upon the rocks, where she became bilged. Another schooner named *Sea Flower* was driven on the beach and wholly lost, together with part of her cargo which consisted of four hundred bushels of corn and one hundred and twenty barrels of flour.

At Salem, the wind did not blow very strongly, and little damage was done in the harbor. A few vessels were slightly injured by chafing against the wharves, and a small schooner was driven up Forest River near the bridge. Several chimneys and two barns in the vicinity of Bridge Street were blown down.

The scene in Gloucester Harbor during this storm has never been equalled in any other New England port. Many vessels sought this haven of refuge from the tempest, and in all as many as sixty were there during the gale. Between three and four o'clock on the afternoon of Sunday, they began to drift, dragging their anchors or breaking the cables that bound them. Upon the beach were many willing fishermen to assist the mariners if it were possible. Within plain sight of them lay a schooner to whose shrouds were lashed three men. On all the coast of New England at that time, it is said, there was not a single life-boat, and no other small craft could live between the wreck and the shore. With full knowledge of this, the shipwrecked mariners bore their sufferings in silence, until finally as the rigging swayed to and fro by the motion of the waves, they were submerged and drowned. As another vessel approached the breakers, two men tried to escape death in their boat; but had scarcely loosed from the vessel when a merciless sea swept them into eternity. Such scenes constantly occurred before the eyes of the kind-hearted Cape Ann fishermen, and they were nerved to exert themselves in the face of the great dangers of the storm. With ropes tied to their bodies, they repeatedly leaped from the rocks and saved many lives.

On Monday morning only a single mast was left standing in the harbor. Twenty-one vessels were driven ashore, three schooners sank, and seventeen were so thoroughly dashed to pieces that in some cases no fragment larger than a plank was left. Twenty vessels still rode in the harbor, all but one without masts, they having been cut away. From each vessel a slender pole stood to bear aloft a signal of distress. They were tossing like egg-shells upon the still raging sea, liable at any moment to part their cables and be driven to sea with all on board. The pieces of twenty-two wrecks were scattered along the shore, scarcely any one of which being larger than a horse could draw. The crowd had staid on the beach all night to give assistance if it were possible. On the following afternoon as soon as it was considered safe to do so, a brave volunteer crew under the direction of Capt. William Carter procured the custom-house boat, and pulled out to the vessels that still floated, taking the weary and suffering seamen to the shore. The shipwrecked men were obliged to jump from their decks into the boat, as the sea was still too violent to enable the gallant little craft to approach nearer. One of the vessels, just after her crew were taken off, drifted out of the harbor and was never again heard from.

But that night the calm, low voice of the Unseen was heard by the elements, "Peace, be still,"—the tempest went down, the wind was taken away, and the mighty waves ceased their madness, sinking into a repose as quiet as that of a child after a hard day's play. The next morning's sun revealed the fragments of the many wrecks strewn along the beach, mixed with spars and rigging. But this was not all, for the articles of the varied cargoes, the personal effects of the seamen,

And the corpses lay on the shining sand—
On the shining sand when the tide went down.

To the shipwrecked mariners was extended every relief and comfort that humanity could devise, and on that evening a public meeting of the citizens was held in the town to adopt means for their assistance. The exact loss of life was never ascertained. About forty lives were believed to have been lost, including the persons who perished by the wreck of a schooner near Pigeon Cove, and twenty were known to have died, though only twelve bodies were recovered. The remains were tenderly cared for. One of the bodies was taken away by friends, and the funeral of the other deceased mariners was held at the Unitarian church on the following Sunday afternoon. All the other churches in the town were closed, the clergymen attending and taking part in this service. The pastor of the church, Rev. Josiah K. Waite, preached a sermon from the words, "Thou did'st blow with thy wind, the sea covered them: they sank as lead in the mighty waters."[1] The people of the town were so deeply in sympathy with the occasion that between two and three thousand persons listened to the exercises. In the church the eleven coffins were arranged in front, and at the close of the services were placed in carriages prepared for their conveyance, being appropriately shrouded in national flags. The vast congregation formed in a procession, which was nearly a mile in length, and followed the remains of the mariners to the public tomb.

---

1. Exodus XV:10.

The dead were Capt. Amos Eaton, Peter Gott and Alpheus Gott, all of
Mount Desert, Maine; William Hoofses and William Wallace, both of
Bremen, Maine; Reuben Rider of Bucksport, Maine; Joshua Nickerson,
Isaac Dacker, Philip Galley, a Mrs. Hilton, and two other persons whose
names are unknown. The remains of Mrs. Hilton were taken to Boston
before the funeral by friends in that city, and later in the season the bodies
of Nickerson and Dacker were removed by water to their homes.

At Ipswich, another sad shipwreck was added to the list, which is
already much too long. The storm was as violent in Ipswich Bay as at
Gloucester, and the schooner *Deposit* from Belfast, Maine, commanded by
Captain Cotterell, was hurried before it through the foaming breakers on
the sandy beach near the lighthouse at midnight on Sunday. Although the
vessel was on the beach, the heavy surf in which no boat could exist was
between it and safety. The waves washed over the wreck continually from
midnight till dawn, and the seven persons in the rigging and elsewhere
about the wreck managed to prevent themselves from being swept off by the
wind and waves—in several instances, however, only to survive that they
might die from the cold and exposure. Before daylight came, the strength of
a boy had failed, and he was lying in the scuppers dead, and a Negro,
becoming exhausted, had lain down and died. At daybreak, only five were
alive. The storm was still raging with unabated fury, and threatened every
moment to dash the remaining persons from their hold. Their feelings cannot be described. Was there no one on the shore to aid them? They
screamed for help;

> And ever the fitful gusts between
> A sound came from the land;
> It was the sound of the trampling surf
> Upon the hard sea-sand.

A man named Marshall was at the beach on that Monday morning, and
discovered the wreck. He gave an alarm, and then he and Mr. Greenwood,
the keeper of the lighthouse, went as near as they possibly could to the vessel. It was apparent that no boat could pass in safety through the surf. But
the piteous cries for help from the sufferers, among whom was the captain's
wife, nerved them to desperate action. Mr. Greenwood dashed into the
water, and after an almost overpowering struggle with the waves arrived at
the vessel. With a rope he hauled Mr. Marshall and a boat to the wreck. The
captain, who was completely exhausted and almost senseless, was first low-

ered into the boat which Marshall was keeping close to the vessel. But a
wave instantly upset it, and threw them both into the surging water.
Marshall went under the wreck, but on rising to the surface caught hold of
a rope and saved himself, but the captain was so exhausted that he was
drowned. His wife saw him as he was buried beneath the billows and her
shrieks rose high above the thunders of the storm. Two of the crew were
helped to the shore, one of them by floating on a boom. Mrs. Cotterell, wife
of the captain, was lowered from the stern of the vessel by ropes, and the two
rescuers standing in the surf received her in their arms as she came down to
the surface of the water. They then waited until a mighty wave came, which
they allowed to carry them all on shore. On the beach was a farmhouse, then
owned and occupied by Humphrey Lakeman, a retired sea-captain, to which
the three survivors were conveyed, and medical aid procured. The two men
that were saved were George Emery and Chandler Mahoney. The bodies of
the lost were taken to the village and properly buried on the Wednesday following. The funeral was held at the South Church, and was attended by a
great number of people, who followed the remains to the cemetery. Sixteen
sea-captains acted as pall bearers. The people of Ipswich had never before
been so affected by any incident. The sadness of the wreck, the dead, the
saved, and the actions of the two noble-hearted self-sacrificing men
touched sympathetic chords in every breast. The crew were all young, and
that fact added to the general sorrow. The expression upon the faces of the
deceased, and especially that of one named Dunham, was peculiarly sweet,
as if they were enjoying a most refreshing and peaceful sleep of the body
rather than that from which they would never again awake. The survivors
remained in the town until they were sufficiently restored to travel, receiving every comfort and attention.

At Newburyport, the tide overflowed the wharves on the river side, and
large quantities of wood and lumber were floated away. Some fifteen or
twenty fishing schooners that were lying at the wharves suffered more or
less damage by chafing, and a large number of other vessels that were
anchored in the harbor were more or less injured.

The second severe snow storm of this month began on Sunday, the
twenty-second, and the next morning the wind was fiercely blowing from
the northeast. The storm continued all through the day, and snow fell in
such quantities that railroads in Massachusetts were blocked, and great
damage was done on both land and sea, many vessels being driven ashore
and more or less damaged. The storm reached as far south as Baltimore,
where snow began to fall as early as Saturday.

The northern portion of Plum Island was so flooded that the keeper of the lighthouse could not get to it. The water flowed quite across the island, in a number of places, making deep ravines, and causing many acres of grass land to be covered with sand. The hotel, which was then conducted by Capt. N. Brown, was entirely surrounded by water and the turnpike road and the bridge were flooded. Sand-hills twenty feet high were carried off and others equally large were formed. The whole eastern shore of the island was washed away several rods in width.

The storm was indelibly impressed upon the minds of the people of Newburyport by the wreck at Plum Island of the brig *Pocahontas*, Capt. James G. Cook, master, bound from Cadiz to Newburyport, it having sailed from Cadiz in the latter part of October. She had set sail first in September, but, being run into by a Spanish ship, was so much damaged that she had to return for repairs. The crew consisted of the officers and nine hands before the mast. The brig measured two hundred and seventy-one tons, and had been built in 1830. Her masts had been carried away by the terrible wind, and she had probably been anchored in the evening, but in the darkness and the blinding snow, the mariners did not know that they were so near the sandy beach. The anchor dragged, and stern first she was driven on the reef, where she thumped until the stern was stove in, the noble vessel at length being torn to pieces. It had been driven upon a reef about one hundred and fifty yards from the beach, at a point half a mile east from the hotel, which was the most dangerous place on the island. Soon after daylight on Monday morning, Captain Brown, the keeper of the hotel, discovered the vessel, and news of the disaster was quickly conveyed to Newburyport. A few minutes later amidst the roar of the storm the cry rang through the streets that a wreck was on Plum Island. A number of humane men from the lower part of the town donned their thickest and heaviest boots, and quickly hastened over the marshes to the sandy island, which was trembling under the tremendous roll of the maddened waves.

The deck of the brig was slippery, the ropes stiff and glazed, and the cries and shrieks of its human burden were drowned by the cruel winds and the roar of the ocean. Tons of water were rushing down the hatchways. When the vessel was first noticed, three men were seen upon it, one of them being lashed to the taffrail, and nearly or quite naked, apparently dead, and two were clinging to the bowsprit. In a short time and before the intelligence of the wreck had reached the town, only one man, who was clinging to the bowsprit, remained, and mountainous waves were rolling over him. Still he clung with a desperate grip. To his rescue, a number of hardy young men, veritable sons of Neptune, insisted upon going through the tremendous sea with Captain Brown's little skiff, the vessel being too far away to throw a life-saving line to it,—and even if it had not been, the man was evidently too much exhausted to avail himself of such means of escape. They hauled the boat over the beach for three-fourths of a mile, but finding it impossible for any common boat to live one moment in that terrible surf, they very reluctantly abandoned their plan. The ill-fated man maintained his position on the vessel for several hours, growing so weak that at one time he lost his hold, but luckily regained it. Still the unpitying storm beat on. The men could only look at each other through the falling snow, from land to sea, from sea to land, and each realized how impotent they all were. Just before noon, the mariner was a second time swept by the heavy sea from the bowsprit, which also immediately followed him, and this time he was seen no more. A few minutes later the wreck was washed in and cast upon the beach. A man was found lashed to the vessel and he was still breathing, but so exhausted that he simply drew a few breaths, and then all was over. The sea had beaten over him so fiercely and continually that his clothes were almost washed off from him. Whether the majority of the crew perished by the cold and exposure or were washed from the vessel by the waves will never be known, as not one of the thirteen souls on board survived to tell the tale. The people were deeply affected at knowing that young Captain Cook, toil-worn as he was, after beating about on a stormy coast for several days, should be wrecked, and perish within sight of the smoke ascending from his own hearthfire. The bodies of several of the unfortunate men washed ashore and were taken up on the beach at some distance from the wreck, the small boat belonging to the brig lying near them indicating that they had attempted to reach the shore in it, probably about daylight. In all, there were recovered the bodies of the captain, first mate, who was Albert Cook, also of Newburyport, and seven others of the crew, who were strangers. Captain Cook's funeral was on Saturday, and after several days had passed, it having become almost certain that no more bodies would be found, the other eight corpses, with the American flag thrown over each of them, were borne into the broad aisle of the South Church in Newburyport, while the bells were being tolled. Amid a concourse of twenty-five hundred persons, a solemn prayer was offered over the remains of these human waifs, untimely thrown upon our shores, and then they were borne at the head of a procession numbering several hundred persons, to the cemetery, while the bells were again solemnly tolled, and flags hung at half-mast from the vessels in the harbor.

At Nantasket Beach, on Monday, at about noon, the bark *Lloyd* of Portland, Maine, bound from Havana to Boston, and commanded by Captain Mountfort, with masts gone, went on shore. The weather was still very thick, and a heavy sea was running, the surf being so high that no boat could put out to its assistance. Four of the crew lashed themselves to the rigging. The six other persons on the vessel succeeded in getting out and launching the long boat, into which they got, but the mighty waves upset it, and they were drowned. Finally the vessel was dashed to pieces, and all on board perished, with the exception of George Scott, an Englishman, who floated on an oar within reach of the people on the beach, and they pulled him out of the water when he was nearly exhausted. Captain Mountfort, who had lashed himself to the rigging, was brought ashore in a boat belonging to a vessel that was lying near, which also suffered from the storm, after three perilous efforts had been made to reach him, and was immediately taken into one of the huts of the Humane Society, every effort to resuscitate his insensible body being made, but in vain. He was the oldest shipmaster that then sailed out of Portland, and was much respected.

During the middle of the week, the weather was unusually fine for the season, but just before noon on Friday, another terrible storm began, this time of rain, which fell in small quantities, however. It was more tempestuous than either of the other storms had been, and the wind came from the east-southeast, increasing during the night to a violent gale, and reaching its height toward morning. It continued thirty hours in all, and brought in the tide to a great height, overflowing the wharves, and doing more or less damage to nearly all of them.

At Portland, Maine, the storm was very violent, and a number of vessels were injured. The tide rose so high that the sea swept over Tukey's Bridge, and the Eastern stage was not able to pass that way.

At Newburyport, Massachusetts, the tide overflowed the wharves, and floated off and destroyed a large amount of property. The damage done to the shipping in the harbor was much greater than had occurred in the other storms. Forty-one of the one hundred and thirty vessels there were more or less severely injured by chafing, collisions and sinking.

In Gloucester, the storm was severer than it was on the fifteenth, the wind being extremely fierce. At times it seemed as if everything would be swept before it. Houses almost tottered upon their foundations, and it was a fearful as well as a sleepless night to the people of the town. The tempest was at its height from four to six in the morning, but all night long the roar of the wind and sea was frightful. Few vessels were in the harbor, and several of those were lost. One of the wrecks was that of the brig *Richmond Packet* belonging in Deer Isle, Captain Toothaker, commander, and bound from Richmond to Newburyport with a cargo of corn and flour. It was driven ashore on a point of rocks and went entirely to pieces. Beside the crew, the captain's wife was on board. When the vessel struck, the captain jumped overboard with a rope and succeeded in getting safely upon the rocks, where he made the rope fast. By its means he endeavored to rescue his wife, but just as he was ready to do so, the brig gave a sudden lurch, and the rope snapped. Later Mrs. Toothaker was let down upon a spar into the water, hoping that upon that timber she would float ashore, but she had hardly reached the waves when a heavy sea swept her from the support. With a loud cry, she went down, and was seen no more until her lifeless body was discovered on the rocks. The crew were all saved.

At Salem, all the wharves suffered more or less, and everything was swept off them. Several vessels were forced from their moorings, there were some collisions, and a few ships and schooners were driven on shore. It was necessary to cut away a large number of masts. A small old house in the lower part of the town was blown down, the roofs of several sheds were torn off, and a number of chimneys injured. At several places on the railroad, the road-bed was washed away for a distance of one or two hundred feet each, preventing the progress of trains through the forenoon of Saturday. The mails from Boston were brought over the road in stages.

In Boston, more damage was done than in the storm of the fifteenth. The injuries to shipping were very extensive, wharves were overflowed, and lumber, wood, coal, etc., were swept away. The Front Street dike, as it was called, was broken down, and water covered nearly all the low land between Front and Washington streets, from the Neck to Northampton Street. It also came into Water Street, and damaged dry goods in cellars to a large amount. The causeway leading to Dorchester, and the lower streets of the city were submerged, so much damage being done that crowds from the surrounding towns came to see it.

The large, beautiful ship *Columbiana*, of six hundred and thirty tons burden, one of A. C. Lombard and Company's line of New Orleans packets, parted her cables at about four o'clock in the morning at Swett's wharf in Charlestown, where she was loading with ice. The wind took her on the flow of the tide, and drove her completely through the Charlestown bridge, carrying away two piers, as though there had been no obstruction there. The vessel then struck Warren Bridge on its side, the mate having succeeded in bringing her into that position. The bridge was considerably injured, but it withstood the shock. The stern then quickly swung around, and struck the wharf which was built out from the draw with such violence that it demolished a dwelling-house one and a half stories in height, that was standing on the bridge, being occupied by the draw-tender. In the house were nine persons, who were in bed at the time, and they escaped without injury. One of them was thrown into the river when the concussion occurred, but was rescued by his companions. The ship was uninjured, in spite of her violent freak.

The storm was so severe at Provincetown, on Cape Cod, that the damage done to the shipping and the property on the wharves amounted to fifty thousand dollars, and many of them were entirely carried away, several persons being injured. Cellars of houses were inundated and a considerable number of the inhabitants were obliged to seek shelter elsewhere. Ten or eleven stores were knocked down by the vessels, two salt-mills were blown down, and many salt works were carried away.

The snows of this winter of 1839–40 were deeper and more severe than those that the old people of that time remembered. In the valleys in the western part of Massachusetts, snow was two feet deep through the winter, and on the Berkshire hills four feet. Many roads remained unbroken on account of it, and people travelled about on snow shoes. In many places the snow was fifteen feet deep, and travellers passed over the drifts in well-trodden paths. In Chesterfield a man died, and the snow was so deep that for four days the family could not get to a neighbor's house for assistance. But the sea-shore witnessed the greater suffering. The month of December, 1839, was indelibly fixed in the minds of multitudes as one of the most awful seasons that they had ever known. If all the disasters that occurred along our coast were known and written out an immense volume would be the result. We do not put it too strongly when we say that upwards of three hundred vessels were wrecked, a million dollars' worth of property was destroyed, and more than a hundred and fifty lives were lost in these three storms. How many widows and orphans afterward sat at the windows of their cottages at Mount Desert and many other places looking for the sails that they knew so well, yet not daring to hope that they would see them again!

> Looking out over the sea,
> From a granite rim of shore,
> Looking out longingly, wearily,
> Over a turbulent, pitiless sea,

For the sails that come no more.
Waiting and watching with tear-wet eyes
Till the last faint hope in the bosom dies;
While the waves crawl up o'er the chill white sand,
Those watchers long for a clasping hand,
And turn away with a thrill of pain,
But often pause to look again
From the rough dark rocks of the sea-beat shore,
For the gleam of snowy sails once more;
Sadly, longingly, wearily,
Looking out over the sea.

Chapter CXV.

THE "OCTOBER GALE," 1841

In the latter part of September, 1841, was a long, unbroken spell of uncomfortable weather, which culminated in a violent and cold storm of wind, snow and rain on the night of October 2, continuing four days. From September 30 to October 6, inclusive, five and sixteen-hundredths inches of water fell. It snowed in northern New England, snow falling at Amherst, New Hampshire, to the depth of six inches. It soon melted, however. It rained in southern New England, though in eastern Massachusetts, there was some snow with the rain, and in the western part of the state snow fell in great quantities, being a foot deep on the hills in Hampden County.

At sunset on Saturday, the second of the month, the wind came lightly from the northeast. It soon freshened and at eleven o'clock was blowing very hard. At midnight it blew a gale, and rain began to fall in Massachusetts and snow in New Hampshire. The violence of the wind continued to increase during the hours of darkness, until it became the cause of disaster on both sea and land. On Sunday morning, the sun rose clear, but it immediately went into black clouds, and the sky looked wild. At eleven o'clock in the forenoon a heavy sea was running all along the coast, and vessels were being thrown upon the rocks and beaches. The wind continued to blow all day, and at eight o'clock in the evening was still a gale. In fact, it did not produce its strongest force until two o'clock Monday morning. At daybreak it seemed as fierce as ever, having veered slightly to the north, but during the afternoon it abated considerably and continued to moderate until Tuesday morning. By ten o'clock a beautiful autumn day was gladdening the hearts made heavy by the destruction of property and lives.

On the land, trees were stripped of many of their small branches and leaves, a great deal of fruit was destroyed, and chimneys and buildings were blown down. On the sea, the gale was so terrific that it tore the newest and strongest canvas into shreds and masts and spars of vessels were carried away. The ocean roared as though with unbridled madness, and its waves ran mountain high, throwing their spray far into the sky, and forming a majestic yet fearful sight. Many vessels were wrecked on the water and on the shores.

In the harbors, vessels broke away from their moorings and collided or dashed against the wharves or upon the shore, some being sunk or afterward found at sea without a person on board. The tide rose so high that on Sunday wharves were covered and marshes submerged for long distances inland.

In the harbor of Portland, Maine, several vessels went ashore and became complete wrecks. At Portsmouth, New Hampshire, the vessel named *Maine*, belonging to Bath, parted her cables and was driven out of the harbor on Monday morning. She was forced into Massachusetts Bay, where she struck on Cohasset rocks at nine o'clock in the forenoon, and went ashore on Scituate Beach, becoming a total wreck. There were on board seven passengers, four women and three men, and the crew which numbered four. The vessel was commanded by Captain Blen of Dresden, Maine, and with him was his daughter Miss Martha I. Blen. The captain, his daughter, five passengers, including all the women and one man, and one seaman perished.

At Cape Ann, only one human life was lost. Since the storms of December, 1839, a lifeboat had been obtained, and it was attempted to use it in this storm, but in getting it off the bottom was stove in. Vessels were snatched as it were from the waves and dashed into fragments among the rocks. The gale was most disastrous at Pigeon Cove. The fisher dwellers there lost fourteen of their entire fleet of sixteen vessels. One of the two that were saved was thrown on the sand and much injured, and the other was at Squam. Many fish houses and fish flakes, together with about sixty barrels of mackerel, two hundred hogsheads of salt, and three hundred empty barrels were destroyed. This great loss of about fifty thousand dollars in value fell upon a class that was little able to bear it, for nearly all they had was invested in the fishing interest, and the vessels and other things necessary in carrying on the business. Public meetings were held at Rockport, Salem, and other places, in behalf of these honest, hardworking and worthy fishermen. The great loss there was on account of the destruction of the breakwater, that had been built in 1832 at an expense of seventeen thousand dollars by individuals in Gloucester, Rockport, Newburyport, and other commercial places.

On the Island of Nantucket, several vessels at the docks were considerably injured, and the tide rose two or three feet above the wharves, running into most of the lower streets. Large quantities of lumber and cord-wood were strewn in various directions. In the village of Siasconset, the high bank or bluff at the front of the hamlet overlooking the sea gave way for some considerable distance, and the residence of Marshall Crosby with two barns was precipitated down the cliff. A man by the name of Hussey fell down the same place and had his thigh broken. But the most disastrous effect of the storm was on the land. The then new and extensive ropewalk belonging to Barker and Athern, and occupied by Joseph James, was swept from its foundation and torn into fragments, leaving only the tar-house and part of the hemp-house standing. A large portion of Isaac Myrick's ropewalk was also demolished. The observatory, two or three barns or carriage-houses, and several chimneys were blown down. During Sunday night, every building trembled under the pressure of the furious elements, but few people were free from alarm and consternation and, as a writer of that time facetiously wrote, "not many slept without rocking."

The greatest loss of life and property in this storm occurred on Cape Cod. The beach from Chatham to the highlands was literally strewn with parts of wrecks. Between forty and fifty vessels went ashore on the sands there, and fifty dead bodies were picked up. At Hyannisport, several vessels were cast on the beach, one of which was the schooner *Franklin,* which first capsized, the cook and a seaman named Newcomb being lost. One of the crew of the schooner *Tangent,* another vessel there, fell overboard from the masthead and was drowned. The schooner *Bride,* belonging in Dennis, was driven ashore and the bodies of the crew, eight in number, were found in the cabin. In this storm the town of Dennis lost twenty-six of her most active and promising men, many of whom were just entering upon manhood, and eighteen of them had been schoolmates, leaving kindred living within a quarter of a mile of each other. The schooner *Forest* of Gloucester, commanded by Capt. Stephen Rich, was lost while mackereling, with its crew of eight men. The schooner *Ellis,* of Plymouth, went ashore on the east side of Truro, a little north of the Highland light, and Capt. Joseph Dunham, the master, and his crew of eight were all drowned. The schooner *Industry,* belonging in Halifax, and bound for Argyle, Nova Scotia, also went ashore near the same place losing three men. Another schooner, *Spitfire,* also belonging in Halifax, was wrecked about half a mile below Race Point. From it were lost the captain, two seamen, and a lady passenger about twenty years of age. The male passengers were saved.

Most of the vessels of Truro, Massachusetts, were on or near the south-west part of George's Banks, and on the night of the second, the crews left off fishing, and made sail to run for the highland of Cape Cod. Mighty ocean currents that they had never encountered before carried them out of their course to the southeast, but being disabled by the gale they were driven upon the Nantucket shoals, which extend fifty or sixty miles into the ocean, southeasterly from the island of that name. These unfortunate mariners were nearly all young men under thirty years of age. Fifty-seven from Truro were lost and buried in the great ocean cemetery.

One of the vessels belonging to Truro was the *Altair,* with a crew of six, of which Capt. Elisha Rich was master. They had been fishing near George's Banks, and were on their way home, when both vessel and crew were destroyed on the Nantucket shoals.

Another of the vessels belonging to Truro, that had been associated with the *Altair* in its trip, and was also destroyed with its cargo and crew, was the *Arrival,* Capt. Freeman Atkins Jr., master. The rest of the crew consisted of eight men.

The *Cincinnatus,* also belonging to Truro, commanded by Capt. John Wheeler, was a large able vessel, and had been fishing, on the second day, in the hook of the Isle of Sable. She started homeward with the rest of the fleet, and was wrecked with many of the other vessels on the Nantucket shoals. The crew of ten men were all lost.

The *Dalmatian,* Capt. Daniel Snow, master, was another of the Truro vessels that went down with all on board on the shoals off Nantucket, having come in with the fishing fleet from George's. There were on deck twenty or thirty barrels of salted mackerel. The vessel was last seen at about eight o'clock Sunday morning, off Cape Cod with the rest of the fleet, apparently in a comfortable condition. Ten men constituted the whole of the crew.

Another fishing vessel, the *Garnet,* of Truro, commanded by Capt. Joshua Knowles, also of Truro, left Provincetown on Saturday, the second, and at sunset was about three miles out from the head of Pamet, engaged in fishing. Soon after he spoke with the *Vesper,* of Dennis, that was returning home from George's Banks. They reported good fishing there, and so the crew of the *Garnet* concluded to go down and try their luck. Heading in that direction, they put on all sail, for the wind was blowing lightly and from the northeast. It soon breezed up, and at ten o'clock the "light" sails were taken in. At twelve o'clock the wind was blowing a gale, and the mainsail was furled. At four o'clock' next (Sunday) morning, they took in the jib. The water now measured thirty-four fathoms in depth, and they supposed they were on the southwest part of George's. Two hours later they double-reefed the foresail, which soon after parted the leach-rope and tore to the luff. The sail was cross-barred, a preventer leach-rope put on as quickly as possible, and the whole was then close-reefed. The gale increased every moment, and at ten o'clock a heavy sea tore away the boat and davits. By sounding they discovered that they were fast drifting across the south channel, and they knew that the shoals were under their lee. Determined to carry sail as long as it would stand, for the purpose of clearing them, if it could be done, to the close-reefed foresail they set a balance-reefed mainsail and reefed jib. The foresail again gave out, was repaired and again set, but as soon as it was up the wind was so terrific that it was blown to ribbons. The mainsail soon shared the same fate, and the jib only was left. It was now about eight o'clock Sunday evening, and they could do nothing more to save themselves. They sounded and found that the water measured fifteen fathoms. They then knew that they were rapidly drifting into shoal water. At the next throw of the line it measured only six fathoms. The sea was breaking over the vessel fore and aft, and the captain advised the crew to go below. All but the captain and his brother did so. They remained on deck, and after discussing the situation, concluded to swing the craft off before the wind, that, if by any possibility they were nearing land, they might have a better chance of escape. The helm was put up, and just as she began to fall off, a tremendous sea, or a breaker completely buried the vessel, leaving her on her broadside, or beam ends. Zach, the captain's brother, was washed overboard, but he caught hold of the main sheet and hauled himself on board. The foremast was broken about fifteen feet above deck, the strain on the spring stay hauled the mainmast out of the step, and tore up the deck, sweeping away the galley, bulwarks and everything else, and shifted the ballast into the wing. A sharp hatchet had always been kept under the captain's berth, to be used in case of an emergency. This he soon found, and to it fastened a lanyard, which was tied to a rope that had already been fastened to Zach's waist, the other end being secured on the vessel. Zach went to the leeward, and when the vessel rolled out of water, he watched his chance, and cut away the rigging. The captain did the same forward, cutting away the jib-stay and other ropes, and by that means relieved the vessel of the spars, sails, rigging, sheet anchor and chains. The crew got into the hold through the lazeret, and threw the ballast to the windward, so that she partially righted. They were now on a helpless wreck. After the great breaker had gone over, the motion of the sea became more regular. With a few of the waist-boards left, and spare canvas, they repaired the deck, and with the remaining anchor out for a drag, made a good drift considering the circumstances, though mostly under water. It was now nearly day light, and the gale had abated. As soon as it was fairly day they knew by the appearance of the water that they were off soundings. On the morning of Tuesday, the fifth, the wind was blowing moderately. They saw a schooner standing by under reefed sails, the wind being northwest. Captain Knowles made every effort he could to attract the attention of the people on board if there were any, but on account of the masts being gone, and the hull so low, they were not noticed, and the vessel, which they had hoped would be the means of their rescue passed out of sight. They then put a stay on the stump of the foremast, set the staysail for a foresail and the gaff-topsail for a jib, to enable them to steer. By ten o'clock in the forenoon the weather had become pleasant and the gale was over. They opened the hatches, and found some potatoes floating on the water in the hold. Fortunately, when the galley was washed away the tea-kettle was in the cabin, so that it was saved. They built a fire on the ballast, boiled the potatoes in the tea-kettle, and had a lunch. This was the first food they had eaten since Sunday morning, and now it was Tuesday noon. Just before sunset a sail was discovered approaching them from the east. They hoisted their flag on a long pole as a signal and used every effort they could to get in her track. They were soon convinced that they had been seen, and that she was being steered toward them. They could see many men in the rigging and on the yards, apparently on the watch. Then within hailing distance the captain inquired what assistance he could give, and the ship-wrecked mariners explained their situation. It was determined to abandon the wreck, and a quarter boat was sent from the rescuing vessel. It was soon alongside, and the crew of ten men, with most of their luggage, were taken away in the first boat-load. The boat returned for the rest of the personal effects of the crew and for the captain, who had remained behind. After they had left the wreck he returned and with his hatchet cut a hole through the bottom of the vessel, letting the water into the hold, which soon filled. He stepped back into the boat, which was pulled away as the *Garnet* settled down to the bottom of the ocean. It had been the home of Captain Knowles for several years, and he had formed such an attachment for the schooner that even the distressing circumstances did not obliterate all regret for its destruction. He was happily surprised when he learned that the vessel which had rescued them was the packet-ship *Roscius,* plying between New York and Liverpool, the first merchant ship of her time, carrying on this voyage four hundred cabin and steerage passengers; and that she was commanded by Capt. John Collins, a Truro boy, formerly Captain Knowles' nearest neighbor as well as a relative by marriage. Another of the officers was Captain Collins' nephew, Joshua C. Paine, also a Truro young man. The rescued mariners were shown every attention while they remained on the ship. They were again surprised when they learned that they were rescued two hundred miles off the highlands of Neversink, New Jersey. They landed at New York on the seventh of the month. There they received the kindest and most generous treatment, and in due time all arrived at Truro in safety.

Another of the Truro vessels fishing on George's Banks on the day before the storm was the *General Harrison,* Capt. Reuben Snow, master. It left the fishing grounds for home with the rest of the Truro fleet, and at about seven o'clock Saturday evening, was several miles off Cape Cod. The vessel was lying there very comfortably with others of the Truro boats, having on its deck some twenty or thirty barrels of salted mackerel. It never reached its port, however, but sank with the other vessels on the shoals of Nantucket, with all on board, the crew being a large one.

The *Pomona,* a small fishing vessel, commanded by Capt. Solomon H. Dyer of Truro, was also returning from the George's, where the crew had been fishing. They were some distance behind the rest of the Truro vessels, and were seen about half-past ten o'clock to the northwest of the fleet off Cape Cod, lying under double-reefed foresail. They stood in toward the shore, evidently intending to come within the Cape. A man was seen to go out on the bowsprit and loose a part of the jib, which they hoisted. The vessel was last seen in the storm at about half-past twelve, when a squall came suddenly over the raging ocean, and it is believed that it was then disabled. The men on board were all lost. The crew consisted of the captain and seven young men, all belonging to Truro. After the storm, the vessel was found bottom up in Nauset Harbor, and in the cabin the bodies of three of the boys were discovered and brought home for burial. Her boat and some other articles were picked up between three and four o'clock, only about two hours after the squall struck her.

Another of the Truro vessels that was with the fleet was the *Prince Albert,* Capt. Noah Smith, master. The boat went down on the shoals of Nantucket, and the crew of eight, all of whom belonged in Truro, perished.

The *Water Witch,* Capt. Matthias Rich, master, was also out in the storm. On the morning of Saturday, the crew were fishing with the fleet, and had caught about half a dozen barrels full of large, fat mackerel. The rest of the fleet sailed for home, and they soon followed but did not overtake them until after sunset. They were then ninety miles southeast by east from Provincetown, and lay to under foresail toward the east, carrying the jib all night. All the other vessels lay to the northwest under foresail only, and at four o'clock next morning (Sunday) bad weather had set in, and there was a smart northeast wind. They wore ship and started for the cape, which was calculated to be one hundred and twenty miles distant northwest by west. At five o'clock, all their sail was put on. Sometimes, on account of heavy seas, they were obliged to swing off the course. The sun rose clear, but it immediately went behind black clouds, showing two sundogs, the heavens having a wild appearance. Between seven and eight o'clock they passed the fleet, which was still lying to the northwest under foresail, two or three vessels having a bob-jib. About eleven, the crew urged the captain to tack ship, but he said it was too late, and that they must make a harbor or run ashore, as he saw no chance to fall to the leeward, and that he had concluded if the highlands of Cape Cod could not be weathered, to run on shore where it was bold, taking the chance of being saved. An hour and a half later, they judged they were nearly up to the land, and were about to make some observations, when a squall struck them, driving the sea completely over the vessel. The jib and mainsail were hauled down, and they lay under double-reefed foresail. The wind was now farther north. At one o'clock the force of the squall had passed, and the heavens had slightly cleared to leeward. The captain was then standing in the gangway, and all the crew were below, as they could not remain on deck. The captain saw land under the lee and well along to windward. The first thought of running on shore, to their almost certain destruction, was a terrible shock to him; but he quickly rallied, sprang on deck and called his men. The jib was set and the vessel fell off so far that the land was now to the windward of the bow-sprit. The captain knew that he had a good sea-boat, having tried her in many a difficult place, and that their race was now for life or death. The mainsail had been balance-reefed before lying to and it was now hoisted. The sail was small, but before it was half way up, the vessel lay so much on its broadside that the halyards were lost, and the sail came down by the run, blowing to pieces. The main boom and gaff went over the lee rail, and they tried to cut them away, but fearing the main top-in-liff would carry away the mainmast, got on a tackle, and pulled the boom and part of the mainsail out of the water. The vessel righted and came up to the wind, making good headway and gaining to the windward under the only sail it would bear—double-reefed foresail and reefed jib, the sea making a break fore and aft. They had now a slight hope that they would weather the highlands. They kept as close to the wind as possible, and at half past three they had weathered the highlands, with no room to spare between them. When off Peaked Hill bars, the jib was blown away, and they just cleared the breakers. But they had weathered! The lee shore was astern, and Race Point was under their lee. They rounded the point, and anchored in Herring Cove at half-past six, as darkness came on. The captain now left the helm, to which he had been lashed for twelve consecutive hours. When morning dawned, theirs was the only vessel in the cove.

The loss in this storm of the fifty-seven young men of Truro was the most serious calamity that ever visited the town. There was scarcely a person but to whom some of them were related; thus making it in the most literal sense a public bereavement. In commemoration of the event, there was erected in the town, a plain marble shaft, rising from a brownstone base, which is inscribed on the front face as follows:

Sacred
To the memory of
fifty-seven citizens of Truro
who were lost in seven
vessels, which
foundered at sea in
the memorable gale
of October 3, 1841.

Then shall the dust return to the earth
as it was; and the spirit shall return to
God who gave it.
Man goeth to his long home, and the
mourners go about the streets.

On the back of the monument is given a list of the names of the lost mariners, with their respective ages, arranged in columns.

Chapter Cxvi.

THE STORM OF 1842

On Wednesday afternoon, November 30, 1842, a snow storm began, which turned to rain about nine o'clock in the evening. The wind had blown moderately through the day, but when night came on it increased until it blew with great violence from the east-southeast, shifting to the east-northeast at two o'clock in the morning, when it quickly subsided. In some parts, a great deal of snow fell, and travel on the railroads was greatly obstructed, fifteen inches of snow being on the ground the next day at Dover, New Hampshire. The storm began early in the morning as far south as Washington and Baltimore, and much snow fell there. The temperature was also low, being at Belfast, Maine, on the day before only six degrees above zero, the coldest November day that had been known there for several years.

At Boston, the storm was much more severe than at any other port in that vicinity. Many vessels were anchored in the harbor when the storm came on, and they were driven from their moorings, being either jammed against each other or the wharves. They were badly chafed and broken, and several of them were sunk. In the very heart of the city the sound of falling masts and of vessels crashing together was heard from time to time above the noise of the storm. It was deemed dangerous to go to the end of the wharves lest some large craft might dash against them, carrying them away. In the night, several sailors were drowned.

Among the many wrecks caused by the storm in the few short hours it continued were two or three that made it memorable. One of them was that of the bark *Isadore,* a new and beautiful vessel of four hundred tons burden, commanded and owned by Capt. Leander Foss. This was its first trip, and it sailed on the morning of the storm from Kennebunk, Maine, for New Orleans. In the blinding snow and the tempest of that night the craft was driven on a point of rocks near Cape Neddock, Maine, called Bald Head, and wrecked. The entire crew of fifteen belonged in Kennebunkport, and all perished. Five were fathers of families, and left in all twenty children. Two were young men, the only sons of widows.

The schooner *Napoleon,* commanded by Capt. James York, sailed from Calais, Maine, for New York, with a cargo of lumber, on the twenty-eighth of the month. The gale struck the vessel out in the ocean on the night of the storm and carried away both masts. She capsized and righted, but was filled with water. The cook, a Scotch lad, was probably lost when the vessel went over, as he was not seen again. The others of the crew remained on deck, in the cold and darkness and tempest, and one after another they lay down and died. The craft was driven about by the mighty wind, but where no one knew or cared. The next day and another night passed away. Death was what they desired, and all but one of them found it. When the wreck had reached a point about forty miles south of Monhegan, it fell in with the schooner *Echo* of Thomaston, Maine. Captain York had survived until within an hour or two of their meeting with the *Echo,* and when the captain of that vessel came on board the wreck only the mate was found alive, he being badly frozen. The other six had all died, and their bodies had been washed away except that of one man, which was jammed in among the lumber in such a manner that it could not be extricated without great danger.

The saddest wreck caused by the storm was that of the schooner *James Clark,* of sixty tons burden, belonging in St. John, New Brunswick, commanded and owned by Captain Beck. It was on a trip from St. John to Boston, and there were twenty persons on board. They left Portland on the morning of the storm, and late that afternoon were driven ashore at Rye Beach, the vessel becoming a total wreck. At six o'clock in the evening, which was soon after the vessel struck, the cabin was stove in, and the people were compelled to remain on deck. The heavy sea dashed over them, and they were washed from one side of the vessel to the other, their clothing being torn off from them. They suffered intensely from the exposure to cold and water, and some died, the first being Mrs. Margaret Stewart's six months' old baby boy, named Willie, who expired in her arms. She had wrapped him so closely for protection from exposure that his death was probably hastened thereby. The mother became insensible and when rescued was found among some lumber almost covered with water. Her arms were stiffened in the position in which she had held her child, and remained so for some time after arriving at the land. She was saved, however, to mourn the loss of her boy. Mrs. Mary Hebersen, a widow of about fifty, accompanied by her daughter Hannah, who was twelve years old, was on her way to an aunt's in Holden, Massachusetts. For hours they kept together in their hopeless condition as well as the waves would permit. At length the daughter, becoming benumbed with cold, lay down upon the deck at her mother's feet and died. While she lay there, her life fast ebbing away, her mother watched over her, and raising her eyes to heaven commended her daughter's spirit to her Maker. This excellent mother was no sooner apprehensive of the death of her daughter than she forgot the tempest and laid herself down by the side of her child. In fifteen minutes her spirit also had fled.

As soon as it was possible, one of the sailors took a long rope, fastened one end of it on the deck, and jumped into the raging surf with the other end tied to him. He fought his way to the shore, and by means of the rope the captain and crew and ten of the passengers, five women, two men, a girl and a boy, and a child sixteen months old, were saved. Only one person, Dennis Mahaney, perished while attempting to reach the shore on the rope. Mrs. Hebersen and Mr. Mahaney were the only adults lost, the rest being children. Five bodies were recovered.

Those most instrumental in saving these people were a Mr. Yeaton and his son, who unweariedly and at imminent peril of their lives assisted in getting them on shore. But for their efforts many more would have perished. Mr. Yeaton's family generously placed everything they had at the disposal of the sufferers. They gave them the use of the whole house and freely distributed their extra clothing among them, both mariners and passengers having lost theirs, except what they wore when rescued, some of them being nearly naked.

Chapter Lxvii.

THE FRESHET OF 1846

The melting of the snow and ice in the spring almost always produces a freshet in some portion of New England. In March, 1846, much damage was done by the rise of the water in several streams in New Hampshire and Maine.

At the great falls in Somersworth, in New Hampshire, on the Salmon Falls River, the dam was washed away on the morning of the twenty-sixth of the month, and on the same day the railroad bridge over the river at Saco, Maine, was somewhat injured, the trains to and from Portland being hindered several hours. On the Androscoggin River the greatest amount of damage was done at the flourishing little village of Livermore Falls, which was swept almost entirely away. Seventeen stores and houses with all that was in them were floated down the river. The rise of the water was so sudden that the people had no time to save any of their property. On the

Kennebec River, the freshet was the most destructive ever known. In Hallowell, the principal street in the lower and central parts of the town was flooded, and the river was filled with floating ice and lumber. At Gardiner, the water rose with great rapidity until it broke up the ice which was two feet thick, and then covered the lower streets of the town, filling cellars, and carrying away lumber and several store-houses, barns and other buildings.

On the Penobscot River there was great destruction of property. At several places the ice had been broken up and great jams had been formed, which caused the water to flow over its banks for a long distance back, doing great injury. As soon as the water was of sufficient height and weight it forced the ice-dam down the stream until it was again blocked, carrying away property as it proceeded on its way. Above Orono the mills were undisturbed; but below that town one of the jams removed from the place called the Basin, at some distance from the channel, a block of seventeen mills, which were among the most valuable ones on the river. They were owned principally by a New York company, but for several seasons had been leased to lumber merchants in Bangor. In the northern part of Bangor, immediately below the forty mills of the "Corporation," or "City mills," another great jam of ice formed, greatly endangering the twenty-two saw-mills and a large number of clapboard-, shingle- and lath-mills below owned by John Fiske of Bangor. A part of the ice soon after gave way, letting down a considerable amount of the water, which relieved the mills.

The Franklin or upper bridge over the Kenduskeag River was carried down the stream, and the middle of Smith's Bridge subsequently followed it, together with a portion of the lower or Kenduskeag Bridge. A large wooden block on the east end of the latter bridge was taken off its foundation, and the water filled nearly the whole of the first story of the market house on the bridge.

The jam gave way about midnight, and passed partly by the city. This let the water down so much that it inundated the lower part of the town, including the whole of Market Square, and Broad, Wall, and Exchange streets and a large portion of Maine Street to the depth of several feet. The deluge came so suddenly that the people in the square at the time were obliged to wade through water a yard deep to reach dry ground. It rose five feet in five minutes, and continued to rise. A temporary ferry was soon established between a point in Hammond Street near the City Hall steps and a point on State Street nearly up to Exchange Street. Smith's block, including the post-office, was submerged almost to the tops of the doors, and it was the same with all the stores on Market Square. The water was sev-

Bangor flood, 1902. Bangor Public Library, Local History–Special Collections.

eral feet deep in front of the old Hatch Tavern and nearly up to the windows in the Exchange. The merchants were busily engaged in removing their goods from lower to higher shelves and floors, the water being all that time from two to four feet above the lower floors. Much property was thus saved. The lumber dealers suffered most of the loss, however, the wharves and piling places being all covered with valuable lumber to the amount of millions of feet which was worth several hundred thousand dollars. The greater part of it was carried away and lost, and the ice was full of boards in every direction. Above the office of the *Bangor Whig*, in the jam of ice were the ruins of forty-four saw-mills, beside shingle- and lath-mills. The ice started, and large piles of lumber were instantly whirled off the wharves in Brewer on the other side of the river. A jam of ice with a mill afloat came down the stream and swept away a bridge just in the rear of the office. The printers removed the presses into the street and carried the type, etc., to the office of the *Democrat,* where they printed the next edition of their paper. The scene was appalling, store-houses began to float down and fill the stream, enormous piles of lumber being among them. Three persons were drowned, the water having come down so suddenly Saturday night that they had not time to escape.

On Sunday afternoon a great deal of lumber and other property was secured. Crowds of people anxiously watched the movements of the water, ice and buildings, and of the men who were endeavoring to save property. So much interest was manifested in the flood that no regular services were held in any of the churches during the day.

At last, a little before seven o'clock that evening, the jam began to make a decided movement. It all passed down the stream with a steady, slow, majestic motion, roaring terrifically as the huge mass was borne along by the mighty strength of the flood. The noble Penobscot Bridge was carried away before it. The next morning the city presented a sad and gloomy spectacle. Signs of destruction were everywhere. Streets were obstructed with lumber and debris. Great cakes of ice were piled in places to the height of twenty-five feet.

Some of the vessels that were being built in the town of Brewer on the opposite side of the river from Bangor were moved from their stocks, many of them being injured, and several houses were more or less submerged in the water.

Chapter Cxviii.

THE STORM OF DECEMBER 1847

The month of December, 1847, was remarkably dry and warm until the middle, when it suddenly changed to wintry weather, and a cold north-easterly storm began. This was on the night of Thursday, the sixteenth, and it continued till about nine o'clock the next evening, when the fierceness of the wind abated, and a snow storm set in, which did not cease until two days had elapsed. The strong wind caused many disasters along the coast. On Ipswich Bar, off the town of that name in Massachusetts, the schooner *Pliant* of Eastport, Maine, commanded by Captain Reynolds, loaded with lumber, struck, and upon discovering their position, the crew abandoned the vessel. Various kinds of craft were wrecked at Cohasset, Nantucket, and other places, but the disaster that caused the greatest general interest in the storm was the wreck of the brig *Falconer* of Belfast, commanded by Capt. Joseph Rolerson, who also belonged in that town. She measured three hundred and sixty tons, was twenty years old, and at this time was transporting a cargo of three hundred and fifty tons of coal from Sydney, Cape Breton Island, to Boston. She also carried a large number of passengers, making with the crew fifty-three persons on board.

The trip was successful until the night of the storm, when Squam light at Gloucester, Massachusetts, was made, which in the thick weather was mistaken for Cohasset light. The captain tacked, and stood to the northward, but when he sighted the Ipswich and Newburyport lights he discovered his error. Not recognizing them, and knowing that no beacons were located at any such distance and direction from Cohasset, he did not know where he was, and with wisdom and discretion born of experience dropped anchor about three miles from shore. Had he been aware of his location he could have run into the harbor in safety. The brig rode through Thursday night, all day Friday and that night, and until about seven o'clock on Saturday morning, when she dragged her anchors, being driven on a sandy reef about three-fourths of a mile from the shore, off the southerly end of Patch's Beach, two miles from the lighthouse. There she became bilged, and the sea made a long continued series of great breaches over her. The leaks increased greatly, and in the cabin the water became so deep that the passengers were compelled to come on deck into the midst of the heavy seas that were constantly sweeping over it, carrying away everything that was movable. The only security that was afforded them was in lashing themselves to the rigging and other parts of the vessel that were still intact and had force sufficient to resist the power of the tremendous waves. This they did as well as they could. The masts had been carried away by the wind, and only the useless hull remained far from shore with tons upon tons of icy waters dashing over it, throwing the spray to a great height. In the cold and wet, suffering with hunger, and without the least hope of rescue, those fifty-three men, women, and children were confined as in a tomb. On that Saturday morning they were all alive, but many of them were nearly exhausted and could not long survive the exposure.

An attempt was made to reach the shore in the boat belonging to the brig, which still remained. Seven persons made their way into it, and turned its bow toward the land, but as they neared the beach they were buried beneath the mountainous waves, and three of them were drowned. The other four fought their way through the surf and were saved.

The keeper of the lighthouse there had watched the vessel as it lay anchored off the shore all Friday night, expecting it would be driven in. On Saturday morning, he saw it on the reef, but was unable to go to it, as there

was no life-boat. If there had been one probably all the people would have
been saved.

The only family living on the beach was that of Capt. Humphrey
Lakeman, whose house was nearly two miles away from the place of the
wreck. As soon as they learned that the vessel had struck, news was quickly
sent to the village five miles away, and many persons came to the beach
through the driving snow, bringing with them thick clothing and invigorating and nourishing supplies for the living, together with articles for enwrap-
ping the dead.

Though a large number of people had gathered on the beach in the pitiless storm, they could do nothing to save the many men, women and children, whom they could dimly see on the wreck through the thickly falling
snow. The only boat that was near was small and leaky, and it was agreed
that it could not possibly resist the power of the breakers. However, something ought to be done; and, feeling the imperativeness of the case, a brave
young sailor, named William Chapman, who had come down from the village with the other people, jumped into the miserable little dory, and pulled
out alone through the deadly surf to the side of the wreck. But he had
hardly reached it and scrambled on deck, when the boat in which he had
come filled with water and sank. He was now without means of getting on
shore again himself, but with hardly a thought of his own desperate condition, he turned his attention to reviving the hopes of the sufferers. His very
presence even gave assurance of assistance, and encouraged them to renew
their struggle for life. Learning from young Chapman's successful passage
through the water that a boat could live in the surf, the men on shore ran
to the lighthouse, and dragged some boats that were there over the soft sand
for two miles to the point nearest the wreck. They were launched and
quickly manned by the Ipswich men, who gladly and courageously volunteered to assist in the performance of the hazardous duty. Back and forth
successfully pushed the boats through the dangerous waters amid the howl-
ing and the gloom of the storm, now mounting the great crested waves, and
then plunging into valleys, where it seemed as if the almost perpendicular
walls of foaming water before and behind them would engulf the craft. By
the humanity of these men, the thirty-six survivors on the wreck safely
reached the shore. As they landed the people put clothing upon those who
had been so long exposed to the cold and wet, and when they had used all
they had brought with them from town they stripped themselves of their
outer garments, giving them to the needy. The survivors were all conveyed
to Captain Lakeman's house as speedily as possible, and everything that he

and his family had was most generously placed at their disposal, all that they could do being done for their comfort. Every exertion was made to revive those that were brought in the boats or had washed on shore, who were in an insensible condition.

Captain Rolerson himself survived only half an hour after reaching land, and his wife and son Charles were also among those that perished. Of the cabin passengers, three men and as many women were lost, and of the steerage passengers seven men and a boy. In all, seventeen of the fifty-three persons perished, most of them by exposure rather than by drowning. The boy was washed overboard from the brig, and his body was never recovered. Thirteen bodies came ashore and were brought to the house on the day of the rescue of the survivors, and the other three were found the next day, after the abatement of the storm. Many of the passengers were poor emigrants coming to the States from the British dominions.

The rescued people were soon taken from Captain Lakeman's house to the village where they were nursed back to health and given every comfort that was in the power of the citizens.

The bodies of the lost mariners that were found and recovered were also taken to the village and placed in the town hall, where on Monday afternoon (December 20) their funeral took place under the auspices of the town authorities. The services, which were rendered by the several clergymen of the town, were very impressive. A long procession then formed, and followed the remains in the sad march to the High Street burying-ground, where they were interred, with the exception of the captain and his family. As the captain was an Odd Fellow the Ipswich lodge took possession of the bodies of himself and his wife and son, and deposited them in a tomb, preparatory to removing them to the place of their late residence, where five children mourned their loss.

One of the men who were saved had a bag of money, which he threw into the boat, when he was taken ashore in the storm, but when near the shore the boat was carried by a wave upon the sand and broken in two, the money being lost. In 1887, some gunners picked up several Mexican dollars on the beach where the vessel was wrecked, which were supposed to have been some of those lost at the time of the shipwreck. The incident created considerable excitement, and in the afternoon of the same day, about thirty young men of Ipswich, with rakes, hoes, and shovels, went to the beach and diligently searched for the missing treasure, but in vain.

Chapter Six.

THE STORM OF OCTOBER 1849

At about six o'clock on the afternoon of Saturday, October 7, 1849, rain began to fall along the New England coast, the wind blowing freshly from the east. At twelve o'clock, a violent gale was blowing from the northeast, and the rain fell in torrents. It continued all day Sunday, and did great damage along the shore, a considerable number of vessels being driven upon the land or bilged. Telegraph wires were prostrated, and communication was interrupted. In Chelsea, Massachusetts, one of the walls of the brick church, belonging to the Universalist society, which was being built on Chestnut Street, was blown down with a terrific crash.

This gale is most noted for the wreck of the brig *St. John* on Minot's Ledge, off Cohasset, Massachusetts. The vessel was commanded by Captain Oliver, and had sailed from Galway, Ireland, with emigrants for Boston, September 5. At about five o'clock on the afternoon of Saturday, October 6, they passed Cape Cod with a light southeast wind. The weather being very thick, they hove to, heading northeast. At four o'clock the next morning they wore ship and stood south. At half-past six, they made Minot's ledge, and, seeing the British brig *Kathleen* there, they ran inside the ledge and anchored. But the violence of the wind and the heavy sea caused the vessel to drag the anchors even there. Fearful that they would all be driven on the rocks, and dashed to pieces, they cut away their masts. But the gale continued to increase, the anchors again failed to hold, and the vessel was cast upon the ledges. The terrible scene was witnessed from the Glade House, but the people found it impossible to do anything. The sea ran mountain high, and as soon as the brig struck, the waves swept over her, washing the unfortunate men, women, and children into the raging ocean. The deck was crowded with the emigrants and a dozen at a time they were carried into the surges.

Shortly after the brig struck, the ringbolt that supported the stern of the jolly-boat in its accustomed place alongside, broke, letting it fall into the water. The captain, second mate, and two boys had but just jumped into it to clear it from the vessel, when about twenty-five passengers also followed them, and it was immediately swamped by their weight. All of the twenty-nine perished, except one boy and the captain, the former swimming back to the wreck, and the latter being saved, by catching hold of a rope that was suspended over the quarter, being pulled on board by the first mate.

The long-boat was then detached, but hardly had this been done when a heavy sea swept over the vessel and carried it away. A number of passengers jumped into the angry waters to swim to it, and they all perished. Afterward, the captain, first mate, eight of the crew and two passengers swam to it in safety, and in it reached the shore, landing at the Glades.

Many incidents, heart-rending and pathetic, occurred on the brig during the half hour that it lay and thumped upon the rocks. Some of them have been brought down to us. One was that of three children, who were by their mother's side when a great wave came over the vessel, and swept the children into eternity. Another is that of Patrick Swaney and his eleven children, who were all washed from the wreck at the same time. Being a good swimmer, he endeavored to save his youngest child, whom he was holding in his arms when he went over into the boiling surge, and struck out for the long-boat in which Captain Oliver and others were striving to reach the shore. But he failed to accomplish his purpose, and the strong man and weak children alike went down.

A smart, fine-looking Irish lad, about fourteen years old, had secreted himself on board the vessel just before it sailed from Galway, and had not been discovered until they were four days out. When the jolly-boat was launched he was one of those that jumped into it, and when it swamped, he swam back to the wreck, getting safely on board. A few minutes later, when the long-boat was washed from the brig, and the captain and others had got on board of her he again leaped into the waves, swam to the boat, and was helped in, landing in safety. He had two sisters on board, who were both drowned.

The other passengers that were saved floated ashore on pieces of the deck; but some of those that were rescued from the water alive soon after died from the effects of the bruises that they then received.

The news of the wreck spread, and in the storm during that Sunday afternoon the shore was lined with people. They were active in assisting the saved, and recovering the dead bodies as they came near the shore. One man came very near losing his life in taking remains out of the surf, many of which were horribly mangled and disfigured. They were laid in a row as they were recovered, presenting a most melancholy sight. Those that attracted the most attention perhaps were the bodies of a woman and her lifeless child of about two years of age securely clasped in her arms. Others were thrown upon rocks, but before they could be secured the sea would carry them back again. Late in the afternoon they began to come ashore in large numbers, two being taken from pieces of the wreck.

The whole number of people on board was about one hundred and sixty-four, of whom fourteen, mostly women and children, were cabin passengers. Forty-five of the passengers were women, and there were fifteen or eighteen children. Of all this great number, only twenty-one persons were saved, and of the one hundred and forty-three that were lost, the bodies of only twenty-seven were recovered, of which there were three of men, twenty-one of women, and three of children.

Chapter Lxx.

THE "LIGHTHOUSE" STORM 1851

Along the New England coast, on Monday, April 14, 1851, began one of the severest storms of rain, hail and snow ever known here. It commenced at Washington, D. C., on Sunday, reached New York Monday morning, and during the day extended over New England. The wind had set in strongly from the northeast some days previous, and on the day the storm began a thick mist slowly gathered. A few hours later it turned to rain, and the wind increased until it blew violently. The moon was at its full, and the water having been blown in upon the shores for several days the tide rose to a greater height in many places than was remembered by the people then living. It swept the wharves and lower streets like a flood, and at Dorchester, Massachusetts, rose nearly seven feet higher than the average tide. Beginning on Monday, it continued about the same on Tuesday, and reached its height Wednesday morning. On Thursday, the wind was still strong, and while it continued to rain on the immediate sea-board snow began to fall a few miles inland. Friday was cloudy and chilly, but on Saturday there was some sunshine. On that night, however, the storm of rain was renewed, the wind blowing from the northeast, and possessing new vigor, but throughout Sunday, snow fell thick and fast, covering the earth both inland and on the sea-shore to a great depth. It was succeeded on the next day by rain. The wind and flood combined did much damage on both land and sea. Wharves were greatly injured all along the New Hampshire and Massachusetts coast, a large amount of property was swept into the sea, and many vessels were wrecked, several lives being lost.

The wind also caused considerable damage inland, fences and trees being prostrated, roofs torn off, and chimneys and buildings blown down. In Lawrence, Massachusetts, a barn was demolished, there being in it five horses, one of which was so much injured that it had to be killed. A man who was in the hayloft at the time was also severely hurt. As a Brighton butcher was passing over the Cambridge bridge, the wind carried himself, his team, and load of calves into the river, and they were carried down to the mill-dam, the calves being drowned but the driver and horse saved. The Lowell bleachery dry-house, three hundred feet long and three stories in height, was blown down, and three hundred pieces of cloth were buried beneath the ruins. The old railroad depot at Wilmington junction and two barns in Tewksbury were demolished, and in Danvers a house and many chimneys were blown down. The steeples of churches suffered in many places. That of the then new Baptist church in Charlestown, was blown down on Wednesday morning, striking the horse and milk cart of a Mr. Locke of Lexington. The horse was killed, and Mr. Locke died from injuries received soon after being taken from the ruins. The steeple also smashed part of a house, but did not harm its inmates. The steeple of the Catholic church at Pawtucket village in Rhode Island, which was one of the tallest in New England, was also blown down; and the then new Episcopal church at the corner of Decatur and Paris streets in Boston was moved from its foundations on Tuesday night, and on the following day was blown completely down.

On all parts of the coast where the northeast wind could exert its force the tide rose over the wharves from one to four feet. At Provincetown, on Cape Cod, many wharves and salt mills were swept away; and in several places people left their houses, which were flooded, water being six inches deep on the lower floors in some of them.

At Boston, the water was three or four feet deep on Central and Long wharves, and the wooden stores on the latter wharf were completely inundated, as were most of the stores at the north end of the city. Many houses were abandoned on account of the flood. Cellars and tenements were filled with water, and a girl was removed from a cellar in Sea Street, in which the water was up to her neck. The lower parts of Washington Street were covered to the depth of two feet, and the basement rooms on Blackstone and Franklin squares were flooded. The water also crossed the Neck near Northampton Street and the city dike above the old South Boston bridge was washed away. The floor of the Eastern railroad station was under water, and around the Boston and Maine railroad depot the streets were covered

Minot's Ledge Rock Light. Oil on canvas by Thomas Birch. Historical Society of Pennsylvania.

to a considerable depth. The Charlestown and Chelsea bridges were so submerged that they were impassable. Rafts were constructed out of planks, boxes, etc., and navigated about the streets by men and boys, the latter enjoying the inundation. Thousands of people from the inland towns visited the scene, which was indeed worth witnessing.

Deer Island in Boston Harbor suffered extensively by the great tide which made a complete breach over the island, covering nearly the whole of it. The sea-wall that had been built there a few years before by the government was washed away; and three buildings were carried out to sea, one of them being the school-house. The boys had a narrow escape. Tuesday night the teacher, finding his own house surrounded by water, immediately went to the boys' house, wading through water a yard deep to get there, and got up the boys, who dressed and otherwise prepared for any emergency. Around the building the water had risen to five feet in height, and about twelve o'clock the roof parted, the house being tossed about by the waves. At daylight, their situation was made known, and ox-teams came to their rescue. With great difficulty they were taken to a new building which stood on higher ground. At ten o'clock in the forenoon the two houses first named,

with their contents, including all the bedding belonging to the boys' department, were carried away. The other houses on the island were left standing,
but damaged, and a large wooden building at the end of the Point was blown
down. Upon another small island called Pleasant Beach, Isaiah Baker had
a three-story public house. It was swept off its foundations, and the sea
dashed over it, breaking it in pieces. Mr. Baker's family and several board-
ers narrowly escaped. Several vessels also went ashore there, and a number
of lives were lost.

At Salem, Derby Wharf was greatly injured, and one of the stores upon
it nearly ruined. Causeways and streets near the harbor, and the floors of
the lead mills were flooded, and North Bridge was raised a little, but not
much injured. The railroad track at Collins' Cove and the railroad bridge
between Forrester Street and Northey's Point were carried away, and the sea
rushed into the tunnel. Great quantities of wood and lumber were floated
off the wharves, and several tanyards were overflowed, being much damaged. Many cellars were filled with water, and several families were obliged
to vacate their tenements.

At Beverly, Water Street was flooded, and the sea washed over Tuck's
Point. At Gloucester, a store belonging to Michael Duley was carried away,
the tide being said to have been the highest there for fifty years.

On the Merrimack River, the freshet was very extraordinary, the stream
being higher than ever before known, with perhaps the exception of the tide
of 1753. It was twenty-two inches higher than it was in December, 1839.
Warehouses and cellars on the lower side of Water Street in Newburyport
were flooded, and much merchandise was damaged by the water. Large
quantities of timber, lumber and wood were carried away and lost. Many of
the wharves were badly damaged, the lower long wharf to the extent of
twelve hundred dollars. The engine and boiler rooms of the Essex mill, situated on the bank of the river, were almost filled with the water, and the
waste house was thrown over and forced from its foundations. Spray was
thrown to the second-story windows of the houses on the upper side of the
street as far as Hale's wharf. Below South Street the river broke in waves
over the whole length of the turnpike road to Plum Island, damaging it to
the extent of four thousand dollars. A number of workshops and outbuildings were floated off by the water, and brought back again in pieces on the
refluent waves. The next day after the storm, the roads were found to be
badly torn up, and strewn with wood, timber and fragments of buildings.
Many families on the lower side of the street, fearing that their houses
would be washed away, removed their furniture and household goods, from

the flooded portions of the city and spent the night with hospitable neighbors. In spite of the storm, many people visited the town, and thousands, a large part of them being ladies, thronged Water Street to witness the ravages that the wind and waves had made.

At Newcastle, New Hampshire, the sea broke through the breaches, and made an island of Jaffrey Point. People gathered their household goods together on the third day of the storm ready to depart to high land, while some thought that another deluge must have come to destroy the world, and that it would finally avail nothing to seek more elevated ground. The effects of the great storm are still visible there.

Roads were badly washed all along the coast, and in many places cars on the railroads could not be run on account of the tracks being swept away by the tide, and in other places because the water was so high that the fires in the locomotives were extinguished by it.

Much damage was done to the shipping, the vessels in the harbors being badly chafed by beating against each other, and some broke adrift and ran aground. In Newburyport, the injury to the wharves and shipping combined amounted to twenty thousand dollars.

During the storm Plum Island presented a desolate appearance. On Wednesday morning, the turnpike from Newburyport to the beach was covered with water and impassable. The sea at one time broke completely over the island, in some parts leaving lakes and ponds when the storm subsided. The brig *Primrose*, Captain Bokman, master, bound from Pictou, Nova Scotia, to Boston, laden with coal, was off Salisbury Beach on Tuesday, the fifteenth. The captain had not been able to take an observation for several days, and supposed that they were in Boston Bay till Tuesday night, when he discovered that they were nearing the reefs at the northern end of Plum Island. The vessel was lying to just outside the breakers on the next morning, and it was evident that she could not long withstand the sea, which was forcing her on to the beach. The wind swept through the rigging terrifically, and the mainsail was soon torn away. The crew's control over the brig was gone. Being driven into the breakers she struck a reef about two hundred yards from the shore and about half a mile below the first relief house toward the Emerson rocks. T.G. Dodge and O. Rundlett, two young men belonging in Newburyport, were on the beach during the storm, and at about half-past ten o'clock in the forenoon they discovered the wreck. The crew could plainly see them on the beach, and communicated with them by signs, as the brig gradually beat on to the sands. The mariners endeavored to throw a line on shore, but it failed to come near enough to be secured until after the young men had stood in the surf for three hours. In the meantime, they had been joined by two men, a Mr. Lufkin, who lived on the island, about two miles below the wreck, and his hired man, who had learned of the disaster and had come to render assistance. This was a little before one o'clock in the afternoon. After another hour's toil, the rope was secured by the four men, and the captain and crew with a single passenger, nine persons in all, were thus rescued from their perilous situation. Great credit is due to the men who persevered so long in their exposure to wet and cold and their exhausting endeavors to save the shipwrecked mariners. The brig lay embedded in the sand till the ensuing July, when she was towed off, her cargo having been taken out by the steamer C. B. Stevens, which then plied on the Merrimack between Newburyport and Haverhill.

At Rockport, several vessels were damaged. In Salem Harbor, there was a large number of vessels, most of which outrode the gale in safety, several schooners being driven ashore and others grounded. The scene on North River near the sea was wild and fearfully grand. At Marblehead, seven vessels were cast on shore, and several mariners lost their lives on Marshfield Beach.

This great storm and tide are known in history as the "Lighthouse" storm and tide, from the fact that in it the Minot's Ledge lighthouse was carried away. Minot's Ledge is one of the rocks off Cohasset, Massachusetts, which before the light was established had sent to destruction many a vessel that had been driven upon them by northeastern gales. The loss of property and life became so great that it would not do to permit darkness to shroud them longer in its dangerous obscurity, and the government constructed a lighthouse on Minot's Ledge, which though only twenty feet across had destroyed more vessels than any other rock on the coast. It was a celebrated structure, great interest being taken in it by the merchants and humane societies of that time.

The construction of this lighthouse was novel. It was considered that it would be much better able to withstand the terrible ocean currents if it were so built that the almost irresistible waves could dash through it. Accordingly a plan for erecting it on pillars was conceived and duly executed. Nine holes, each measuring nine inches in diameter, and five feet deep were drilled into the rock in a circle. In these holes were placed nine wrought-iron pillars which towered forty feet above the ledge, and on them rested the lighthouse proper, which weighed thirty tons. The first floor was simply a platform, which was called the deck, on which the keeper's boat, the only means of communication with the land, was kept. The second floor was fifteen feet higher than the first, and on that was the store-room, which was fifty-five feet above the ledge, and the lowest sheltered part of the structure. This room was fifteen feet high. Next above that was the living room of the keepers. It was an octagon in form, and measured ten feet in diameter, and the same in height. Then came the lamp-room, which was seven feet high. The lamp itself was the best that could be obtained, having twenty burners, with silver-plated concave reflectors two feet in diameter. From the upper floor a cable stretched to a buoy that was moored outside the breakers, and on it was a large wooden box called the chair, which was slipped up and down, being the only means of communication between the boat and the house. Situated a long distance from the shore, the boat was the only means by which the keepers could get to the main land. The extreme height of the structure was eighty-seven feet. To the ordinary observer the edifice seemed fragile, and little able to cope with the tremendous waves, but to those who better understood the laws of mechanical construction it was firm and strong, abundantly able to bid defiance to the winds and waves and to laugh at their assaults. It stood there a solitary and grim sentinel of the sea, with a forehead of flame.

A few years after its erection the ledge became cracked where the holes were drilled, which was probably caused by the vibratory motion of the pillars when the violent gales and the vast waves crowded against them. In its construction, where the most strength was required the braces were of cast iron, which would easily crack when severely strained. In the January before this storm, John W. Bennett, the keeper of the light, philosophically told visitors that it was very doubtful if it stood through the winter. The pillars had become so loosened in the rock that when a heavy sea struck them the house shook so violently as to throw a person off his feet. One of Mr. Bennett's assistants was tossed from his berth to the floor, and a barrel of water that stood in the living room was emptied of two-thirds of its contents. When the sea was very rough the entire structure oscillated, and seemed to throb and tremble like the movement of an immense steam engine. The keeper complained of its insecurity at several different times, but it was allowed to remain in its dangerous condition.

When this storm came on, Mr. Bennett was absent, having been ordered to Boston by Collector Greely to purchase a new boat. He returned on Tuesday afternoon, but found the sea so wild and dangerous that the boat could not be put out to the lighthouse. He had two assistants, Joseph Wilson and Antoine Joseph, who had been left in charge of the light. Wilson was an English sailor, modest and unassuming, about twenty-three years old and unmarried. He was an agreeable companion and always faithful. In March, some one had asked him about the danger of staying there, and he bravely replied, "Yes, sir, I shall stay as long as Mr. Bennett does, and when we leave the light it will be dangerous for any others to take it." Antoine Joseph was a Portuguese and belonged in Corvo, one of the western islands, being about twenty-five years of age, and having some relatives in Cohasset. He had a mild disposition and good habits, and was faithful to his trust.

The lighthouse was last seen standing at about half-past three o'clock on Wednesday afternoon. Amid the horrors of the storm, the young men were compelled to remain in their fatal rooms. There was no escaping to the shore through the hell of waters. As soon as darkness came on, probably at about five o'clock on that stormy evening, they lighted the lamp as usual, and its warning rays beamed over the raging ocean. But that which saved others was powerless to save itself. The light was last seen burning at ten o'clock that evening by several persons, and at about the same time the lighthouse bell rang with great violence, alarming the dwellers on the shore for the safety of the youthful custodians of the light. The bravery and faithfulness of these young men, who were careful to perform their full duty, even while they knew the certainty of their fate, and felt the pillars snapping asunder beneath them, and while the emotions of anguish that can neither be described nor imagined, were surging like billows through their souls, constitute them heroes of the highest order. The entire structure was undoubtedly carried over at once, and the men went down to death and a tomb beneath the surges, their bodies never being found.

At four o'clock next morning, Mr. Bennett was on the beach. The lighthouse no longer lifted its head above the waves, and no vestige of it remained, but instead fragments of the building were strewn along the shore, among them being parts of the living room and of the lamp. Portions of the bedding, Mr. Bennett's clothing, and other things that had been kept in the lighthouse were also there. One of the lifebuoys came ashore, appearing to have been lashed to the back of one of the men, but the waves had probably washed it off from him. Another one had apparently been used. For two miles along the beach were scattered pieces of the woodwork of the structure and of the furniture. On Saturday, after the storm had cleared away, and the waves had quieted, some six or seven of the iron pillars or supports of the lighthouse were seen standing, and they leaned toward the west. They came only three or four feet above the surface of the ledge, and appeared to have been broken off squarely, as though they had been made of cast iron.

A vessel bearing a temporary light, under the charge of Mr. Bennett, was immediately anchored off Minot's Ledge to serve as a beacon until a new lighthouse should be constructed. This was done soon afterward, it being erected after the pattern of the famous English Eddystone, and there it stands to-day, its light shining out brilliantly over the dangerous rocks and reefs as soon as night comes on.

Chapter lxxi.

THE TORNADO OF AUGUST 22, 1851

On the afternoon and evening of Friday, August 22, 1851, there was a heavy thunder shower in eastern Massachusetts, during which several houses were struck by lightning, and other damage was caused by the wind which swept with a speed of more than two miles a minute in a northeasterly direction from Worcester to Rockport. For some days previous a southwest wind had prevailed.

In Quinsigamond village in Worcester, at about five o'clock the wind was very furious, tearing up fences, trees, crops, etc., and carrying off roofs of buildings. It then proceeded to Wayland, where the shower was severe, and hardly had it begun than there occurred an extraordinary flash of lightning. The people thought that some building in the town must have been struck, and a few minutes later they saw rising in the southwest a dense black column of what seemed to be smoke. It was soon discovered that it was a cloud, which rose rapidly until it seemed to be a mile in height. It appeared to rise entirely above the earth, and to stand on legs, which touched the ground, extending over an area of about forty rods square. At some places along its route it became single and resembled an elephant's trunk, though it appeared differently elsewhere. Some said it was like a tall wide-spread elm tree; others, an inverted cone; and still others an hourglass. The upper portions of it seemed to vibrate, and to move from side to side like an elephant's trunk or a waterspout at sea, and among the projecting points below were fitful gleams of lightning. The whole cloud whirled as it came over the town on its disastrous trip to the sea. It was the most violent and destructive tornado that was ever experienced in that section. At the northern part of Malden, its force was principally lost, and the column divided at a point about half-way between the earth and the cloud above, the upper part being dissipated, and the lower half settling down into an irreg-

ular mass, which soon disappeared. The force of the wind, however, was not
wholly gone, for it wrought some slight injury at Lynn and Rockport.

The topography of the country, it is believed, has much to do with the
origin and destructiveness of tornadoes. Prospect Hill in Waltham, an emi-
nence four hundred and eighty-two feet in height, was probably the cause
of the terrific whirling force of this wind. There were two opposing air currents of different temperatures, one coming from the northwest and the
other from the southwest. They acted suddenly against each other, after a
sultry calm of some duration, and shortly a third gyratory motion made its
appearance between them. The surface of the ground over which the tornado passed in Waltham and Arlington, where the force was greatest, was
quite undulating and diversified.

In Waltham, the damage done to property amounted to four thousand
dollars, but the wind was most severe in what was then called West
Cambridge, but which has since been incorporated as the town of
Arlington. About two o'clock, as the tornado neared the place, a long continued roll of thunder was heard in the northwest, where there appeared a
very black bank of cloud rising slowly to the height of fifty degrees, and
stretching from west-southwest to east-northeast. The air was calm, sultry
and oppressive. Not the slightest breeze was blowing, not a leaf moved.
There was a dead closeness, a remarkable want of elasticity in the air, and
many complained of lassitude. An old sea-captain told his wife about an
hour before the awful devastation occurred, that if he were at sea he should
expect a waterspout. People felt that something was about to occur, but they
did not know what. A deathlike stillness prevailed throughout nature, which
for about two hours seemed to remain still, and then the tornado burst with
terrible fury, destroying houses, stone walls, fences, gardens, etc., and
endangering human life. Large orchards were completely destroyed, great
trees were uprooted, twisted, shattered, carried long distances and tossed
about like straws. Oaks, walnuts and maples from two to two and a half feet
in diameter were treated in the same way. Others were uprooted and carried
a hundred feet. A great number of houses had their chimneys carried away,
and were also unroofed, the fragments being carried thousands of feet. A
two-story brick house was entirely demolished, and pieces blown away,
hardly a trace of it remaining. Cars were also blown from the track. A man
and a horse were lifted, whirled around, and then set down about a hundred
yards away. The track of the wind narrowed as it came near the Medford
line, but the fury increased, injuring several persons, and demolishing
strongly built houses as if they were made of paper. Roofs were taken up as

by suction, and carried into the cloud, being transported in some instances for miles. When the column of cloud and wind caught up the buildings into its huge mouth, it ground them to the smallest fragments, as a mill grinds what is put into it.

Many wonderful incidents occurred in Arlington. The large grocery and dry goods store of Messrs. Fessenden, Whitmore and Company was levelled to the ground. Mr. Fessenden was the only person in the building at the time, and he was buried in the ruins, being extricated in an insensible state. His head and face were badly cut and bruised, but he was finally restored to his normal condition. Two men were blown entirely across Mystic River, and others were carried considerable distances, receiving serious injury. In proceeding to Medford the tornado passed over Spy Pond, where two ice-houses were destroyed. In one of them was a man with a horse and chaise. The noise of the wind startled the horse, and the man took him by the bridle. As the building fell, however, the horse started, dragging the man out of it, but the carriage was crushed by the falling timbers. Colonel Douglas of Cambridgeport, with two friends, was sailing on the pond, and the wind lifted the boat upon one end, perpendicularly. The members of the party grasped a tree, they being near the shore, and held on until the boat righted. This disaster was caused by the water at one end of the boat being lifted in a column upwards of a hundred feet in height, and carried to the shore, where some boys, who were playing were covered first with water and then with earth, being finally blown on to the railroad track, completely coated with mud. It not only prostrated the grass and corn, but partly buried them in the earth, making the fields look as if a heavy roller had passed over them. A committee appointed for that purpose appraised the damage in Arlington at twenty-three thousand, six hundred and six dollars.

The wind passed through Arlington from the west-southwest to the east-northeast, but when it reached the Mystic River, it took a more northerly course, and kept it till it reached Malden. It passed through the northern part of Medford near the railroad depot, a few rods south of "Wear" Bridge, demolishing several houses, barns and other buildings, and damaging many others, and seriously injuring several persons. It destroyed property there to the extent of eighteen thousand seven hundred and sixty-eight dollars, as appraised by a committee appointed at the time for that purpose. The track of the wind in this town was from forty to seventy-six rods in width, and through much of the course the ground was plowed up by the wind in places from one to two feet in depth. Parts of roofs, furniture, agricultural implements, lumber, trees and chimneys were strewn up and down the streets and in the fields. At the "gate," three large and elegant houses were blown down. Miss Brooks' large barn, built of heavy timber and plank, was taken up and carried fifteen feet before it was torn to pieces. The two-story residence of James. M. Sandford, the station agent, was carried twenty feet and blown to fragments, while his son James, who was eighteen years of age, was passing from the barn to the house. It was blown toward him, and his feet became entangled in the partly ripped-up sill of the doorway. One of his legs was torn open from the knee to the ankle, the bones were crushed, and the foot became a shapeless mass. He lay under the timbers three-fourths of an hour before they could be cut away, a work that he directed himself. Both legs were amputated, one above the knee, and the other just above the ankle. At the station a heavy baggage car, standing on the side track, was driven along the rails one hundred and sixty-five feet, and then taken up and carried sixty feet, nearly at right angles to the track. A stone wall three and a half feet in height was also levelled even with the ground, and the stones were scattered a rod or two on each side, badly injuring one of the shoulders of Luke Costello and fracturing the skull of George Maxwell. Five or six persons were also more or less injured in the town by falling buildings, and two men at work upon a new house were thrown several rods, one of them being considerably hurt. Timothy Fagan's house was unroofed, and his wife's ribs were badly jammed by her body being crowded into an opening in one side of the house. A Mr. Nutter's house was also unroofed, and his sick wife escaped injury, though the bedstead on which she was lying was torn apart, and a beam fell upon it. The wife of a Mr. Caldwell, who resided on a hill, while standing in the doorway of her house, was caught up and carried across the fields and over fences and trees about five hundred feet, being safely deposited by the side of a neighbor's barn, without injury, except some slight bruises. She knew nothing of her experience in the air. In another house a woman was sitting with her child in her lap when the building suddenly shook. She thought of no danger, but in a moment or two there was a tremendous crash overhead, and on looking upward she saw the sky, the roof of the house having been carried away. A moment later she was slightly injured on the shoulder by a falling timber. The house of a German farmer named Huffmaster was completely shaken to pieces, and he was buried beneath its ruins, receiving a violent contusion of the brain, which proved fatal. A Mr. West, who was building a house for a Mr. Haskins, saw the cloud coming from Arlington, and watched it anxiously. As soon as he saw it destroy a new house west of the Lowell railroad station, he sprang out of the house where he was at work, and ran, as he says, "for his life," to shelter himself behind a wall only five rods distant from the place from which he started. He had scarcely reached the shelter when the house he had left was totally destroyed. One more instance of the terrible power of the wind in this town is that of a pine tree, ten inches in diameter, which was broken off, carried several hundred feet into the air, and then thrown through the roof and windows of Dr. Kidder's house.

The tornado was also felt in the northern part of Malden, and then it swept on to Lynn, where, at a locality called Wood End, a boat was blown out of a pond, a brush heap carried bodily a distance of several rods, and apple trees eight or ten inches in diameter torn out of the ground. Accompanied by a terrific noise, it pursued its way to the upper part of Swampscott, where it uprooted several trees, moved a house slightly from its foundation, carried away a porch from another house, and scattered pots and kettles.

It was last heard from at Rockport, on the extreme point of Cape Ann, where the wind uprooted trees and forced the tide in to a considerable height, thus doing much damage to property in stores.

The day following the catastrophe crowds of people flocked to the scene of the principal desolation at Arlington and Medford.

At the time of the tornado a great deal of rain fell in Lowell, Massachusetts, about seventeen miles to the north of Arlington; and as soon as the wind had passed showers of rain fell violently and in great quantities for a few minutes all along the northern side of its track, but none fell on the southern side. In Waltham, the northern and eastern sides of the house in which the principal of the high school lived were covered with mud, while on the other sides none was seen. No rain had then fallen in the town, and there was no water near the house. Other houses were wet, but not muddy. The water and mud were probably brought from a distance.

Chapter Lxxii.

THE STORM OF APRIL 1852

The winter of 1851–52 was very severe. Snow came late in the season, thus making the spring backward. In New Hampshire, a great snow storm began on the fifteenth of April, and continued till the next day. Saturday, the seventeenth, was pleasant, with bright sunlight; but on the morning of the next day an easterly wind began to blow and a drizzling rain fell. The wind constantly increased in strength and the rain in volume until the water fell in torrents and a terrific gale was blowing. The storm continued until the next Tuesday night, and it was but a little less severe than the great storm of the year before, being productive of much damage to property and loss of life even as far south as Virginia.

This rain melted the snow that fell on the fifteenth, and the rain water together with the melted snow greatly swelled the streams, causing a freshet in many of them. The earth was saturated, almost beyond known precedent, and cellars were flooded everywhere. The Kennebec River in Maine was extremely high, the water being eight feet deep on the wharves at Hallowell, where it continued to rise until the morning of Friday, the twenty-third. The Saco River also overflowed its banks at its mouth. In New Hampshire, the water was over the bridges at Auburn Village, and other places. The Nashua River reached its height on Tuesday, and caused much damage. The mills at Dover and Great Falls were stopped by the water, and the trains at Newmarket could not be run as the water was so high above the rails it extinguished the fires in the locomotives. The freshet was as high in Massachusetts as it was farther north, the water in some places being two feet above the Nashua and Lowell Railroad two weeks after the storm. The Merrimack River was never known to rise so high before; at Lowell and Lawrence all work in the mills having to be suspended on account of the flooding of the lower stories. Water ran eight feet above the dam at Lawrence, and the southern end of Andover Bridge was swept away. Two houses were carried down the river on the twenty-second, and at Groveland people boarded them in boats, and saved the furniture. The roads near the mouth of the river were almost impassable and the wharves at Amesbury and Salisbury point were five or six feet under water. In most of the manu-facturing towns in Worcester County the dams and bridges were swept away.

Shipwreck. Oil on canvas by Thomas Birch. Brooklyn Museum of Art.

In Winchendon twelve bridges were washed off, and every one of the nine bridges over Miller's River in that town was either carried away or rendered impassable. The freshet was also high in Rhode Island and Connecticut. The Connecticut River was very much flooded, and that part of the city of Hartford which lies east of Front Street was completely inundated, the cellars and, in Charles and other low streets, the first floors of the houses being filled with water. At Masonville, in Thompson, a woman was drowned.

The strong wind caused a large number of disasters on the ocean during the storm. The brig *Spartan* of Boston, while returning from Surinam with a cargo of three hundred hogsheads of molasses, was driven ashore on Plum Island at midnight on Monday. The crew of nine persons was saved; one of them being sick with yellow fever, and most of the others unable to walk. Mr. Lufkin, a farmer, who lived on the island, in the greatness of his heart took a cart and conveyed them all to his house, where he cared for them in spite of the terrible disease. The cargo was scattered along the beach, and the vessel was quickly dashed to pieces by the powerful waves. Other vessels were driven ashore at Nauset Point and Alderton and on Chatham, Duxbury, Marshfield, Scituate, Salisbury and Hampton beaches.

The fatal shoals of Cape Cod lying off the coast at Truro again caught several vessels and sent them to destruction with many human lives. A Danish brig struck the bar, and went to pieces, all hands being lost. Among others were a ship named Inez, three barks, the *Josepha, Queen* and *Solway,* and two English schooners. The most interesting of these disasters was the wreck of the bark *Josepha,* which belonged in Gloucester, England, and had sailed from Bristol for Boston March 19, with a cargo of railroad iron, white lead and skins. It was commanded by Captain Cawsey, and the whole crew numbered nineteen men, all of whom were young. The craft was six years old, of about six hundred tons burden, and heavily and substantially built of larch and other woods from the north of England, being ironed with heavy braces. The ocean voyage was short and prosperous, and they made Cape Cod light at twelve o'clock Monday night, April 19. In the thick fog and the easterly gale they took a southeasterly course to get clear of the land. After running out far enough to accomplish their purpose, as the captain thought, they backed and sailed in toward the shore intending to enter Cape Cod Bay. The fog was so thick they could not tell where they were, but when they tacked, to their surprise and horror, they discovered upon sounding that the water was only fifteen fathoms deep, and that they were right on the breakers. The vessel struck on the outer bar off the head of the marshes about half a mile north of the Highland light. This was at about three o'clock on Tuesday afternoon. She was soon on her beam ends and after a few more of the violent and powerful seas that were running on the bar had struck her, the starboard quarter was carried away. The crew knew that the bark could not hold together very long in that tremendous sea, and they launched the pinnace, but it was instantly dashed to pieces, and the long boat, which they next got out, met with the same fate. A few minutes later the deck gave way from the stern to the foremast, the main and mizzen masts fell overboard, and the larboard side fell in. What was left of the vessel lay about three hundred yards from the shore, and the sea was continually washing over it. While she was in that condition, at about five o'clock in the afternoon, three boys who were walking on the beach saw her as the fog lifted a little. They immediately informed Mr. Hamilton, the keeper of the Highland lighthouse, and with the life preservers, India rubber coats, caps, etc., belonging to the Humane Society, he hurried toward the beach. A messenger went to Pond village, Truro, a mile away, and shouted through the streets, "A ship ashore, and all hands perishing!"—a cry that always caused the men of Cape Cod to spring to their feet and hasten to the beach. A large number assembled. They could see the spray from the waves fly over the foremast, which remained standing, and plainly distinguish several men clinging to the larboard side of the vessel, their heart-rending cries for assistance being heard above the thunder of the storm. The life-boat was kept a mile away, but even had it been there it was doubtful if it could have survived the mighty surf. But the piercing cries rang on, and the men of Cape Cod could never permit such calls to continue without risking their lives to rescue the mariners. The rocket belonging to the Humane Society that was used for throwing a line to a wreck was tried and burst. Jonathan Collins, who had just arisen from the tea-table, procured the lighthouse dory, and against the entreaties of the people present started to go out in the boat to carry a line to the wreck. This was about seven o'clock. David D. Smith took his watch from his pocket and handed it to a neighbor, but as he was about to step into the boat to go with Collins, a brave young man, named D. H. Cassidy, only twenty-three years old, who had been married but a few days, pushed Smith aside and took his seat in the boat. They pushed out into the mountains of foaming waters, on, on through the raging seas, until they had got within about fifteen yards of the wreck, when the boat capsized, and both men perished. The evening had long since set in, and the darkness of a stormy night shrouded land and water. Nothing could be done to save the dying men. Fires were built on the beach, and companies formed to patrol the shore to discover and lend assistance to anyone that might come ashore. The strong heavy timbers of the vessel were heard crashing asunder, and all believed that some of the men must soon be washed on the beach but that they would be alive no one dared hope. About eleven o'clock, the patrol found a man kneeling before one of the fires. It was one of the crew named George Chitney, who informed the patrol that when the foremast gave way the broad side of the bark went with it and that he and John Jasper, who was then lying at the edge of the water, being much bruised about the feet and in a dying condition, clung to the timbers, and though washed off several times, the rigging catching in the railroad iron held them for an hour and a half, they being at length washed ashore. Both the men were taken to the lighthouse, where they were kindly cared for, and only those two out of the crew of eighteen were saved. The body of Cassidy was found and buried at North Truro. Only six other bodies were recovered, and they were interred at Provincetown.

Chapter Lxxiii.

THE FRESHET OF NOVEMBER 1853

About the middle of November, 1853, a great rain storm caused a freshet all through New England. On Sunday, the thirteenth of the month, rain fell apparently as heavily as it had since the deluge. The darkness in the churches was very great, and many of the pulpits were lighted artificially, while in others the clergymen could hardly see to read, or discontinued the services. Some of the churches in Boston were closed, and a newspaper of that time said that the congregation of the Brattle Square church heard an excellent sermon though they hardly saw the preacher, and that they sang the hymns beginning:

"Mark the softly falling snow, and the descending rain," and "Hear what God the Lord hath spoken,/Oh, my people, faint and few."

A bridge of some thirty or forty feet span on the Vermont Valley Railroad between Dummerston and Putney, Vermont, was carried away. In Maine it was the greatest freshet that had occurred in the Penobscot River for twenty years. The boom at Veazie broke, and a large number of logs floated away. The village of Kenduskeag was badly flooded, a dam was carried away, and a teamster was drowned in the road there.

The Connecticut River and its tributaries were greatly swollen, and much damage was done on the Housatonic, Naugatuck and Danbury and Norwalk railroads. The Agawam meadows were under water, and the bridge at Mittineague was carried off. The railroad bridge at Seymore, and a highway bridge at Ansonia, both over the Naugatuck River, went off together with other bridges in that region. The western end of the bridge at Ansonia abutted on high ground, while through the village of Ansonia on the eastern side of the stream water ran rapidly and at great depth. On the bridge were several persons, who were watching the water on that Sunday evening when the middle pier fell, throwing the people into the water. A young lady, a young man and some other persons were drowned, and others clung to the abutments, to stumps and roots of trees, and to bushes until they were rescued. Cries for help were heard from several places in the water, but there was no boat to help them, and if there had been the water was raging so fiercely that few would have dared to risk their lives to go out to them. The shrieks of the drowning became heartrending, and several of the citizens of

Ansonia ran their horses to Birmingham, two miles away, to procure a boat. This was speedily obtained, and hauled to the place, four brave men stepping into it and pulling out into the maddened stream amidst the floating trees, bridges, and timbers. There was great excitement as the light in the boat was watched, darting down on the current. At the southeastern abutment of the bridge were found ten or fifteen persons, unable to escape. They were brought ashore, the water bailed out of the boat, and the crew started again for those farther down the stream. But clinging to bushes and other supports for two and a half hours had exhausted their strength, and timbers had swept them down the current. A number were rescued, but not all, several being drowned.

Chapter lxxix.

WINTER OF 1856–57

The winter of 1856–57 was one of the severest winters ever known in this climate, and is the last very rigorous season that has occurred in New England. It began much earlier than usual, and continued far into the spring. There were thirty-two snow storms in all, three more than the average number for a score of years, and the snow fell to the depth of six feet and two inches, the average depth for twenty years having been but four feet and four inches in eastern Massachusetts.

The preceding summer had been hot, and the weather was pleasant nearly all the time to the middle of December, though considerable snow had fallen and there had been some sleighing. Extreme cold weather, however, began on the night of the seventeenth of the month, when the thermometer fell in Massachusetts to twelve degrees below zero, and in Maine to sixteen below. They next day the temperature was scarcely above zero anywhere in New England, 'it being the coldest day that had been experienced since December 16, 1835. During the remainder of the month the weather was very inclement for the season, with strong and boisterous winds. On the night of the twenty-third there was a violent snow storm, which extended over a large tract of country, and during which snow fell to the depth of four or five inches on the level, making good sleighing. During the storm, the strong wind caused several wrecks on the coast.

January opened with a snow storm on the third, accompanied by a violent southeast wind. Snow was not twelve inches deep on the level, and sleighing was good. The railroad companies were more or less hindered by the snow which blocked their tracks and prevented the cars from running. The temperature became colder and colder, being from the sixth to the eighth below zero and almost unbearable because of the strong piercing wind which prevailed and which penetrated the thickest clothing. The whole country was afflicted by the rigor of the season, the west especially suffering terribly from it. The roads were still drifted, and mails and trains from the south and east were greatly delayed. In New Hampshire, on the twelfth, the thermometer indicated nineteen degrees below zero, and there was a very severe snow storm prevailing, accompanied by a gale that caused damage to the shipping along the coast.

> *O the long and dreary winter!*
> *O the cold and cruel winter!*
> *Ever thicker, thicker, thicker*
> *Froze the ice on lake and river,*
> *Ever deeper, deeper, deeper*
> *Fell the snow o'er all the landscape,*
> *Fell the covering snow and drifted*
> *Through the forest, round the village.*

Provisions were sold at extremely high prices, and poor people suffered much for want of good and necessary food. Contributions for their benefit were taken in many of the churches in the cities.

On the night of Saturday, January 17, and also the next day, the cold was severer than it had been during the winter. At Salem, Massachusetts, the temperature was twenty below zero on Saturday night, and five below on Sunday noon. At Lowell, Massachusetts, on Sunday morning it was twenty below, and at noon six. By evening, however, it had risen to twelve above zero, and snow had begun to fall. The wind was strong and from the northeast, and as the night advanced the storm increased until it became one of the severest and most violent that had been known for very many years. For several hours after sunrise the next morning the wind continued to be very cutting, and it was hard to face. The violence of the storm ceased before eleven o'clock in the forenoon, but snow continued to fall in flurries all through the day. Snow fell to a great depth, drifts on the northern side of Essex Street in Salem, Massachusetts, being from eight to twelve feet deep. Business was necessarily almost entirely suspended everywhere, and the streets were so blocked that no draught animal made an appearance during

the day, milkmen, bakers and butchers making no attempt to distribute
their supplies in the ordinary manner. A Sabbath stillness prevailed in the
city as well as in the country. No cars could be run, no mails came or went
during the day, and scarcely any one travelled about the streets. The snow
was too deep to be pathed in the old-fashioned ways by oxen, either with a
log or with the Swedish heater. Not quite as much snow fell in Maine during this storm as in Massachusetts, but in the south it came in remarkable
quantities, being at Washington, D. C., two feet deep. The wind forced the
snow into every crevice and cranny, and large drifts were deposited in barns
and other buildings that were apparently water-tight. The streets in Boston
were piled full of snow, and three days afterward many of them had not been
broken out. Several people were nearly smothered or frozen to death, the
cold during the storm being most intense, and the wind drove the snow into
the faces of those that were travelling. Snow shoes were found to be necessary to pedestrianism, and many of the old ones were hunted up and
brought into use again.

The violent wind which prevailed during this storm wrought many disasters on both sea and land. The steeple of the church in the village of
Campello,[1] Massachusetts, blew down, crashing through the body of the
church into the cellar. The steeples of the Episcopal and the Second
Congregational churches in Waterbury, Connecticut, met with the same
fate, as also did the spire on the Congregational church in Fairhaven,
Massachusetts, which was one of the tallest in the state. A house in New
Bedford, Massachusetts, was also completely demolished by the wind. The
gale was unusually severe on the ocean, being very disastrous to the shipping; many vessels were driven ashore and several lives lost. At
Provincetown, on Cape Cod, it was one of the worst storms ever experienced in that vicinity, the wind blowing a hurricane from ten o'clock
Sunday evening until twelve o'clock Monday night. Seventeen of the twenty
vessels in the harbor were driven ashore. Another vessel, the schooner
Bonita of Eastport, Maine, which had sailed from her home port before the
storm, had anchored at Cape Ann on account of the wind. She parted her
cables and, drifting across Massachusetts Bay in the thick snow storm, was
finally driven on shore at Provincetown, about half a mile east of Race
Point, on the night of the nineteenth. After striking, the sea made a complete breach over the vessel, washing overboard a man, who was drowned
before he could be rescued. Another man perished on board, being buried

---

1. A part of Brockton.

under the floating rubbish of the cabin. By the strenuous and noble efforts of the people of Provincetown, four of the crew were saved. In the steerage the water had risen above their waists, and the captain had lashed himself to the bit heads, while others of the crew clung about the gaff and main-mast. The mate succeeded after great exposure and suffering in floating some yarn through the surf to the beach, where it was secured by the inhab-itants, who attached to it a small rope and to that a small hawser which were successively pulled on board the wreck by the mate. To the hawser he fas-tened the captain, who was very much benumbed, and threw him overboard. The other two of the crew that remained alive were then fastened on and thrown overboard. He then tied the rope around himself, and all four were successfully hauled through the surf, a distance of more than a hundred feet. The captain was severely frozen and nearly exhausted before he was cast into the water, but by the excellent nursing of the rescuers, he, with the rest of the men, was finally restored to health and strength.

During and immediately following this storm, the temperature descended to an extremely low point, and remained there for a whole week. Sunday and Monday, the eighteenth and nineteenth of the month, are sup-posed to have been the two coldest days known in New England during this century. The "Cold Friday" of 1810 was more blustering, but the tempera-ture was not so low. At sunrise on the morning of the nineteenth the mer-cury congealed at Franconia, New Hampshire, and at Montpelier and St. Johnsbury, Vermont, it was fifty degrees below zero, the coldest ever known there. The following are some of the degrees below zero that the ther-mometer indicated at the same time in the different places named. In Maine, at Portland, twenty-nine; Bangor, forty-four; and at Bath, fifty-two. In New Hampshire, at Keene, twenty-four; Nashua, twenty-eight; Dover, thirty-one; and at Manchester, thirty-five. In Vermont, at Northfield, forty. In Massachusetts, at Boston, sixteen; New Bedford, twenty; Fall River, twenty-six; Worcester, twenty-six; Salem, twenty-six; Lowell, thirty; Malden, thirty; Taunton, thirty; and at Springfield, thirty-three. In Rhode Island, at Providence, twenty-six; and at Woonsocket, thirty-five. In Connecticut, at New Haven, twenty-seven; Hartford, thirty-two; and at Coventry, thirty-two. The temperature continued to be as low as it was on the nineteenth until the twenty-sixth. At Auburn, Maine, on the twenty-third it was twenty-two below zero, and at Weare, New Hampshire, forty below, and although the temperature was lower than it was on "Cold Friday" the day was much more bearable as there was no wind. This was not true in all parts of New England, however, as in some sections a brisk northwest

wind prevailed throughout the day, causing the thermometer to descend at
Lawrence, Massachusetts, to thirty-two degrees below zero; at Amherst,
New Hampshire, to thirty-five; at Northfield, Vermont, to forty; at White
River Junction to forty-three; and at Bangor, Maine, to forty-four. Long
Island Sound was frozen the whole width for the first time as far as known.
The twenty-fourth was thought to have been the severest day ever experienced in New Hampshire, the thermometer at Amherst descending to
thirty-seven degrees below zero. The air was very thin and peculiarly transparent and light, and the sky therefore remarkably clear. A strong northwest wind blew all day. At Franconia, New Hampshire, the temperature was
forty-nine degrees below zero, and it was the severest day ever known there.
At Auburn, Maine, it was forty below, and at Manchester, Massachusetts, it
was thirty-seven. On the twenty-fifth, the weather had moderated a little,
being then at Auburn, Maine, only six degrees below zero, and at the same
place on the next day two below. This was the coldest week ever known in
New England, and the severest January there had been at least for ten years.
During this spell the harbor of Portsmouth, New Hampshire, was frozen
over, a thing that was never known to have occurred before. In fact the reign
of this rigorous weather continued from December 20 to January 27, and
during all that time snow did not melt on the roofs of buildings in the
greater portion of New England.

On the twenty-seventh of the month, it began to thaw, and rain fell.
Two heavy rain storms followed, one immediately succeeding the beginning
of the thaw and the other after the lapse of a week. The rain fell in the
greatest quantity on Sunday, February 8, when a vast amount of snow was
carried away, causing freshets on the ninth and tenth in all parts of the
country. At Norwich, Connecticut, the destruction of property on the
Shetucket River was very great; and the heavy timber from Lord's and
Lathrop's bridges (which were carried away) was driven down the stream
with fearful power. East Chelsea was submerged in 1807, but at this time
the water front of Norwich was swept over by the raging flood. Below the
city the river was blocked by ice, which caused the water to be thrown back
upon the wharves and buildings of Water Street, suddenly deluging the territory.

The freshet was followed by fine weather, though the temperature was
often below zero. The snow was still very deep in Vermont, and sleighing
was good throughout New England. One of the most powerful and destructive slides of snow that ever took place in New England occurred on
February 22, on the side of a hill at Castleton, Vermont, completely

demolishing the barn and wagon shed of Merlin Clark. His residence was also in its course, being a few rods farther down the hill, and that also would have been destroyed had not the barn and shed lessened the force of the avalanche. As it was, the doors and windows of the house were broken, and the rooms almost filled with snow, ice and water. A child that was lying in a cradle in one of the apartments was completely buried by the snow, but was rescued without injury.

During the latter part of February the weather was mild, and on the first of March, bluebirds, blackbirds and robins appeared in Massachusetts, three weeks earlier than usual; but on that afternoon snow began to fall again, and the mercury descended to a point below freezing. The wind also rose, and before midnight was blowing most violently.

The weather during the spring was very changeable. March 31 and April 1 were mild and genial days, the temperature being as high as sixty degrees above zero; but at eleven o'clock in the evening of April 1 a change rapidly occurred. A blustering snow storm set in, which continued through the remainder of the night. The next morning the thermometer had fallen to seven degrees below zero. On the third of the month three inches of snow fell during a piercing gale of wind; but the sixth was very warm, the temperature being fifty-four degrees above zero, the wind south, and the weather dull and foggy.

On April 20 and 21, there was a severe rain storm, which flooded cellars, and carried away every bridge in Bartlett, New Hampshire. Vessels chafed at wharves along the coast, and many were driven ashore. At Salem, Massachusetts, snow fell for several hours, and at Deerfield, in the same commonwealth, there was still good sleighing.

This was one of the coldest winters ever known in the south as well as in the north and west, and it is said that the first snow storms known to have occurred in the city of Mexico was experienced this winter, on the night of January 31.

Chapter LXXV.

THE GALE OF SEPTEMBER 8, 1869

On the afternoon of Wednesday, September 8, 1869, occurred the last violent gale that New England has experienced. In the early part of the afternoon the weather was warm and pleasant, but at about half-past three the wind began to breeze up from the southeast and rain commenced to fall. The wind increased in force until five o'clock, when it blew a hurricane and continued raging until between eight and nine o'clock in the evening. It was accompanied by a heavy fall of rain, which came down in sheets, flooding the streets and greatly refreshing the earth after a long drought. A warm still atmosphere succeeded the wind, and the next day the weather was fine.

The storm was a very narrow one, being less than fifty miles wide. It passed over Narragansett and Buzzard bays in a northerly direction, and when it reached the coast, at Boston, its course changed to the northeast, following the shore as far as Cape Ann. It then swept across the ocean to the coast of Maine, and was felt but a short distance below Portland. The city of Fall River, Massachusetts, was in the middle of the storm belt, but the extremity of Cape Cod escaped the raging elements, and it was only an ordinary storm at Lowell, Massachusetts, and at Nashua, New Hampshire.

Great damage was done on both land and water. Telegraph wires, trees, fences and chimneys were blown down in every direction, and a great amount of fruit was destroyed. Many roads were blocked with fallen trees, and several tall factory chimneys were blown to the ground. In Boston, the famous Coliseum building was wrecked, and with it its great organ and big drum. A fatal accident happened to Granville M. Clark, who lived near the building, at the time it was blown over. He was just entering his residence when he heard that a person had been injured in the fall of the Coliseum, and he started to go there, but a furious gust of wind tore up the wooden sidewalk on which he was walking, and the timber was hurled against him so violently that his skull was badly fractured, his lips severely cut, and one arm broken. He fell bleeding and insensible, and died shortly after seven o'clock. The beautiful spire of the Hanover Street Methodist Church was blown down, and several fine church edifices in the city were severely injured. In Chelsea, Massachusetts, a tenement block was entirely blown down, and another house was lifted from its foundations. The spire of the First Baptist Church in Lynn, one hundred and sixty feet in height, also fell, nearly crushing the western wing of the church. A house on Marblehead Neck was blown down, injuring two men, one of whom died the next morning. At Salem, John Grover was carried some distance by the wind, and had one of his shoulders broken. In Peabody, Thomas E. Proctor's large building, two hundred feet long, was blown over, a two-story house was moved from its foundation, and two or three other houses were blown down. At Beverly, two houses and several other buildings were blown over. In Hamilton, the wind blew down Francis Dane's great barn, which was one hundred feet long.

The gale was also disastrous on the ocean, vessels dragged their anchors in the harbors and elsewhere, several being driven ashore at Marblehead, Massachusetts, and at Kennebunk, Boothbay, Portland and Orr's Island in Maine. At Gloucester, the scene on the beach was most exciting, wrecks being strewn along the shore. Fortunately there were but few craft in port at the time, else there would have been greater loss. The crews of several vessels were saved by means of the lifeboat, after repeated attempts had failed on account of the fearful power of the sea. A brave crew of seven men volunteered for the hazardous service, and another man risked his life to carry a rope to one of the vessels, by means of which the men were saved. Several other heroic acts were performed at this port during the gale.

The schooner *Helen Eliza,* belonging in Rockport, Massachusetts, with a crew of twelve men, Edward J. Millet, master, was near Portland, Maine, when the storm came on, and the captain decided to take refuge in that harbor. They had sailed within sight of Ram Island when a thick fog settled over the coast, followed by the rain and wind. Cables broke and sails blew away. The men saw Portland Light, and concluded to run to it, but could not make the channel. With anchors gone, in the terrible sea, the hurricane drove them on. Captain Millet stood at the helm till he was killed, it is supposed, by a blow from the main boom. The schooner struck on Peak's Island, smashing its bow, and instantly killing five of the crew. Having divested himself of all his clothing but his trousers and shirt, Charles Jordan, one of the survivors, ran into the hold, but had scarcely reached it when a tremendous sea tore off the deck, and he was swept into the raging waters. He regained the wreck, and clung to it while he got his breath and rested. An empty barrel was floating near the vessel, and he swam to it, using it as a support. The waves ran fearfully high, and as he was driven toward the shore he passed two of his shipmates who were clinging to a plank. He was carried in the direction of a rocky bluff, and was almost exhausted in trying to keep the barrel in position, the undertow becoming very powerful as he approached the shore. The waves would heave him toward the ledges, and then bury him in their treacherous waters, but at length he grasped the rocks, and in their crevices he put his fingers, holding on until he could regain strength to drag himself up their steep and jagged sides. He finally reached the top, becoming completely exhausted. He heard one of the men calling, but they were seen no more. Mr. Jordan discovered that he was on a ledge, at some distance from the shore, and after a short time he again plunged into the raging waves to make another struggle in the surf. His strength was fast leaving him, and he apparently made no headway; moments seemed hours; but he finally reached the shore, and drew himself beyond the breakers. It was about nine o'clock in the evening, and after a while he found a house, whose inmates furnished him with clothing, nourishment and care. He was the only one of the crew that was saved. Four bodies were found, and their funeral was held in the First Congregational Church at Rockport on Saturday of the same week.

Chapter Lxxvi

THE TORNADO AT WALLINGFORD, CONNECTICUT, IN 1878

During the last of July and the first of August, 1878, showers with thunder and lightning occurred almost daily, and on some of the days there were several disastrous ones. For two or three weeks there seemed to be more and greater thunder showers than the people of New England had ever experienced. Wind blowing with the force of a tornado frequently accompanied them, especially those that occurred on the eighth and ninth of August.

On the afternoon of Friday, the ninth, in all sections of the three southern New England states there was great destruction of property by lightning, and several persons were killed by it. Rain fell in great quantities, falling in Boston to the greatest depth ever known, and in several places wind was very disastrous. The tornado that occurred at Wallingford, Connecticut, was the most terrific and resulted in the greatest destruction of life and property that was ever caused in New England by such means.

Rain began to fall at about six o'clock, and in a few minutes it increased to a deluge. Heavy black clouds gathered over the village, making it dark as night, and lightning illumined the gloomy masses, while thunder continually rolled and crashed along the clouds. When the shower was at its worst, without a moment's warning, a fearful tornado swept across the northern part of the town, from west to east, accompanied by hail. The wind swept before it the rain and every movable thing that lay in its track, heavy and light articles being alike carried away and destroyed. Wooden houses were unroofed or blown off their foundations, some only a few feet, others an eighth of a mile. Its track, which was less than half a mile wide and about two miles in length, lay over what is known as the "sand plains," about a quarter of a mile north of the railroad station, and near the line of the New York, New Haven and Hartford Railroad. For a slight distance on either side of it some damage was done, especially to chimneys, but it was not to be compared to that which occurred within the track. The wind came and went almost in an instant, but in that time many strong, healthy persons had been swept into eternity, and desolation had come upon the town. Such a frightful scene had never before been witnessed by the inhabitants. Immediately after the destruction took place, fire burst out among the ruins in many places, being occasioned by burning lamps and stoves, and for a time it seemed that a terrible conflagration would add to the horror of the scene; but the rain which continued for about an hour fortunately extinguished the flames. At eight o'clock, the sky was clear and the moon shone brightly and serenely over the scene.

The tremendous force of the wind and the awful desolation it caused can perhaps be conceived when the reader learns that thirty-four persons lost their lives, twenty-eight more were severely injured, and that one hundred and sixty buildings were wholly ruined, which with the other property destroyed amounted to two millions of dollars in value. Among the buildings wholly demolished were forty dwelling houses and fifty barns. The latter were in some instances raised clear of the hay contained in them, which was left standing. Trees and fences were torn away, and hurled through the air as though nothing but straws. The damage to property and the loss of life were caused by the force of the wind alone, many persons being killed by the falling houses.

The town was in a state of uproar and consternation, and the greatest excitement prevailed. Immediate assistance was needed from other places, but there were no means of communication. The telegraph poles and wires were blown down, the cars would probably be late, and the distance to Meriden, the nearest town, was six miles. Little John Hoey, only twelve years old, thinking that the trains would be delayed, rode on horseback to Meriden for help. At seven o'clock, the steam cars arrived, and by them a message was sent to Meriden. On the express that left that place at half-past seven came seven physicians and other assistance, and systematic work was immediately begun. The dead bodies were searched out and brought together, twelve being laid on the children's desks in the Plains schoolhouse. The town hall was transformed into a hospital, and those who were seriously wounded were conveyed thither, being placed in charge of the physicians and professional nurses. There were wounded persons of both sexes, young and old, some with broken arms, legs and backs and fractured skulls, and others suffering from concussion of the brain and internal injuries. The scene throughout the place will never be forgotten by those that witnessed it. A guard of one hundred and sixty men was immediately placed over the desolated district.

Twenty-five of the dead were buried in the town cemetery on Sunday, the eleventh, an immense throng of ten thousand persons being present at the sad services, which were conducted by Rev. Mr. Leo of Winsted, assisted by Rev. Messrs. Slocum and O'Connell of New Haven and Mallon of Wallingford. There were two thousand carriages in the procession that followed the remains to the cemetery.

The disaster was not only sad and distressing on account of the loss of life and personal injuries, but in the great loss of property, buildings, furniture and goods, which belonged principally to the working-men, entailed upon the community many privations that had to be met. In several of the towns and cities around, public meetings were held to raise funds to assist the sufferers from this terrible catastrophe. The Catholic diocese immediately responded to the wants of the people, all those that died being of that faith, except Mr. Littlewood, and assistance came as freely and in as large amounts from Protestants.

Many wonderful incidents were related of fearful deaths and narrow escapes. Over the lake at the Wallingford community two clouds appeared to come together, and reaching down to the water drew it up in an immense spout seemingly two hundred feet high. A man was out on the lake in a boat, and when he saw the fearful commotion he jumped into the water, and swam ashore; but had scarcely done so when he saw his boat carried into the air and lodged on a hill. Four persons belonging to the family of John Munson were buried in the cellar when the house was blown down, and it was a good while before they could be dug out of the ruins. Two of them were slightly injured and the other two escaped. Michael Kelly, who was driving in a buggy, was blown in his team some thirty feet over a precipice, and both himself and horse escaped with slight injury. A boy named Matthew Mooney was struck by the wind as he was standing on the railroad track, and was blown fifty feet, being almost beheaded. A woman was lifted a hundred feet in the air, carried along seven hundred feet; and then dropped to the earth, her remains being found horribly mangled. A Mrs. Huxley had her child in her arms when she was picked up, both being dead and almost scalped. Frederic Littlewood was found dead by the side of the road, where he was killed by flying timbers. He was one of the many men that were on their labors for the day. In the Catholic cemetery, the largest monuments were torn up and trees were uprooted. The wooden church of the Catholics, and the new brick high school building were both crushed to a mass of ruins. To this scene of disaster and desolation there was a constant stream of visitors for several days after the catastrophe.

Chapter lxxvii.

The Yellow Day of 1881

On Tuesday, September 6, 18981, occurred a darkness which overspread New England almost all day. It was similar to the famous "dark day" of 1780, but on account of the intense brassy appearance, which everything assumed, it will go down in history as "the yellow day."

The smell of smoke had filled the air for several days, indicating its presence in large quantities. People generally at the present time have but little doubt that all the dark days here were caused by smoke. They have all occurred when the ground was bare, and either in the spring or autumn. With reference to the source of the smoke, various opinions were given: some believed that it came from extensive forest fires which, it was said, were then raging in Canada and the West; others thought it might be due to an active volcano in the interior of Labrador, while still others supposed it came from the immense peat bogs of the Labrador barrens, which in dry seasons burn to the rocks, the fire running over them faster than on a prairie. In two or three days time it has sometimes swept from Hudson Bay to the Gulf of St. Lawrence.

On the morning of "the yellow day" there was no apparent gathering of clouds, such as occurred on the "dark day" of 1780, but early in the morning the sun and sky appeared red, and toward noon every part of the sky assumed a yellow cast, which tinged everything, buildings, ground, foliage and verdure, with its peculiar novel shade. All things were beautiful, strange and weird, and it seemed as if nature was passing into an enchanted state. It was at first intensely interesting, but as the hours dragged on, and but slight change occurred the sight became oppressive. The wonderful spectacle will never be forgotten by those who witnessed it.

The day was warm, and the air was close and still, being in some sections most densely charged with moisture. The darkness continued until near the time of sunsetting, when the red sky and sun again appeared, and the darkness lifted.

The effect of the darkness upon animals was similar to that of the "dark day" of 1780, though in but a slight degree, some of the poultry retiring to their roosts. Lamps were lighted in shops and offices to enable people to see to work or read or write, their flames being white as silver, and gas-jets appeared like electric lights. Work was suspended in many places, partly on account of the darkness, and partly because of the gloom. In many schools a recess was taken during the darkest part of the day, and in several instances the scholars were dismissed.

People were considerably excited in some places, thinking that a tempest or some extraordinary commotion of the elements would follow, causing dire disaster. Others thought that the earth was passing through the tail of a comet. Still others felt that it might be the last great day of darkness, though they were not very solicitous for themselves or others; and some Adventists thought that the end of the world was approaching, when they would meet their Lord, although few of them believed it strongly enough to make any preparation for the glorious event. There were some persons who suggested that it might be a token of divine sympathy for President Garfield, who was then dying at Elberon.

The darkness prevailed over a large part of New England, being noticed as far northwest as White River Junction in Vermont, some distance into Maine, westward to Albany, New York, and south into Connecticut, where it cleared early in the afternoon.

Chapter Lxxxviii.

CYCLONE AT LAWRENCE, MASSACHUSETTS, IN 1890

At about nine o'clock in the forenoon of Saturday, July 24, 1890, a cyclone swept down upon the southern portion of the city of Lawrence, Massachusetts. Rain had begun to fall in torrents a few moments before, and after the sky had lighted up momentarily dark clouds rolled together, and the terrible whirling wind dashed through the city in an easterly direction, without a moment's warning. The path of the cyclone varied in width from fifty to three hundred feet. The noise of the wind was not very loud although it was heard some distance away, the principal sound attending it

Lawrence, Massachusetts, July 25, 1890. Immigrant City Archives.

being that of falling houses. During its progress the air was filled with
boards, shingles, limbs of trees, and debris in general, whirling round and
round. It was all over in a minute, the air was quiet again, as though inno-
cent of having done any mischief.

The cyclone struck the city at a point a little west of Broadway, which
is the main thoroughfare leading from Lawrence to Andover by way of the
bridge near the great dam. On that side of Broadway very little damage was
done to houses, but many trees lost large branches, which the wind threw
about in profusion. The Catholic church on the other side of the street, at
the corner of Broadway and Salem streets, was somewhat damaged, having
some of its windows broken, losing in some cases entire sections of them
and, at the rear end, the roof of one of the transepts. Continuing across the
overhead railroad bridge on Salem Street, the wind first demolished the
house of Deacon William F. Cutler on the corner of Salem and Blanchard
streets, leaving it a mass of ruins fit for nothing but kindling wood. There
were three or four persons in the house at the time, and they all escaped with
slight injuries. A daughter of Mr. Cutler would probably have been killed
had not a piano protected her from falling timbers. Another daughter,
named Helen, eleven years old, who was near the house, was blown down the

embankment at the eastern end of the bridge, and then struck by a timber, receiving a concussion of the brain. She lived but a few hours. The house next to Deacon Cutler's, which stood near it, being occupied by Dr. Birmingham, only suffered the loss of a few shingles, a single chimney, and some broken windows. The railroad bridge was also slightly injured.

To this point the wind had taken an easterly course, but now it changed a little to the north, following Springfield Street, where the devastation was greatest. That street ran in the same direction as Salem Street, and lay beyond it. Most of the houses on the street were either blown down, rolled over upon their sides, had the sides torn out, or were otherwise damaged.

The cyclone then crossed Union Street and came upon a grove of trees many of which were twisted off at the trunk or taken up by the roots. Just beyond this point a very pretty street extended through a grove, among the trees of which the wind wrought great havoc, many of them being torn up and twisted off. In Portland Street, some half a dozen houses met the same fate as those on Springfield Street, and some of the trees were injured. At that point the wind seemed to have spent its force.

In many cases the houses were completely demolished, in others the roofs were lifted and blown off, leaving the buildings in their original shape. In at least one instance one of the walls of a house was ripped off, leaving the interior of the rooms exposed to view from top to bottom, but otherwise as they were before the wind came. In another case a house was turned upside down. Many houses were moved partially around and twisted out of shape. In some instances shingles were stripped from the roofs, as though done preparatory to re-shingling, leaving the roofs intact. The houses on Springfield Street were utterly spoiled, even where the general outline of their shape remained. In illustration of the whirling motion of the wind, large and well-built houses were moved from their stone foundations, sometimes in the direction of the cyclone's course and frequently in the opposite direction. One house on Market Street was moved from its foundation westerly, while another which was but a few rods distant was carried to the east. In numerous instances boards were seen lodged in trees.

In one house, the wind caught up a lighted oil stove that stood on the floor and raised it to the ceiling as gently as a toy balloon would rise, and as carefully deposited it in the place from which it was taken without injury. The wind struck the rear end of a wagon, turning it partly around, but the man who was riding in it whipped up his horse, and thus escaped injury.

Michael Higgins, switch-tender at the Salem Street railroad bridge, was blown with the switch-house more than one hundred and ten feet, and was found with his neck broken. From the ruins of her residence on Portland Street were taken the dead bodies of Mrs. John Collins and her four-year-old child, also the remains of Hannah Beatty, a girl of ten years.

Mrs. Jeremiah O'Connell was extricated from the ruins of her home on Springfield Street, in which she had been crushed to death. Her daughter, Mamie, aged fourteen years, was also taken out the ruins, her neck being broken and her body mangled. When the wind had abated, a bundle was found rolling down the street. It was at first thought to consist of rags, but a few minutes later, cries issued from it, and an investigation revealed Mrs. O'Connell's baby girl. Her body was covered with dust and plastering, and had been but slightly injured. How the child came in that situation the wind only can tell.

Mrs. Lizzie Holdeworth, who resided on Springfield Street, was among those that narrowly escaped death. She was sitting in her house when she heard a crash, and then knew nothing more. When she came to her senses, she was lying in the ruins of her home, being fastened down by timbers between two stoves. A beam lay across her forehead, and held her head down, her lower limbs being also pinioned. Her tongue was between her teeth, and it was impossible to move it. In this terrible situation, she could not call for help. She seemed to gain in strength, and at last heard the rescuing party chopping at the boards and timbers which held her down. As soon as she was taken from the ruins she again became insensible, but revived on the way to the hospital, where she was made comfortable.

Probably the most pathetic of several touching incidents of the cyclone, is that concerning James Lyons' family, who resided on Emmet Street. Mrs. Lyons was in the yard when the terrible clouds appeared, and she rushed into the house. Her husband was in a field a short distance away, and he immediately started for home. He came in sight of the house as the mighty wind lifted it bodily from its foundations and ruthlessly tore it to fragments. He himself was forced to the ground, and when the wind abated, he arose and hurried to the ruins of his house, among which with the assistance of some more fortunate neighbors he began a search for his family. As some heavy timbers in the front room were lifted, the remains of his wife were revealed with a beam lying across her forehead, which had probably caused her death. Mr. Lyons was almost frantic with grief, and was calmed by his friends with much difficulty. In a few moments the muffled cries of an infant attracted their attention, and further search revealed a baby girl almost hidden and protected by her mother's body. Her arms were tightly clasped about the inanimate form of the woman, and in piteous cries she lisped, "mamma, mamma," but the call received no answer.

The cyclone either demolished or seriously injured seventy dwellings. Many families, of course, lost their homes, but it was in the warm season, and that made it easier to bear than if it had occurred in the winter. Most of these people were the owners of their houses, and the loss proved almost total as none of it was covered by fire insurance. The whole amount of damage was estimated at about one hundred and fifty thousand dollars. It is perhaps wonderful that of the large number of people who were in the path of the cyclone, only eight were killed. Fifty-one others were more or less hurt, and several of them afterward died from their injuries.